COMMUNITY POWER AND
GRASSROOTS DEMOCRACY

OTHER BOOKS BY MICHAEL KAUFMAN

Jamaica Under Manley: Dilemmas of Socialism and Democracy
Beyond Patriarchy: Essays by Men on Pleasure, Power and Change (ed.)
Cracking the Armour: Power, Pain and the Lives of Men
Theorizing Masculinities (co-edited with Harry Brod)

COMMUNITY POWER AND GRASSROOTS DEMOCRACY

The Transformation of Social Life

*Edited by Michael Kaufman
and Haroldo Dilla Alfonso*

ZED BOOKS
London & New Jersey

INTERNATIONAL DEVELOPMENT RESEARCH CENTRE
Ottawa · Cairo · Dakar · Johannesburg · Montevideo · Nairobi · New Delhi · Singapore

Community Power and Grassroots Democracy was first published in 1997 by
Zed Books Ltd, 7 Cynthia Street, London N1 9JF, UK, and
165 First Avenue, Atlantic Highlands, New Jersey 07716, USA,

and the International Development Research Centre,
PO Box 8500, Ottawa, ON, Canada K1G 3H9.

Typeset in Monotype Garamond by Lucy Morton, London SE12
Printed and bound in the United Kingdom
by Biddles Ltd, Guildford and King's Lynn

A catalogue record for this book is available from the British Library

Library of Contress Cataloging-in-Publication Data
Community power and grassroots democracy : the transformation of
social life / edited by Michael Kaufman, and Haroldo Dilla Alfonso.
p. cm.
Includes bibliographical references and index.
ISBN 1-85649-487-X. — ISBN 1-85649-488-8 (pbk.)
1. Community development—Latin America—Case studies.
2. Political participation—Latin America—Case studies.
3. Community development. 4. Political participation. 5. Social
movements. I. Kaufman, Michael, 1951– . II. Dilla Alfonso,
Haroldo.
HN110.5.Z9C6259 1997   96–39524
307.1'4'098—dc21   CIP

ISBN 1 85649 487 X (Hb)
ISBN 1 85649 488 8 (Pb)

Canadian ISBN 0 88936 784 1

Contents

Part Two: Theme Studies

Acknowledgements

Finishing work on this particular book is a bitter-sweet experience. Over the course of seven years a group of us worked together on an ambitious project that brought together colleagues from seven, eight, nine countries. Our aim was simultaneously to build a research network that spanned North America, Central America, the Caribbean, and, eventually, South America (and four different native tongues – Spanish, English, French, and Haitian Creole) and to conduct a novel bit of research on a co-operative and collaborative basis. Sometimes months would pass when we were unable to communicate among ourselves – so bad were phone and mail connections in some cases. Seeing the project come to an end brings an immense sense of satisfaction, but also sadness, as a period of our lives comes to an end without a clear idea when we will see each other or have the pleasure of working together again.

This work has benefitted from the contribution and dedication of so many individuals. In particular, I would like to thank Sheilagh Knight, who worked tirelessly at CERLAC as the project administrator during its most difficult two years. I would also like to thank Liddy Gomes, the tireless CERLAC administrator and a source of advice and help on matters large and small. I am indebted to Lizeth Alvarez and Sabrina Blackstad, the persons-of-all-trades at CERLAC during the project, and Barbara Anderson, our original part-time project administrator. Former CERLAC Director Alan Simmons played a key role in encouraging me through the difficult first stages of this project and generously giving both his time and invaluable advice. All my colleagues at CERLAC were a source of ongoing encouragement, but let me mention Liisa North, who for two years during the project was the Acting Director of CERLAC; Peter Landstreet, who was, for a period, Deputy Director; and Meyer Brownstone and Ricardo Grinspun, who were Directors during its completion. All were tremendous in their ongoing help.

This project would have been impossible without the very generous support of the International Development Research Centre (IDRC) in Ottawa and the Ford Foundation in New York. At the IDRC, I would like to thank Andrés Pérez, who helped in the original formulation of the project, Guillermo Thornberry, Esther Beaudry, and particularly Christopher Smart, who took over relations with our project during its most critical stages and provided not only support and encouragement, but many insights as well. At Ford, I would like to thank Michele Heisler, who participated in one of our initial workshops, Cynthia Sanborn for her ongoing backing, Rebecca Nichols, as well as Penny Alex and Peggy Greves. The Social Sciences and Humanities Research Council provided valuable assistance for one of our workshops and for the research of the project co-ordinator. Thanks also to Robert Molteno and the staff at Zed Books.

In addition to the many colleagues who contributed to the specific research projects and whose names are mentioned elsewhere in this volume, I would like to thank various individuals who contributed to the development of the project through participation in workshops, preparation of papers not included in this volume, and through early support for various projects: Barry Adam, Amparo Arango, Jonathan Barker, Deborah Barry, Julio Barrios, Meyer Brownstone, Almachiara D'Angelo, Hugh Dow, Norman Girvan, Andrew Goodman, Xavier Gorostiaga, Eddy Greene, Claremont Kirton, David Lewis, Laura MacDonald, Antonio Ruiz Meléndez, Brian Meeks, Malena De Montis, Steve Patten, Magaly Pineda, Luis Suárez, C.Y. Thomas, José Manuel Valverde, as well as the individuals who provided fine translation at our three project workshops.

Patricio Mason in Chile did the primary translation of the articles on Cuba, Dominican Republic, and Haiti. Lilly Nichols translated the Costa Rica article. Haroldo Dilla and I did additional translation; I was responsible for the editing.

I would also like to thank my partner in those years, Maureen Simpkins, and our son, Liam, for their loving encouragement. My own research for most of those years was made possible by a Canada Research Fellowship, provided by the SSHRC. I would also like to thank my colleagues and their families in all the participating countries for their tremendous hospitality and warmth during numerous, but usually far too brief, visits.

Haroldo Dilla would like to express his great appreciation to his wife Teresa and daughter Charlene, who, along with his mother, form a triumvirate of strong women in his life. He would also like to thank his colleagues and staff at the Centro de Estudios Sobre América for their support and help, as well as the IDRC for its support for his project and for his own research while holding a year-long Pearson Fellowship in Ottawa in 1989–90.

Haroldo and I would like to dedicate this book to community leaders and all those active in organizations of community power, not only in the countries studied in this project, but throughout the world. As researchers we may write about, reflect upon, and encourage their work, but it is they who are remaking their lives and remaking history for us all.

Michael Kaufman
Toronto, Canada

Foreword

Rosny Smarth
Prime Minister of Haiti

It has given me immense pleasure to read *Community Power and Grassroots Democracy*, the result of a multi-country research project and the outcome of years of perseverance by researchers in eight countries and by the team at the Centre for Research on Latin America and the Caribbean (CERLAC) under the direction of Michael Kaufman.

The welcome initiative by CERLAC to co-ordinate this research has resulted in a book of inestimable value about new forms of collective action that have blossomed throughout much of the Third World

In *Community Power and Grassroots Democracy* we are able to follow a range of popular organizations and initiatives in grassroots democracy in their formation and their evolution, with their diverse courses of action and modes of internal functioning, and in their ideological articulation and political action. Together, the chapters in this book give us the ideological and methodological tools to understand that underneath their contradictions and ambiguities, their weaknesses and stumbling blocks, there lies an ensemble of organizations and practices with astonishing vitality and remarkable social and political productivity.

In effect, these organizations and associative practices give all the signs of a new mode of political action that embodies profound sociocultural transformation. They respond to the sometimes anxious search for a true citizenship that is rising in the hearts of the people in my region and elsewhere. And the search by so many directly challenges us all to work actively towards a new social and political order: an order that no longer centralizes decision-making, knowledge, and the fruits of production in the hands of a small minority. An order that, to the contrary, unites and harmonizes the work of all citizens and renders them able to act in a manner that is congruent with their rights and abilities.

This book shows without doubt the contribution of these collective organizations. They represent a point of convergence for the interests of diverse groups and, at the same time, a space to conduct dialogue, to exercise serious contestation, and to organize people to resolve the problems of daily life. In brief, they are centres for apprenticeship, and for the construction and exercise of a democracy based on the responsible and effective participation of diverse groups of people.

This book gives us an interpretative trail that is profound and sometimes surprising of social phenomena that, at first sight, are, at least sometimes, quite unusual. It informs us that one of the essential characteristics of these new forms of community action is precisely that they are somewhat inaccessible and escape many of the categories of traditional social and political analysis. It helps us remember that, although they are only in the process of emergence, they are already organizations with distinct characteristics, which, in consequence, force us to discover distinct approaches to uncover and understand their origins and activities.

Community Power and Grassroots Democracy is a wonderful beginning to this process of intellectual and political discovery.

Port-au-Prince, Haiti

1

Community Power, Grassroots Democracy, and the Transformation of Social Life

Michael Kaufman

I spotted the young girl out of the corner of my eye. She was barefoot and sat on the concrete step in front of a small, run-down house. She wore a clean print dress and was playing with a doll that had lost most of its hair. There was nothing special about the girl, but I thought about her because she seemed so content. It was the simple contentment of a child at play, but in my mind I projected ahead a decade or two and thought that her life was going to be better than that of her parents.

I was in Port-au-Prince, Haiti, and it was in the heady and optimistic days in 1990 leading up to the election to the country's presidency of the radical priest Father Aristide. Several years before, the dictator had fallen, and although remnants of the old regime clung to power, there was something new and powerful stirring in the neighborhoods of the city and in the farms and villages across the countryside. People were creating grassroots organizations that, for the first time in 200 years, seemed to have the potential of turning common people into the shapers of their own destinies. Although I knew my association was fanciful – the stuff of novels rather than everyday reality – the girl in her contentment seemed to represent what lay ahead.

In its specifics this was the story of one country. But it is a story told in different ways, with different voices, in different chapters, throughout much of the world. It is a story of a search for forms of democracy that allow people in their communities and workplaces to control their lives and livelihoods. It is a tale of empowerment, of grasping the tools of political action, of group discipline, of economic and social will.

It is not, unfortunately, a simple story with fairytale endings. One need look no further than Central America and the Caribbean to see that. In Haiti, popular organizing had not gone far enough to prevent the military from overthrowing Aristide in 1991. In Nicaragua, attempts to build organizations of community power were undermined by war, economic crisis, scarce resources, political sectarianism, and a view of the central state as the ultimate means for social change. In Jamaica, most community councils of the 1970s failed to survive an economic crisis, a change in government and a reorientation of social priorities in the 1980s. In Cuba, new, democratic forms of municipal organization have had to compete with bureaucratic and centralist tendencies. In the Dominican Republic, explosive forms of popular organizing in the *barrios* have so far failed to coalesce into ongoing organizations capable of developing a new vocabulary of social action. In Costa Rica, the success of grassroots efforts to create new communities through land invasions and pressure on the state to provide housing has meant the development of stable communities in which social activism becomes less and less necessary.

The real end of each story, however, has yet to be told. We can sketch a tale of struggle and change. But the only thing that has definitively ended are today's chapters. The accumulation of experience, the development of new possibilities, the creation of new priorities, the shaping of new social actors, the building of new skills and self-confidence, are but raw materials for stories yet to be written.

Although half of the chapters in this volume refer specifically to experiments in grassroots organization in five different countries – Chile, Costa Rica, Cuba, Dominican Republic, and Haiti – these pieces and the broader theoretical chapters have a wider historical and geographic sweep.[1]

All the articles, directly or indirectly, emerged from a co-operative and collaborative research project that involved researchers in the Central American and Caribbean countries, as well as researchers working in Canada, Uruguay, and Chile. In most cases, the period under investigation was from sometime in the 1970s, when most of the experiments began, through the early 1990s, when our collaborative research project came to an end. The research, which will be described in detail in the second part of this introductory chapter, involved more than ten research centers in a co-operative project. The aim of our work was, for the first time anywhere, to do a comparative examination of the process of grassroots mobilization and the development of community-based forms of popular democracy.

The experiences in these countries have been very different in their origins, structures, developmental impact, relation to central governments, and in their areas of successes and failures. What they held in common was an attempt to extend participation and democratic decision-making. In some countries, governments initiated these efforts; in others they began at a grassroots level with or without any support from the government but usually in direct confrontation with the state.

The richness of this experimental base has stood in stark contrast to our limited understanding and scant evaluations of these attempts. While many agencies and theoreticians acknowledge the potential of community participation in the process of development, no attempt has been made to study these actual experiences in this region systematically at the individual and, particularly, at the comparative level. This parallels the weakness of comparative studies in other regions of the world.

The overall research issue was the role and potential of organizations of community participation as effective participatory, decision-making, and administrative structures capable of responding to the problems of a community and a nation. What role were they playing or might they play in the process of social and personal empowerment, economic development, and socio-political transformation? In the end, our research became a study of the strengths and weaknesses, the limits and potential, of community democracy in the Third World and beyond.

The central contentions of this chapter – ones that emerged in the course of the project – are these: participatory democracy represents both a goal of social change and a method of bringing about change. In particular, the community represents a potential locus of change that offers the possibility of bringing together individuals in a unitary way that overcomes divisions based on sex, age, political orientation, and, to a certain extent, class and ethnicity. Nevertheless, efforts towards popular power based in the community face enormous obstacles in the form of the power of central bureaucracies, party and state apparatuses, lack of skills and organizing traditions, the impact of national and transnational economic and political structures and activities, and a range of existing social divisions. The impact of differences of social, economic, and political power is what I term differential participation and is the theme of Chapter 7.

I now want to explore a series of themes concerning democratic theory and community-based forms of popular participation, and then go on to summarize the themes and goals of the project as a whole and very briefly summarize the focus of the various research projects and their results.[2]

The Theoretical Framework

Participation and power

The practical and intellectual roots for organizers and researchers of community-based participation lie in the search for a road to rebuild community life and the more secure (if far from idyllic) human relationships shattered by industrialization, urbanization, internationalization of capital, colonization, and proletarianization. Its roots also lie in the progressive decomposition of the two prevalent development paradigms of the twentieth century – centrally planned socialism and market-driven capitalism.

The failings of the capitalist market model, all too evident in the underdevelopment of most of the Third World and in what we might think of as the overdevelopment of the First World, has stimulated an interest in finding forms of development that actually reach the majority of the population. Advocates of capitalist development thought that structural economic crises, the endemic social problems, and the political instability of so many Third World countries could be conquered through technological and economic solutions that would boost growth and development. Their solutions were diverse, including large state investment, import substitution, the encouragement of small business, and the enactment of so-called free-market policies. The aim was to promote growth and profit-making that would spread in the fashion of nineteenth- and twentieth-century capitalism in Europe and the colonial settler states of the US, Canada and Australia. As has been analyzed exhaustively over the past 30 years, the model has not met its expectations, although certain nodes of growth do exist.

As for state socialism, as an economic model it has been undermined by its own social and political contradictions. One aspect of its politico-economic model – the virtual equation of socialism with democracy – has been the source of many problems: seize the state in the name of the people (the curious concept of dictatorship as democracy), nationalize the means of production, and, in a snap, as if Marx were Merlin, you'd have the rudiments of a new democracy, a people's democracy, a workers' democracy. In spite of the often grim workings of the Moscows and Pekings, and the Pragues and Warsaws, the obvious inequalities and lop-sided development of the capitalist world, and certain material gains in countries such as Cuba, helped maintain a faith in this model.

What this model ignored – as had been pointed out for many decades by those of us who felt that the Soviet Union, China, and Eastern Europe were neither particularly socialist nor particularly democratic – was that democracy was a precondition for socialism as much as some sort of socialism was a precondition for an extension of democracy. The problem, as has been explored in an increasing number of books and articles since the early 1980s, has been to understand the articulation of the two and how one constructs a deeply socialist democracy. There are many takes on this riddle, but they have in common the notion that new structures need to be built that allow forms of popular participation, indeed popular power, to operate directly. Forms of direct control – such as workers' ownership and control of the workplace and the economy through co-operatives, public ownership, and networks of workplace and community committees – would play a key role in the extension of democracy. In some versions, forms of direct democracy would be combined with a revamped liberal democratic electoral and party structure; many versions now recognize the possibility, even the necessity, of mixing public owner-ship with some forms of private business and a market economy.

One of the problems has always been how to realize these goals. What structures are viable in large, complex societies? What experiments provide a useful pathway of empowerment? What strategies might take us along the pathway towards this future? Here the fundamental problem has been how to build inclusive structures of social, economic and politi-cal power, ones that overcome inequalities and could fundamentally shift the basis of social power.

Our own research venture did not pretend to be able to answer all these questions, but rather set out to look at one level at which answers might be articulated: that is popular participation at the community level. The conceptual framework that emerged was one which sees the resolu-tion of problems and the answer to the questions as pertinent to a process of transition, transformation, and empowerment.

These four words – process, transition, transformation, empowerment – are key to this approach: 'process' suggests that change is ongoing and, implicitly, difficult and full of conflict and struggle. The particular organi-zations we study are not of interest as fixed entities – this is not research into organizational structure – but in the sense that they are part of the creative flux of change. 'Transition' suggests that this process is not sim-ply one of modernization and development, but is a process leading to an alternative future. This prospective future may not be well articulated and is indeed unknown, but it is an alternative in the sense that it is a future substantially freed from the nightmare of the present – a present typified in most countries by the existence of waste, greed, and corruption alongside malnutrition, inadequate housing, poor health care, illiteracy, alienation, unemployment, racism, sexism, and fear. The word 'trans-formation' suggests that this process of transition is not simply one of quantitative or linear improvement, but a substantial and qualitative shift in the political, economic, social, and cultural relations of the day. And finally, 'empowerment' refers both to a method of change and to a definition of these new relations.

Indeed the problems we are talking about have to do with relations and not just living conditions. The problem in most of the countries of the region we studied, as elsewhere in the world, is not simply that the conditions of life are onerous. The problem is that those who suffer the most under the status quo – and the sufferers are easily a majority of the population – do not have ready-made means to change either their lot in life or the societies in which they live. They do not have access to effective means of political power. They do not have access to sufficient means of economic production. They do not have the education, the training, or, in many cases, the self-esteem and self-confidence to engage in a successful process of change. What is more, other classes, other social groupings have defined for them and for all of society what is important and how society should be structured and managed. In some cases any attempt by these individuals and groups of individuals to bring about change is met with harsh repression.

The common denominator of all these factors is a lack of power by the majority of the population – a lack of power to identify problems and mobilize the society's resources to solve them. If we take a historical and even anthropological view, we can see that this current situation is a result of an ongoing process by which certain groups of the population have gained more and more control of the means of political, economic, and social power. These groups might be particular classes, castes, ethnic, national, or color groupings, one sex, or a combination of many of these. Thus a process of change must necessarily be a process of empowerment of the majority who lack power.

I start off with these points because of the theoretical weaknesses that have plagued both the literature on participation *and* the actual attempts to develop popular participation. Such a framework allows us to ask the fundamental question as to whether the organization plays a role – or has potential to play a role – in changing the fundamental social, political, economic, and social relations that have created inadequate living conditions in the first place.

As many social theorists have noted, 'participation' is a broad and often vague concept. It can refer to everything from voting to participating in a vote fraud, from participating in a neighborhood committee that has power to direct a process of local change to participating in a hired gang that beats up those who lead such a local committee.

To a certain extent the framework I have just described appears consistent with that taken in some other studies. For example, the Popular Participation Program of the United Nations Research Institute for Social Development (UNRISD) defines participation as a means, particularly by those currently without power, to re-distribute 'both the control of resources and of power in favor of those who live by their own productive labor.'[3]

One study of popular participation in West Bengal modified the UNRISD definition and referred to popular participation as 'collective efforts to increase and exercise control over resources and institutions on the part of groups and movements of those hitherto excluded from control.'[4] However, like any one-line definition, this can only hint at a range of issues, problems, and conflicts. Such 'collective efforts' of change have distinct political, economic, social and cultural dimensions. Society isn't divided neatly into those who have power and those who don't; for example, even within dominated groupings there are power inequalities – inequalities based on sex, age, color, sexual orientation, and so forth. And there are differences within the camp of 'those excluded from control' between the urban poor and the peasantry, between blue-collar, white-collar, and those such as teachers and nurses.

Furthermore, such 'collective efforts' at change are not merely an effort by one group to grab the reins of society, but must of necessity include a redefinition of social priorities and social organization. The notion of 'control of institutions' can mask the need for new social institutions altogether.

The authors of a study by the World Employment Program of the International Labor Organization note that popular participation can contribute to a basic needs strategy 'by playing a part in the definition of basic needs; by enhancing the generation of resources to meet basic needs; by improving the distribution of goods and services; and by satisfying the psychological desire to participate in decisions which affect people's lives.'[5] These points are valid, but, as with much of the literature on participation, do not sufficiently emphasize the need to shift relations of power. Rather, the stress in this ILO document is on a series of institutions that may augment the power of certain groupings in order to provide specific things or a sense of participation, but not necessarily change the fundamental social relations of power.

Another problem with one-line definitions is that participation/empowerment is both a goal and a method of change. As a goal, popular participation refers to a society in which there no longer exists a monopoly of the means of political, economic, cultural and social power in the hands of a particular class, sex, social stratum, or bureaucratic elite. As a method of change, participation is a means to develop the voice and organizational capacity of those previously excluded; it is a means for the majority of the population to identify and express their needs and to contribute directly to the solving of social problems. As a method, participation is a prefiguration of a future society based on new principles of socio-economic and political organization.

Perhaps what is fundamental in any analysis of popular participation is not to get lost in the myriad different organizations and activities. The key question is whether these organizations constitute meaningful participatory institutions of empowerment. Much of the literature on the subject speaks of the ability of the population to influence and indeed control the processes of both decision-making and implementation. But I think we can go beyond this. For me the key is whether *the mass of the population has the means to define the terms and nature of its participation.*

This has several implications. One is that for people to have this capacity, a society must meet a number of preconditions: a population must have the economic, cultural, political and social means to define what is desirable, what is good, and, in a sense, what is the nature of their reality – that is, what Antonio Gramsci defined as hegemony. Such a precondition has, in different terms, been called social justice. Of course, we must acknowledge not only that social justice is a precondition for participation, but that participation is a precondition for social justice. There is no absolute level of either social justice or participation; rather, there are degrees of each and the development of each remains inter-related and intertwined.

The second implication of this analysis is, as C.Y. Thomas points out, that those interested in new relations of political and economic power have not concretely defined the norms and rules of behavior of new relations of power. We have not adequately codified the basic principles of alternative institutions. And we have not developed the measuring rods to assess these new relations, or a process, of empowerment. The question, therefore, is what is the practical content, what are the necessary and sufficient features, of a hegemony of the majority?[6]

Third, the notion of a population having the capacity to define the terms of its participation suggests we must historicize the concept. The quest for defining the terms and nature of social participation is a process that changes over time. Specifically this means that neither activists nor researchers are dealing with fully formed, fully successful, or pristine organizations. Rather, organizations and structures embody a process of change. The expression of a mass impulse for empowerment can take radically different forms, which themselves change over time.

Historicizing the idea of participation places emphasis on the process of change, the dynamics of empowerment, and the conflicts that this process generates. This includes the conflicts not simply between those who have and those who do not have power. It also includes conflict within the group that lacks power, such as conflict between men and women or young and old. These conflicts affect the capacity of a group to define a new hegemonic discourse.[7]

This emphasis – on the ability of the mass of the population to define the terms and nature of its participation – relates to other assumptions that emerged within this research project. For example, it relates to the contradictory role of the state and political leadership in the process of empowerment. What political conditions, what political culture is most likely to encourage and allow the development of this self-definition and the development of institutions of popular participation? Are there conditions where a central state actually fosters this process, or, conversely, when does support from the outside actually undermine a process of local empowerment?

Community and community power

There are, of course, many institutions that potentially allow some form of popular participation: voluntary associations such as political parties; organized groups of women or youth; groups based on color, ethnicity, tribe or religion; consumer groups; self-help groups; peasants organizations; and neighborhood associations. There are representative bodies, structures of workplace democracy, trade unions, and co-operatives. With such a range of institutions, why the interest in community power? Let us first look at what type of organizations our study focused on, and, second, consider why these institutions are worth studying with both care and enthusiasm.

There isn't only one type of organization that falls under the rubric of organizations of community power and grassroots democracy. Even within the countries of our research project, the organizations we ended up studying ranged from those supported by governments and integrated into the political structure of the country to groups that were organized against the existing political system. There were groups focused on a particular concern (such as housing) and those with wide responsibility for community affairs. There were groups that operated with some patronage functions for the national government and those that maintained an uneasy relation with the government to receive funding for the organization's activities. There were highly structured groups and loosely structured, leaderless, largely spontaneous efforts.

They all had several things in common. First and foremost, they were all organizations based at the community level. By community we meant a geographic community – in our case, a village, an urban neighborhood, or a city. These organizations were based on common interests where people lived and, in some cases, where people worked. They were not based on political affiliation – although partisan politics might play a role in their operation in some cases – nor exclusively in the workplace, nor relating exclusively to a particular sub-group within the community, such as women, youth, workers, or an ethnic, religious, or color grouping. Taken together, they were potentially unitary bodies able to express and articulate the felt needs of people in relation to everything from the provision of housing, food, water and roads, to the distribution of land, the creation of meaningful employment, matters of security, and particular problems experienced by women. In a nutshell, they were mass organizations open to anyone in a given community. The other common feature was that these organizations represented an attempt – explicitly or implicitly, consciously or unconsciously – to capture more power for the population at the grassroots level. Some were quite advanced and self-conscious in this orientation. Others were taking the first steps in that direction. Some had been successful, others not.

They were not groups of symbolic participation or of bureaucratized 'community development' schemes. They were mass membership, community-based organizations that attempted to be groups of real empowerment. Such organizations are of interest for several reasons: the most obvious have to do with the nature of social organization and social structure in the region. Most adults in most countries of the Third World are not proletarianized workers who of necessity spend the majority of their waking time away from their community. In North America or Europe a primary source of identification and potential power is the workplace. In Central America and the Caribbean (with the exception of Cuba) most of the adult population are peasants, artisans, small crafts producers, self-employed, those hustling for a living, women engaged in domestic labor for themselves or someone else, or unemployed altogether. Even for those employed in a traditional industrial or agro-industrial setting – the majority of adults in Cuba, for example – the existence of strong family and community networks remains a central facet of life.

This first point – that is, the reality of social organization in the region – suggests that we need to look at the indigenous experience and not to Eurocentric models of social change. We need to think no further than the traditional, European Marxist model, which stresses the centrality of the proletarianized working class and workers' councils in the process of change. One of the realities of the process of change in the region is the complex character of class coalitions and new forms of struggle. Of course I am not positing a new dogma: that is, that the community is the only locus of change. Rather, I am suggesting that the experience in the region suggests that the community is one of several critical loci of organization and change.

The second reason for our interest in community organizations is that it seems that it is at this level that ordinary people can best articulate a holistic concept of their needs. That is, they are no longer focused simply on working conditions or pay, but on basic needs, on children, on cultural and spiritual needs, as well as on work.

Why community level?

Furthermore, at this level, people are directly aware of community problems and unused resources – that is, they are able to match development plans with existing and potential resources. Self-interest intersects with self-reliance and self-management to produce possibilities for development. An approach to change that stresses community-based forms of popular participation potentially addresses problems of political patronage, the aloofness and rigidity of bureaucracy and the political directorate, and the limited resources of the state.

A third reason for our interest in organizations of community power is that the process of change in the region has created important experiments in community organization. In Nicaragua, for example, the precursors of the Sandinista Defense Committees were critical in the overthrow of the Somoza dictatorship. In Haiti, loosely organized neighborhood committees played a key role in the mobilizations that forced Duvalier to flee the country and led a process towards democratization. In all the countries we studied, there were attempts to develop new forms of political and social power at the community level.

A fourth reason has to do with the project of deepening democracy – in particular, the relationship of new forms of organization and decision-making (such as that at the community level) to forms of representative democracy. There is, of course, debate in the region, as elsewhere, as to the importance of traditional forms of electoral democracy. My own thought is that the right to form political parties and to vote in representative elections has been an acquisition won by working people, women, and oppressed groups in many countries of the world. Although the electoral arena is subject to manipulation and is activated only once every few years, and although parties as now conceived reproduce the hierarchical, competitive, and authoritarian structures of patriarchal and class societies, the system does create space for dissent, for organizing and for the expression of various group interests.

At that same time it is important to recognize the great weaknesses in all systems of representative democracy – hence the need for new forms of democratic expression to complement representative institutions. New forms have the potential to devolve decision-making in a society and, to whatever extent possible, put the means and responsibilities of decision-making into the hands of the population, especially where they live and work. Particularly in the context of many Third World societies, the community seems an ideal location for new means of democratic decision-making.

This, then, is the theoretical framework that informed this multi-country research project. Some aspects of this framework informed the project from the start, while most emerged during the course of the research.

The Research Projects

Let me now introduce the project as a whole and provide an introduction and summary of the individual country studies and the various theme studies.

The history of the research project

From the start, our research project was an effort in co-operative and collaborative research. It developed, rather slowly, through a series of separate consultative meetings starting back in 1986 between myself and researchers based in Jamaica, Nicaragua, Guyana, Costa Rica, Guatemala, and later with others from Cuba, Haiti, El Salvador, Dominican Republic and Grenada. The project was organized by the Centre for Research on Latin America and the Caribbean (CERLAC), York University, Toronto, where I was Deputy Director from 1987 until 1990.[8]

In the end there were six country studies – Cuba, Costa Rica, Dominican Republic, Haiti, Jamaica, and Nicaragua. All research was conducted by colleagues and research centers based in these countries.[9] In addition, there were a number of thematic and other country studies published in the form of working papers. Several of these appear in this volume.[10] Partly as a result of local control of the research projects and partly as a result of the great diversity of local situations and participatory experiments, the objects of research varied significantly from country to country. Although we had thought differently at first, in the end this was not a study where strict comparisons or a common research methodology would be possible. Rather they are complementary studies, with some common aspects of research methodology in harmony but not lockstepped.

Research issues

The central research issue we articulated from the beginning was the role and potential of organizations of community power to be effective participatory, decision-making, and administrative structures capable of responding to the problems of a community and of playing a role in the process of empowerment, development, and transformation. Through the process of consultation, we came to include as possible components in this definition their role and potential:

- as guarantors of meaningful participation at the community level and in relation to national politics and economic decision-making;
- in economic development and harnessing untapped economic and human resources (including youth and the unemployed);

- in challenging traditional sex roles and other forms of discrimination and oppression;
- in the development of a new social consciousness;
- in the provision of social services (including education, health care, housing, child care, and public works);
- in reducing sectarian political tensions;
- and, in some cases, in the provision of community self-defense.

A more general research issue was the relation of institutions of community control and development to the larger political and socio-economic environment. The importance of central state support for these projects was to be assessed, as was the importance of integrating social, economic and political goals for the work of community bodies.

We expected we would have to assess the usefulness of the terms and categories that had been used in the literature in the field. These terms included co-operation, co-determination, self-determination, devolution, deconcentration, decentralization, self-help, and community development.

We set out to examine the factors which could retard or reduce the effectiveness of decentralized community-based institutions. These included lack of clear guidelines or boundaries; inadequate linkages with central agencies; a clash between the framework of community-based development and the overall developmental model of the country; the inability of the state to balance demands for the devolution of political power with national processes of decision-making; conflicts with those who wield political or bureaucratic control at the state level; weak local management resources; the existence of forms of political, class, ethnic and sexual polarization that threaten community unity or that marginalize the role of certain groups; and the creation of institutions that are inappropriate to the specific social, cultural, economic, and political environment. An understanding of this overall environment within which changes were attempted was seen as a critical variable.[11]

Part One: The Country Studies

Costa Rica: the struggle for housing

The Costa Rican struggle for housing was a community-based effort that began in the late 1970s and lasted through the 1980s. Various 'fronts for housing' were formed, each having different political ties and different relations with the government. The local housing committees that they sparked, however, maintained their autonomy and adopted a variety of forms of organization and struggle. The first half of the 1980s was a period of land invasions and road blockades. This struggle paid off in

1986 when newly elected president Oscar Arias signed an agreement with the housing fronts to provide more housing. The housing committees underwent a transformation, from groups mobilizing people in struggle to members of new communities actually building housing and leading communities in close collaboration with the state.

The project of the Centro de Estudios Para la Acción Social (CEPAS) was led by Silvia Lara with the collaboration of Eugenia Molina. Unlike the other centers in this network, CEPAS had carried out studies of the housing organizations in the mid-1980s, but had not conducted any community-based research. The focus of this research project was in-depth and protracted field research in four communities, representing a range of experiences and socio-economic conditions.

Among the conclusions reached by our researchers were the following. As opposed to the dominant analysis among Costa Rican researchers (and the initial assumption of this project), these organizations had limited potential for developing popular democracy and participation. The motivation for involvement by the population in the committee was simply to find housing. Collective action was a means to this end, but, once achieved, seldom seemed necessary any longer. Victory led to the demobilization of the participants, particularly since work in the committees represented a third work shift (in addition to the normal work day and household labor). Participation in mobilization and then construction of housing was often a real burden, occupying all of a family's free time for as long as six years.

Sometimes the more authoritarian groups were the most effective, especially in a context where patron–client relations with the state often brought rewards. The main context for democracy in these groups was in the election and control of leaders – something parallel to the existence of national structures of representative democracy. By and large, they were not particularly democratic in their internal organization; levels of participation depended on the phase of struggle and organization; participation in meetings was often quite passive. Nevertheless, there existed a higher degree of rank-and-file control over the community leadership than at any other level of Costa Rican society; community organizations had little bureaucracy and could respond spontaneously to changing situations.

Whatever the limitations of this effort, the committee was extremely successful in meeting its objectives, new communities were created, and there was a tangible experience in the value of collective struggle.

Cuba: organizing locally for 'people's power'

Commencing in 1976, Cuba launched a municipal government structure, the Local Organs of People's Power, *Poder Popular*, based on direct elections to Municipal Assemblies. A unique feature of this structure was that Assembly members were not representatives, but rather delegates who were required to report back regularly to district meetings and who were subject to recall. The electoral process itself involved a high level of community participation, including in the processes of nomination and selection. The municipal assemblies controlled a wide range of social services and local economic activities, especially in the service and construction fields.

The project of the Centro de Estudios Sobre América, a non-governmental center in Havana, was headed by Haroldo Dilla and included the participation of Gerardo González plus several research assistants. It was the first time that any systematic public research had been done not only on local government but on any level of Cuban government. After looking at twelve possibilities, the researchers selected four communities, representing a spread of geographic, population, and socio-economic conditions. Within each, interviews and observation were carried out both with municipal leaders and in five to seven electoral districts, again chosen to reflect different socio-economic characteristics and leadership types. Their ambitious project studied the nomination and election process; the decision-making and accountability process in neighborhood assemblies, neighborhood committees and organizations; and the functioning of local government structures, including the municipal assembly and bureaucracy.

Given the broad mandate of the research project, conclusions were similarly wide-ranging. To summarize only a few: a climate of freedom and lack of interference typifies the electoral process; the high percentage of representatives who are members of the Communist Party seems to result from a range of factors, particularly the overall credibility of these individuals in the community, and not from party manipulation or control; ongoing accountability meetings draw large participation – 50–60 per cent of the community – but have yet to go beyond individual accountability and the expression of demands to actual community control and empowerment; a number of structural and ideological factors produce a disproportionately low percentage of women and young delegates; much power resides with local bureaucracies and the executive committees of the assemblies. All in all, our colleagues concluded that the system represents a significant step towards increased democracy at the local level, with structured and active elements of popular participation, but it remains limited by paternalistic, verticalistic, and bureaucratic tendencies.

Dominican Republic: neighborhood councils and popular movements

From the 1970s through the 1980s, a number of different popular movements in the Dominican Republic coalesced, many of which sought to have a political base within communities of the urban poor. The Comité para la Defensa de los Derechos Barriales. the Comités de Lucha Popular. the Consejo de Unidad Popular, the Frente Amplio de Lucha Popular, and the Colectivo de Organizaciones Populares all had a strongly ideological political character. They were often allied with particular political parties of the left or had their own quasi-party character. For most of them, their influence focused on one or two *barrios*. Distinct from these were *juntas de vecinos*, neighborhood organizations, which started in the late 1970s as state-supported groups but which often developed an autonomous and very effective character.

The project of the Equipo de Investigación Social (EQUIS) of the Instituto Tecnológico de Santo Domingo was headed by Cesar Pérez and involved various other researchers and assistants at different times. Its primary foci were: to produce an inventory of the activities of the popular movements over a 15-year period; to organize and take part in a series of workshops among leaders of the various organizations as a sort of balance-sheet exercise; and to carry out an in-depth study of a neighborhood committee in one community.

Their study of the popular movements concluded that they were limited by their own ideological political character and ties with political parties and, particularly, by the fact that they were essentially outside organizations that sought to build a base within communities. Even where they had this sort of base, they didn't function as community organizations *per se*, and as a result had suffered a drop in support in recent years. Their problems were compounded by a tendency to focus on their national political agenda – particularly on issues relating to the cost of living and the strategy of national general strikes – rather than the type of community issues that had the strongest resonance in the *barrios*.

Some of the neighborhood councils, on the other hand, broke from the political agenda of the state and the governing party, and evolved as functioning and effective neighborhood organizations. In the community of Máximo Gómez, for example, a local group effectively mobilized the community and made real gains in terms of bringing in a water supply, garbage collection, and road pavement through the use of tactics of confrontation – including pickets of government offices and road blockades – as well as through dialogue and negotiation with officials from the government and state institutions. Although youth were active in community mobilizations and community assemblies, the leadership tended to be made up of adults over 30. There was a high participation by women in both leadership and activities. The effectiveness of this group lay in its roots within the community and its ability to respond to community needs; its weakness was the lack of a wider perspective and strategy for the transformation of Dominican society.

Haiti: popular organizations and the first steps to democracy

Although the roots of Haiti's popular organizations (POs) go back to the 1974–80 period, with the beginning of a human-rights-oriented organization of journalists, it was the blossoming of Christian Base Communities and Radio Soleil (in 1982) that was the immediate antecedent to the POs. In the countryside and in the cities, there was a series of mobilizations that culminated in the flight of Baby Doc Duvalier on February 7, 1986. Popular Organizations quickly sprang up in cities, larger towns, and the countryside, with the goals of routing *macoutes* and *duvalierists*, of cleaning and beautifying neighborhoods, and of working to provide public services, health care, and education.

The project of the Centre de Recherches Sociales et de Diffusion Populaire (CRESDIP) was led by Luc Smarth, with the support of Rony Smarth and the assistance of other researchers and research assistants. In the context of a country without previous research institutions (CRESDIP was one of a handful of centers formed after 1986), CRESDIP carried out germinal research into the POs, charting, as they were developing, the scope and nature of these organizations. Given the sometimes dangerous and chaotic conditions in the country, and the near-total absence of local research projects involving large-scale interviews or surveys, the project (and consequently the chapter on Haiti in this book) has a pathbreaking, more descriptive character than the others.

The organizations themselves emerged as a direct challenge to two centuries of corrupt leadership. Their leaders and members were critical of the political parties of all stripes and of the professionalization of politics. They had a very strong base in the communities and their home was in the streets. They talked of a new way of doing politics. Some were widely based in a community; others focused particularly on women, students, artists, vendors, or the unemployed. Most were led by committees and had assemblies every couple of weeks in their communities. Their capacity to mobilize, and their strong defensive role, were seen in their prevention of the coup on January 7, 1991. They also played an important community role, organizing cultural and educational events.

They were plagued by problems. They often had a somewhat ephemeral character, distrusting leaders and organization. Some of the leaders were sectarian towards other groups or progressive political leaders. Only three organizations gained a national dimension and all were debilitated by lack of financial resources. Their spontaneous approach to politics and distrust of institutionalization had the negative effect of leaving them without a political strategy and organized resources. This weakness was seen in their inability to withstand the onslaught of the army in the successful coup of September 1991. Nevertheless, the POs represented an important step in the development of a new, democratic political culture in Haiti.

Chile: women and local-level participation

Traditional studies of popular participation are often gender-blind. This problem is particularly glaring in cases where the overwhelming majority of members of participatory organizations are women. In such cases it is obvious that the almost exclusive participation of one sex or the other is not a major factor in the constitution, activities, and impact of such a group.

Veronica's Schild's chapter draws on her research into neighborhood organizations in the *poblaciones*, the poor neighborhoods in Chile. She sees these organizations as spaces where women are contesting existing relations of class and gender power; they are an opportunity for participation and political learning, as women begin to question the routines and norms that govern their everyday lives. At the same time, relations between members and their largely middle-class women animators include conflict based on the class-based realities of their lives and the way that their class differences shape their gender.

Jamaica: community councils, self-mobilization, and the state

This study is not included in this volume, but let me mention its general contours. Although Jamaica's community councils had antecedents in the late 1930s, they came into prominence during the Michael Manley years of the 1970s. They were seen as a means actively to involve the population in decision-making, to mobilize local resources, and to contribute to economic and social development. Although there were over 400 councils by the end of the 1970s, involving tens of thousands of members (at least on paper), they had never been studied.[12]

The project of the Institute of Social and Economic Studies at the University of the West Indies in Mona involved various researchers, including Maxine Henry-Wilson and Ian Boxhill. It set out to look at why the councils were formed, who formed them, how they were structured, the nature of citizen involvement, their relationship with other levels of government, and their impact. The researchers did an inventory of the councils — making the first accurate count of the councils and visiting communities across Jamaica to establish which ones actually functioned and which ones still existed at the time of the research. Initially, three councils were studied – one in a parish capital, two in rural villages; at a later stage, three communities were studied in greater depth.

Among the conclusions reached by the researchers were these: the councils suffered because of a top-down approach; too much was riding on the national government and on direction from the national leadership – there was inadequate self-mobilization. Many saw themselves as groups to press for government support for one project or another. At the same time, individuals working for the state bureaucracy who had responsibilities for the councils were not adequately trained as community animators; nor did they have the time or resources to engage in community-building exercises. Councils tended to function on a hierarchical basis, with many members investing time with the hope of future gain.

Participation was evenly divided between men and women, leadership was largely middle-class, and, by the time of the research, youth often felt alienated from the councils (although this was likely to have been different in the 1970s). Few councils had access to the economic resources (including land) that would allow them to contribute to economic development. National political polarization was a factor in undermining the councils. Nevertheless, where there were vibrant councils, there is usually a legacy, such as a community center or a basic school, which citizens proudly point to as their own accomplishment. Overall, they suffered from a lack of organic, developed relations to the process of regional and national decision-making and planning. In other words, they had very little power.

Nicaragua: local committees, defending the revolution, the government, or the state?

Again, while this study isn't represented as a chapter in this volume, let me briefly summarize the research project. The Sandinista Defense Committees (CDS) emerged during the insurrection of 1979 and were seen as an important means to involve people at the neighborhood level in the process of self-government and mobilization. They were mainly urban, and their tasks were to defend the revolution, including through community patrols, and to develop local community projects.

The research project of the Instituto de Investigaciones Económicas y Sociales (INIES) was led by Luis Mora Castillo, whose researchers included Ixy Jaime Martínez, who played a central role in the project during its early stages. INIES sought to develop a diachronic analysis of the evolution of the CDSs and an analytical account of their demise.

Their work included a scrutiny of CDS documents and the national press, interviews with national and local CDS leaders, research workshops, a national survey, and field research in two communities (Monimbó, where the precursors of the CDSs emerged during the revolution, and *barrio* Ariel Darce in Managua).

In the first years of the revolution the CDSs received considerable local support. Weekly meetings drew large turnouts, particularly from women, and the CDSs played an important role in the literacy programme, food distribution, and health promotion, including an ambitious vaccination programme.

Control and direction of the CDSs came from the national leadership of the Sandinistas. Thus, these local organizations were not able to express autonomous and local needs, but became the expression of the national political agenda. During the period of revolutionary ascent (1979–81) the CDSs enjoyed considerable support, but as fatigue, economic crisis, and destabilization set in, the CDSs were hampered by their static, partisan link to the FSLN and, after 1985, quickly lost their social base. They were seen as appendages of the party and the state, and not the means for local social power. Attempts to transform the CDSs in 1989 came too late to have a significant impact, paradoxically at the same time that the institutionalization of representative democracy opened up new possibilities for the expression of community interests.

Part Two: The Theme Studies

Men, women and differential participation

Participation does not exist in the abstract. Participation is defined through specific institutions, processes, and ideological and cultural factors. It is defined through the individuals and groups of individuals involved (or not involved) in a participatory process. Within any participatory structure, overall forms of social inequality and oppression are usually reflected and maintained. This is what I call differential participation. With a quest for participatory mechanisms of empowerment comes the necessity of overcoming the structured inequalities in social power.

My study of differential participation has two aspects. The first locates the source of the problem in structures of inequality, the second in the hegemonic definitions of power that exist within patriarchal society. It looks at solutions to the first within the framework of participatory democratic or critical liberal democratic theory, while suggesting that solutions to the second require a redefinition of power and the development of radically different structures of social power. It concludes by looking at how not only women but also men are negatively affected by the very structures in which they have differential power and privilege.

Questions of decentralization

Because it can have so many different goals, decentralization of the state is not a unitary concept. Decentralization is usually seen as a means for the empowerment of ordinary citizens, their organizations and communities. In this sense, decentralization becomes an indispensable part of a popular alternative that can confront neo-liberal privatization on the one hand and the omnipotence of the central state (as was common in the Soviet bloc) on the other.

At the same time the history of decentralization also includes examples where the weakening of the central state left it more vulnerable to outside control or where some measures of decentralization were actually a mechanism for the consolidation of authoritarian power.

Haroldo Dilla's chapter examines a range of meanings and problems associated with decentralization, especially in relation to the devolution of power to the local level and the construction of popular alternatives.

Competing theoretical paradigms: new social movements and resource mobilization

In recent years, the study of social movements – a term which might include at least some experiments with organizations of community power and grassroots democracy – has been dominated by two distinct theoretical paradigms. One, the *new social movement* approach, was developed in Europe; the second, *resource mobilization* theory, emerged in North America. Although both seek to understand a range of contemporary social movements, they are usually seen as competing approaches.

Eduardo Canel suggests that the differences in theory are largely accounted for by the fact that they occupy two different, but complementary, levels of analysis. His chapter analyzes the two approaches, looks at what makes them distinct from traditional social theories, examines their differences, and then suggests the possibility of integrating the two. Although covering a broader sweep than the issue of community-based forms of popular power, the issues raised are important for enhancing our understanding of grassroots organizing and popular democracy.

Conclusions

With such a diversity of organizational types and social situations examined in this book, it is difficult to reach simple and uniform conclusions.

In a sense, the theoretical assumptions enunciated at the beginning of this chapter form some of the conclusions of the book as a whole. Community-based forms of popular participation cannot represent the sole locus of social organization for change; they are constrained by limited availability of resources, by the impact of outside political and economic forces, and by the very cultural, economic, social, and political factors that have required community action in the first place.

On the other hand, while not being a panacea, they represent an important locus of organization and mobilization: one that is capable of being a vehicle of empowerment, education, and outreach; one that can (but does not necessarily) challenge hierarchy and oppression among the oppressed. In short, they can be a successful vehicle for change and part of the goal of a qualitatively more democratic society.

Research on such organizations is still in its infancy. One or two of the studies presented in this book represent the beginning of this process, as they attempt, for the first time, to record a range of organizations and activities. Others were able to take the second step, to look at the internal dynamics of these organizations and to study in greater detail the role of community members and their relation to the larger political realm. Differential participation, the role of leaders, relations between community organizations and the state, changes measured over time in self-consciousness and self-esteem of participants, and implicit or explicit organizational norms are topics that would benefit from future in-depth studies.

Together, these chapters affirm the need to develop broader, more inclusive theoretical paradigms for understanding and advancing community-based forms of popular power. At the same time, the analysis presented here recognizes the specificity of any project of democracy-building and local empowerment: such processes are subject to cultural and historical conditions, and are part of the changing internal life of a community and of national political-economic life. There is no single democratic experience or form which is a blueprint for future action at the community level; indeed, grassroots democracy itself isn't one thing. While these democratic experiments share a desire for enhanced participation and social justice, the means to obtain these goals will flourish – or wither – in ever-novel forms. Our hope is that this book will contribute to both understanding and encouraging such a process.

Notes

1. The Chilean study was not formally part of our research network; it was done, along with the theoretical chapters, as a related theme study. Of the six country studies that I refer to occasionally, two – those on Jamaica and Nicaragua – do not appear in this book.

2. Generous funding for the project was provided by the International Development Research Centre in Ottawa and the Ford Foundation in New York. The IDRC provided approximately three-quarters of the total costs from project development through the follow-up stage. The Social Sciences and Humanities Research Council in Ottawa provided some funding for one project workshop and supported my own research through its Canada Research Fellowship program.

3. Andrew Pearse and Matthias Stiefel, *Inquiry into Participation – A Research Approach*, (Popular Participation Program, the United Nations Research Institute for Social Development, 1979), p. 5.

4. Kirsten Westergaard, *People's Participation, Local Government and Rural Development*, CDR Research Report No. 8 (Copenhagen: Centre for Development Research, 1986), p. 25.

5. World Employment Programme of the ILO, *Popular Participation in Decision-making and the Basic Needs Approach in Development: Methods, Issues and Experiences* (1978), p. 8.

6. C.Y. Thomas, personal communication.

7. See Chapter 7.

8. The first workshop, held in Kingston, Jamaica, in November 1987, was hosted by the Institute of Social and Economic Research (ISER), University of the West Indies, and was co-sponsored by CERLAC and the Managua-based research network, Coordinadora Regional de Investigaciones Económicas y Sociales (CRIES). Funding was provided by the International Development Research Centre (IDRC) in Ottawa.

The IDRC funded the studies in Costa Rica, Cuba, Jamaica, and Nicaragua, and the Ford Foundation funded those in Haiti and the Dominican Republic. Both Ford and the IDRC supported project co-ordination and communication.

A second workshop was held in Havana in the fall of 1989, funded by the IDRC. A final workshop was held in Toronto in June 1991 with funding from IDRC, Ford, and the Social Sciences and Humanities Research Council.

9. CERLAC's role was to act as a co-ordinator, facilitator, and catalyst for the project, but not to control the actual research in any country. One goal of the project was to facilitate research co-operation within the two regions, between Central America and the Caribbean, and between Canada and the regions. At the same time, by having funding relations directly between the foundations and the national research centers, we sought to prevent the type of Northern domination of research processes that have typified many North–South academic relationships.

10. In addition to those in this book, some of the theme studies, published as CERLAC Working Papers, were: Andrew Goodman, 'Organizational Characteristics, Organizational Democracy, and Social Change' (May 1991); Laura MacDonald, 'Community Development and Participation: A Review of Some Relevant Literature' (November 1988); Steve Patten, 'The Transformation of Liberal Capitalist Society and the Role of New Social Movements' (February 1991).

I would particularly like to mention the working paper by Hugh Dow and Jonathan Barker, 'Political Participation and Development – Africa and Latin America: A Bibliography on Latin America and Africa' (September 1992), which has since been published and can be ordered from the Centre for Urban and Community Studies, University of Toronto, 455 Spadina Ave., Toronto, Canada

M5S 2G8 for Canadian $13 or US $11.

11. In addition to these points and the obvious goal of understanding a number of diverse experiences, we defined three research goals: (1) to disseminate widely the findings nationally and internationally with the goal of achieving a policy impact; (2) to contribute to the development of research capacity in the region with respect to studies of popular participation and forms of democratic organization; (3) to contribute to research co-operation within Central America and the Caribbean, and secondarily between Canada and the region

12. For a discussion of the Jamaican community councils, see Michael Kaufman, *Jamaica Under Manley: Dilemmas of Socialism and Democracy* (London: Zed Books, 1985), chapter 8.

Part One

Country Studies

2

Participation and Popular Democracy in the Committees for the Struggle for Housing in Costa Rica

Silvia Lara and Eugenia Molina

In Costa Rica in the early 1980s, popular organization and the struggle for housing indicated growing social discontent, which culminated in a call for a profound transformation of Costa Rican society. Even though the housing problem was by no means new to the country, the systematic organization of parts of the population into Committees for the Struggle for Housing was a novel phenomenon, which started in the late 1970s. The shortage of adequate housing in Costa Rica was one aspect of a dramatic deterioration in living conditions experienced by broad sectors of the population. The aggravation of unemployment, underemployment and low wages, coupled with excessive increases in rent, a deterioration of purchasing power, and the high costs of land and construction, all made it impossible for families to obtain adequate shelter. Aggravating the problem were inadequate state intervention and support payments to families with scarce resources.

The housing committees emerged as an innovative tool of grassroots organization and community-based struggle. These organizations emerged spontaneously and maintained simple, informal, non-bureaucratic forms of organization in which all family members participated regardless of experience. Members often came from the poorest sectors of the population and represented territorial rather than trade-union interests. It was not long before these organizations began to dominate the public scene with their activist methods involving protests, land invasions and the mobilization of grassroots communities.

This chapter summarizes our study of the limitations and potential of the housing committees as well as the role of democracy and participation in their development. The first section looks at their relation to existing institutional and policy frameworks, the state, and political parties. The second part analyzes their organizational practices with respect to democracy and participation. Finally, we look at the work of their leadership and its impact on the committees.[1]

We conclude that, for the housing committees, effectiveness in obtaining housing stands above any specific consideration for developing participatory and democratic practices. The specific ways of being effective are, of course, strongly determined by the conditions and opportunities offered by the social system and the political conjuncture. Even though the struggle has successfully focused on winning better living conditions for the poor, community members have, through these struggles, pressed the system for a greater and more extensive democracy.

Studying the Struggle for Housing

The housing committees played a pivotal role in popular organization and the articulation of popular demands in Costa Rica during the 1980s. Their emergence converged with ongoing debates about the changing nature of social movements in Latin America and elsewhere. These debates were motivated by the rise of a broad range of new actors – youth, women, settlers and indigenous people – who became protagonists in Latin American social struggles and collective protests during the 1980s. Some believed that these social movements already were, or would inevitably become, alternative social actors and political forces in the region.[2] The local character of the new movements was interpreted as an indicator of their participatory nature, grassroots origins, and democratic character. Consequently, it was assumed that these movements constituted the embryo of more democratic social practices at the local community level. Great emphasis was placed on their non-institutional nature as well as their autonomy from traditional political actors. With this analysis came a new conception of social change, in which traditional institutional politics was displaced by greater interest in values, cultural production and civil society. The terms of debate couldn't have been more different from older notions of the assault on state power, the vanguard, political parties, or the centrality of the working class and peasantry. The new social movements were quickly interpreted as being an essential ingredient of any strategy for change, since by their nature they opened new spaces, helped forge new identities and solidarities, and introduced innovative social and democratic relations, which were seen as gradually paving the way for the transformation of daily human relations, leading to a qualitatively more open and democratic society for all.

Although many theorists would join Norberto Bobbio in assuming that direct democracy is 'materially impossible ... especially given the growing complexity of modern industrial societies',[3] it is possible that the neighborhood and the local community – the communities built by the Committees for the Struggle for Housing – offer a place where extensive and intensive democratic organization is possible. They might be places where face-to-face interaction that is both humane and manageable is possible thanks to the straightforwardness of local customs and a common experience of shared poverty.

To analyze these and related issues, this study focused on different levels and forms of participation, leadership, division of labor and decision-making, and on how these forms either weakened or enhanced popular democracy and participation in communities. Special attention was paid to the efforts and roles of leaders and their influence over their communities' organizational practices and modes of protest. We looked at length at relations between the housing committees and external agents, such as political parties, the state and the housing fronts. Four communities were selected for inclusion in the study.[4]

La Guarari

The origins of this community, named in honor of an Indian chief, go back to 1982 when a group of 300 families formed a united front and were soon joined by an equal number in their fight for adequate housing. They obtained land in 1985 and in the next six years built streets, sidewalks, sewers, street lighting, and 295 houses. Three hundred families still live in shacks. The community is directed by the COPAN (Coordinadora Patriótica Nacional) housing front.

Carmen Lyra

Named after a renowned Costa Rican storyteller of the 1930s and 1940s (a Communist Party member and defender of the poor), the community was initially organized by only 10 families, although today it comprises 564 families. It acquired land at the end of 1987, and between 1988 and 1990 built the 564 houses and the surrounding infrastructure. During their struggle, community members maintained close ties with ANAVI (Asociación Nacional de Vivienda), a housing front associated with the Communist-led Vanguardia Popular.

Oscar Felipe

Named after the son of Costa Rica's ex-President, Oscar Arias Sanchez, its roots go back to 1986, when a group of 14 families invaded a piece of state-owned property. A year-and-a-half later, half of the 200 families living on this land were transferred by the government to an empty lot, which they named 'Oscar Felipe'. Before long, this community consisted of 321 families. Between 1988 and 1990 the community worked industriously to construct the infrastructure and the houses which compose the settlement. They did not maintain regular links with any housing front, but instead established direct contact with state officials and the social democratic party, Partido de Liberación Nacional, in power between 1982 and 1990.

El Nazareno

Since the land invasion that led to the creation of this community occurred during Holy Week, the community is named after one of the principal biblical characters in Easter festivities. The land invasion was carried out by a group of 100 families in March 1986. Between April 1987 and mid-1990, the community devoted itself to the construction of adequate housing. During an earlier phase, the organization of the community was linked to the FCV (Frente Costarricense de la Vivienda), one of the housing fronts, but relations were severed soon thereafter.

Institutional Politics: Relations with the State and Political Parties

Part of the framework that led to the formation of the housing movement was the initial belief that the demand for housing should not be channeled through political parties and/or more permanent and established community organizations such as the ADCs (Community Development Associations). Many settlers associated political parties with corruption, opportunism and personal interests, while the ADCs were regarded as organizations deeply penetrated by partisan interests, and which had shown little responsiveness to community needs. Nevertheless, given the enthusiasm, explosiveness and reach of the organization and struggle for housing, political parties could not afford to be left at the margins. The social effervescence of this new movement offered fertile ground for political parties to widen their social base, even if it meant they would have to intervene surreptitiously through the so-called 'housing fronts', which were to play a key role in the subsequent development of the housing movement.

In November 1980, the small Trotskyist OST (Partido de Organización Socialista de los Trabajadores) created a coalition called the National Patriotic Co-ordination (COPAN – Coordinadora Patriótica Nacional). The fundamental purpose of COPAN was to form an organization composed of a politicized mass membership, which would be directed in a co-ordinated manner and play a decisive role in a broader strategy of societal transformation.[5] In June 1981, only seven months after COPAN's emergence onto the scene, the Democratic Front for Housing (FDV – Frente Democrático de la Vivienda) was created. The FDV was closely linked to the social democratic PLN (Partido de Liberación Nacional), one of the two major parties in the country. The objective of its leaders was to prevent growing popular discontent over the shortage of adequate housing being channeled through an organization (such as COPAN) whose ultimate goal was a complete transformation of Costa Rican society. Therefore the primary objective of the FDV was to maintain a certain degree of stability in Costa Rica's political system, by ensuring that solutions were found within the existing political framework. (In 1983 many of the FDV's top leaders resigned as a result of partisan differences. In 1984, these dissenters formed the Costa Rican Front for Housing, the FCV, which remained linked to the PLN but to another grouping as well.)

Although its political and consciousness-raising activities had until then focused mainly on peasant and labor organizations, the small communist Vanguardia Popular tried to create its own housing front as a way of extending its efforts to include settlers and local communities. The initiative nevertheless failed, due to the growing fragmentation suffered by the party during those years. Such was the case at least until 1986, when one of the party's factions created the National Association for Housing (ANAVI – Asociacion Nacional para la Vivienda). Among ANAVI's principal objectives was the continuity of popular organization around the issue of housing, making the struggle for housing a political and educational experience for those involved, and developing ways of working with grassroots organizations which wouldn't reproduce the clientelistic relations that characterized other housing fronts. These fronts came to local communities and appeared before the housing committees without revealing their partisan links, pretending to be there as a result of their leaders' own personal interests.

Undeniably, the housing committees were the principal protagonists in the organization and struggle for housing, with FDV and COPAN playing particularly important roles. They not only became important meeting places and forums for the co-ordination of the housing struggle, but in the process also reached beyond the confines of local activity and the organizational atomization so commonly regarded as one of the principal limitations of trade unions, peasant or other communal organizations. A great mass of people organized under these umbrellas. Their numbers and the belligerence of their fight turned the movement into a powerful political force, capable of exerting tremendous pressure on the state to respond to the housing needs of impoverished sectors of the population. Nevertheless, it is important to bear in mind that a committee linked to one of these fronts did not necessarily adhere to their party line or political project. One reason, of course, was that the link to the parties was unknown to the majority of the committees. The top leaders of the fronts simply served as intermediaries between the state and the committees in negotiations.

The housing fronts were not the only ones to intervene. The land invasions also attracted the attention of high-level party leaders, public officials in search of popular support, non-governmental organizations, charities, religious sects and academics. The organization and struggle for housing constituted a truly new phenomenon and novel working laboratory, as did the communities born out of the land invasions.

In addition to maintaining close (albeit sometimes hidden) ties with established political parties through the housing fronts and partisan leaders, the housing committees believed that the solution to their housing problems also depended on developing a close working relationship with the state itself. Although at first (between 1980 and 1986) the state was incapable of meeting the housing demands of thousands of organized families, it coped by tolerating the land invasions that were taking place. In fact, the 1982–86 PLN government ceded vast expanses of state property so that families which could not be allocated elsewhere in the short term could settle and build shacks, without the state having to resort to dislodging them. In 1986, however, state housing policies and the organization and struggle for housing took a dramatic turn as the Oscar Arias government (1986–90) came to power. During his electoral campaign, Arias had promised to construct 80,000 houses during his four-year administration, a promise which, along with his theme of peace, was a major reason for his electoral triumph.

Following the electoral victory, three factors shaped the development of the housing movement. The first was a formal agreement between the new government and the housing fronts (COPAN, FDV and FCV) a few days before the official transfer of power. In this agreement, the fronts agreed to oppose further land invasions as well as to obtain their committees' collaboration with state institutions. This would come in return for the development of a massive housing construction plan for the benefit of their members. The agreement meant the end of the FDV, whose leaders felt that their objectives had been fulfilled, and a complete transformation of COPAN from an organization of political struggle for popular demands into a kind of private construction enterprise which collaborated directly with government in the development of public housing projects.

A second factor was the change in housing policy and forms of institutional organization, which opened the door to construction projects aimed at satisfying the housing needs of low-income Costa Ricans and, at least to some extent, modified the profitability criteria and expected rates of return on investments that had caused a housing deficit among the poor in the first place. One component of institutional change was the creation of the Special Housing Commission (CEV – Comisión Especial de Vivienda). As part of its institutional policy, the CEV took government officials away from their desk-bound routines and assigned them daily duties in the community. It was not long before these officials began to play an active leadership role and in some cases even replaced the local directorship in the housing committees.

The third determining factor was the adaptation and transformation of the housing committees from pressure organizations and sources of conflict into state-collaborating organizations in the construction of public housing.

When the housing committees turned to political parties and the state in search of effectiveness, angry local disputes occurred between persons guided by partisan interests and those primarily guided by the interests of the community. Recognizing such problems, the housing committees set out to maintain organizational independence from both political parties and governmental institutions. But at the same time as they maintained their organizational independence, they established close ties with political parties, officials, and governmental institutions. A great part of their success in obtaining housing was traceable to these ties, proving that engagement in institutional/traditional politics continued to be a basic strategy and a fundamental area of work in the struggle to improve living conditions.

Certainly state intervention as well as that of political parties through the housing fronts was oriented by its own interests and purposes. Even so, it is worth noting that the relations which were established were by no means unidirectional. The housing committees developed a great sense of creativity and practicability as they learned to take advantage of the relationships they formed. They learned to change their political banner depending on who visited them and to negotiate with whomever had more to offer. On the other side of the coin, some of these committees were fighting precisely for the institutionalization of their demands and needs and their integration into the status quo. In this sense, it is not accurate simply to speak of a strategy aimed at controlling them. Tapping their ingenuity and pragmatism, these organizations searched for relations that would permit them to meet their immediate interests while retaining their own decision-making power.

Retaining their decision-making power, however, was not always easy. The government of Oscar Arias imposed a series of conditions under which the committees were expected to operate. By promising to address their demands but at the same time threatening not to help those groups that did not accept their conditions, the government succeeded in prohibiting public protests and land invasions. Given their urgent need for housing and the long, previously fruitless struggle of the families involved, many of the housing committees had no choice but to accept the requirements, ways of operating and types of solutions offered to them by the state, thereby changing from protest organizations into supporters of state action.

This give and take between the community organizations, the housing fronts and the state – or, in particular, the capacity of the communities to retain their decision-making power – wasn't easy. Threatened and afraid to lose their support, the communities sometimes had to accept decisions that came from the outside. Nevertheless, the relationship of the three was relatively democratic. Following a similar line of thinking, Norberto Bobbio claims that,

> Insofar as we can speak of a democratization process today, it is possible to say that this process does not consist so much ... in a transition from representative democracy to direct democracy, but rather in a transition from political democracy, in the strictest sense, towards social democracy; that is, in an extension of ascending power which, until recently, had almost exclusively occupied the space of the great political society ... towards the space of civil society and its diverse articulations, ranging from school to the work place.[6]

From Bobbio's perspective, it is possible to speak of a transition from the democratization of the state to the democratization of society as a whole.

Anatomy of a Community

When, in July 1983, ten families met in the small town of Turrialba to form a committee to obtain housing, they began a seven-year struggle. This story of the Carmen Lyra community is an example of the long struggle necessary when there are scarce resources. It has much in common with other stories: land invasions, evictions, public protests, highs and lows in popular participation, prolonged and frustrating negotiations with the state, as well as intense and exhausting efforts by families to construct their own homes. Notwithstanding these common features, the struggle waged by the Carmen Lyra community proved to be particularly harsh and difficult. The presence of a community leader who was also a left-wing activist; the absence of contacts with influential state institutions, government officials and the major political parties; together with the belligerence and confrontationalism that characterized this community's relationship with the state – these factors put the Carmen Lyra Housing Committee's needs at the very bottom of the government's list of priorities. But in the end even they were successful.

The original ten families began to hold meetings in the open air, in the park across from the church, and the group grew steadily. A board of directors was created and assigned the task of overseeing all petitions made to governmental institutions as well as publicizing the composition and demands of the housing committee. These tasks were undertaken mainly by a man who organized and led the group, a well-known leader of the communist Vanguardia Popular. In the group's weekly meetings, he would inform members of any progress made during the previous week.

The number of families participating in each meeting varied dramatically – some meetings would attract more than 100 families, while at others only 20 would turn up. The levels of participation depended largely on how the families perceived the administrative and institutional gains made by the committee. Since the majority of families did not know one another and committee meetings provided the only venue for interaction, the four or five organizers constituted the only source of permanence for the organization at this time.

In 1986, after three years of meeting in the park, a change occurred in the working dynamics of the committee. President Oscar Arias's electoral promise to build 80,000 houses during his administration caused the number of participating families to swell. By the end of that year, close to 600 families took part in the meetings. By March of the following year, after a year of unsuccessful negotiations with the government – and fearing they would be excluded from the government's plans to construct the new homes – the committee decided to change its form of struggle and invade a parcel of unused government land. Committee leaders we interviewed proudly described the transition:

> We left at three in the afternoon and arrived at three-thirty, ready for the march. But instead of six hundred families, at this point we were as many as a thousand. As a result, the march was incredible. Turrialba had never seen anything like it. People walked with pieces of cardboard, sheets of metal and megaphones in hand; men and women swung knives in the air. As the public saw us go by, everyone applauded.

The group arrived at the plot of land outside of town, climbed over the hill, quickly cleared the debris, and started putting together their shacks with cartons and pieces of metal. It wasn't long before the police threatened to evict them. To resist, they seized the municipal government building and took the alderman hostage. This, however, did not stop them from being evicted. One of the leaders recalls the eviction:

> Over 500 troops arrived, armed with tear gas and M-16s. At one o'clock in the morning, we received news that the eviction was already planned and that the police feared we were armed. As a result, they were ready for a major shoot-out and had prepared for an insurrectional-type operation. When they actually arrived at four in the morning, our initial suspicions were confirmed: first they sent in troops wearing gas masks, who threw tear-gas bombs; these were immediately followed by an armed unit.

After they were evicted from this lot, they decided to take the city park, where they erected shacks using cartons and plastic. They quickly improvised a common kitchen. Once again, they were thrown out by the police and had no choice but to take refuge in the church across the road. An intervention by the communist congressman in the General Assembly enabled them to leave the church without being arrested as well as to rescue those who had been captured during the eviction. Fifteen days later, after the government had failed to meet their demands, they again took to the park. They were evicted by police yet again, and once more took refuge in the church. After two days, however, they were forced to leave the church – this time because the local priest refused to continue giving them refuge.

In August 1987, after waiting four months, the families had still not received a positive response from the government. And so the leaders decided it was time to exert more pressure, and called a meeting in the park. To the surprise of the organizers, this time only a few families showed up, a sign that the experience of the invasion, the seizure of the park, and the evictions had been too much for the families. In the process many had lost hope. In spite of this, they were still encouraged by the solidarity demonstrated towards the housing committee by the people of Turrialba and its social organizations. The leader of the committee sent a communiqué to the Minister of Housing and to President Arias, threatening to paralyze the town if the government failed to meet the committee's demands. The government eventually decided to negotiate, and, after a series of disagreements, agreed to purchase the plot of land and to initiate the design of a new community. Thanks to the success of these negotiations, the committee was once again able to secure broad participation by families in the town. In December, however, the government still hadn't purchased the land; in response, the committee decided to reoccupy the plot demarcated for their use. Finally, the government was forced to buy the land.

Between 1988 and 1990, the 564 families which now composed the core membership of the committee devoted themselves to the construction of their houses, while a private construction company was hired to build the infrastructure of streets, sidewalks, street lights, drainage and sewerage. Whole families spent their Saturdays and Sundays completing their houses; during the weekends the site resembled an ant-hill as over 400 workers labored from sunrise to sunset digging holes, mixing cement, and putting up walls. However, by its last year, participation in construction started to decrease and only a small group worked in an organized manner, with the rest devoting themselves mainly to their own houses.

The construction process took much longer than expected. Construction was often paralyzed by ongoing conflicts between the committee and government institutions over control of the project and decision-making, as well as by constant delays originating in the institutions which provided funds to purchase building materials. The families occupied their houses in October 1990.

The Struggle for Housing and the Articulation of a Democratic Norm

Within the struggle for housing, the nature and degree of participation varied widely, depending on specific circumstances – the political contacts of a particular community, the approach taken by the leadership, and particularly the distribution of work and tasks within the committee, which depended primarily on the stage of the struggle.

Generally, there were three distinct phases of struggle, although they did not necessarily occur in this order. The first entailed petitioning and negotiating with government institutions; the second involved the occupation of land – be it as a result of a land invasion or negotiation – and the formation of a community; and the third revolved around the construction of the houses and the surrounding infrastructure. While relations with state institutions are necessary during the last two phases, the first is a phase where dealing with the state is the only organizational task.

In the four communities studied, the phases of work were as follows:

Guarari Institutional dealings. Occupation of negotiated territory and establishment of community life. Construction of housing.

Carmen Lyra Institutional dealings. Failed invasion. Institutional dealings. Occupation of negotiated territory. Institutional dealings. Construction of housing. Transfer of families to new community.

Oscar Felipe Land invasion and establishment of community life. Institutional dealings. Occupation of negotiated territory and establishment of community life. Institutional dealings. Construction of housing.

El Nazareno   Land invasion and establishment of community life. Institutional dealings. Construction of housing.

During each of these phases, the tasks undertaken and the levels and forms of participation and organizing work differed.

When each group went through its phase of institutional dealing and negotiations, its energies were almost exclusively devoted to visiting officials in the appropriate public institutions, focusing particularly on the government's response to the community petition. The immediate objective was to convince them to speed up the required paperwork and to ensure that the community was working towards meeting any prerequisites. During this phase, the community needed to establish political contacts with high-level government officials in order to press effectively for their demands at a later date.

To conduct these institutional dealings, it was important to have a person who was familiar with public institutions, their institutional dynamics, and functionaries, as well as having contacts who could facilitate access to those who administered the paper trail. It was best if such a person was politically connected or at least knew how to reach those politicians in a position to intervene on behalf of the organization. Because these were communities where people had little or no previous organizing experience, it was often difficult to find a person with these attributes. Usually the group's leader was backed by one or two assistants who gradually developed the required leadership skills through on-the-job learning. In the meantime, the other members of the organization simply waited to see what the leader accomplished.

At this time, participation was limited to attending the meetings called by the leader to report on the progress of the organization's petitions, as well as to maintain a sense of unity and permanence. At these meetings, participation was passive and principally limited to listening to the leader's report. If they lasted too long, attendance was lower at future meetings. To address the problem of declining attendance, the leader of the Oscar Felipe community organized raffles in which domestic appliances could be won by attenders; this was so effective that it became impossible to fit everyone into the building where meetings were normally held.

In other cases, meetings were more like a circus, with two hundred or more people gathered, most standing up in the open air with children of all ages running around and playing through the crowds. To some extent, the informal nature of these meetings created a less rigid and more spontaneous atmosphere, which was conducive to broad participation. At the same time, the dispersed and sometimes unfocused crowd made it difficult for people to concentrate on what was being said. Furthermore, the fear of speaking up in such a large gathering tended to inhibit active participation. Invariably, participants later referred to these meetings as 'long and boring,' which they attended only because they were formally required to do so. For them, participation made more sense when they knew beforehand what topics would be discussed and what decisions made, such as preparations for a land invasion or a public march, the initiation of construction projects, the size of lots to be distributed or the type and cost of houses to be built on them.

When a committee was created not through a land invasion but through institutional dealings – as was the case with Carmen Lyra and Guarari – participation in the initial phase was even more difficult since people did not share a common group experience and barely knew each other. This made it hard to create the trust needed for participation. Work in the organization was very irregular; people came but then left when they could get no concrete results to keep them there permanently. At some meetings one group took part, at the next another; the leader soon became the only source of permanence.

In contrast, participation was essential during a land invasion because the success of the action depended on everyone's involvement; the same holds true during an eviction threat since effective resistance requires the force of numbers and group cohesion. Under these circumstances, participation acquired a clear meaning for people. When marches or protests were staged, everyone's participation was a decisive factor in demonstrating the force the organization represented; numbers were one of the key sources of power that these organizations held.

When a property was invaded the organizational dynamic was entirely different. During this phase, tasks became diversified, which, in turn, required different forms of organizing as well as other levels and forms of participation. It was necessary to clean, prepare and demarcate the property, start up vegetable gardens, find sources of water and electrical connections, create sanitary conditions and address general health problems, provide transport services and schooling for children, and prepare for the possibility of a last-minute eviction. It was clear to everyone that broad participation was crucial to these tasks, that their successful completion would have concrete and immediate benefits to all those involved, and that the leaders could not accomplish this alone. Normally, the leader organized commissions (work groups) which became accountable for specific tasks, thereby contributing to a broader participation and delegation of responsibilities. This was one of the most participatory moments in the life of the organization.

However, once assured of their permanence on the land, once the shacks had been built and service and access problems had been at least partially resolved, the organization entered another phase. During this second phase, institutional dealings with government were resumed and participation declined, although this changed sometimes when a protest or march was organized as a pressure tactic.

Participation revived when the organization reached the phase of building community houses, and a wide range of construction tasks needed to be completed. Once the houses were finished, however, even if communal tasks remained incomplete, people were much less willing to participate in common efforts, preferring instead to devote themselves to putting the finishing touches to their own homes.

Exactly what type of participation are we talking about? We indicated earlier that in periodic general meetings, participation meant attendance and not necessarily playing an active role. When people participated in communal tasks, including those related to house construction, a type of boss–worker relationship often developed between leaders organizing the work and the grassroots members. Each family was required to donate a certain number of hours of collective labor, with this input strictly monitored through registry sheets kept by the leaders. Those who did not put in the required hours had no right to benefit from the products of community labor. If a household head was unable to work, a son, daughter or another relative had to put in the time. If this was not possible, then the family paid someone to do the work. Although people were aware that the houses and infrastructure would not be constructed unless they all participated and contributed through their work, the truth was that if they did not have to participate, they did not do so. Leaders needed to resort to strict control measures, coercion, pressure, and various incentives to ensure participation, especially when it came to communal tasks.

In the community of El Nazareno, to give an incentive to become involved in the work commissions formed after the invasion, whoever participated had the right to choose the site of their own lots, while others were arbitrarily assigned lots by government officials in charge of the project. Many people participated. In Carmen Lyra, because of a conflict with community leaders, an official from the state institution in charge of the project – the Comisión Especial de Vivienda – erroneously informed families that they were not obligated to help with construction work as they had done in the past since the hired construction company was expected to do all the work. Even though the official was removed from her position and the misinformation was quickly corrected, doubts as to the real need to participate were never completely dispelled. People slowly began abandoning their jobs until, in the last few months, only a small group of people showed up for work. Nevertheless, in each of the four communities, approximately 10 per cent of all families were always willing to participate and collaborate, regardless of the material benefits, since they were motivated by their desire to fulfill their personal commitments to the community.

However, for the majority of families in the communities participation meant a third work shift. In contrast with other social sectors, these families had to build their own houses, sidewalks, drains, streets, schools, and churches in addition to completing a 10–12 hour regular work shift and their regular domestic responsibilities. For them, work in the community was simply a survival strategy, and the less time and effort the better.

After five or more years participating in a committee, one or two years of devoting weekends and free time or even sacrificing full-time paid employment for the benefit of the community and house construction, these families had neither the desire nor the energy to continue participating in the organization. The fatigue caused by continuous work for the organization was tremendous and signified a heavy burden and sacrifice for the families.

In spite of these limitations, in contrast to traditional organizations, the experience of participation in grassroots and local organizations such as the housing committees was direct and intense. Self-sufficiency in order to meet needs implied broad participation in communal tasks and house construction. This allowed members to feel a greater sense of identification with both the organization and fellow members, thereby enabling the establishment of solidarity, neighborliness and a sense of collaboration.

It was clear that for these organizations, participation was not conceived as a politically formative or (re-)educational experience. 'Raising people's political consciousness' or changing the system was not of interest to them, although it was of interest to the housing fronts who may have worked with them. In fact, our interviews indicated that participants (other than the odd militant in a left-wing party) did not see any correlation between the real problems they faced and the prevailing social order. Rather, poverty was seen as a phenomenon which was as natural as rain or sun – nothing could be done to change it or avoid it – and social differences were seen as a product of the natural order of things in dichotomous opposites: good/bad, above/below, poor/ rich. Their struggle, therefore, was not against the status quo but rather against exclusion; they demanded to be included in the status quo by pressuring government institutions. Participation, rather than being an objective, was a necessity which became a decisive factor under specific circumstances.

Democratic and Participatory Practices:
Objectives and Successes

One-third of household heads in Carmen Lyra and as many as two-thirds in the El Nazareno and Oscar Felipe communities were single women. In Oscar Felipe, we found that 75 per cent of households earned barely the minimum legal monthly wage; in El Nazareno it was 62 per cent, and in Carmen Lyra 31 per cent.[7] In other words, those who formed the housing committees were persons of modest means whose priorities were work, food, and a roof over their heads. These women and men had resorted to collective action because they had been unsuccessful in finding individual solutions to their housing needs. But as soon as they were able to find a solution to their problems, they did not hesitate to relegate collective action to a secondary place in their list of priorities. For these people, the organization and struggle for housing was fundamentally a personal survival strategy and not an activity with greater democracy and participation as an end in itself; the means utilized to obtain housing were not as important as the achievement of the goal itself.

One might assume that although democracy and participation were not the goals of the housing committees, in practice they would naturally develop democratic and participatory forms of organization. Yet, by observing their organizational practices, we concluded that because the committees were not formed or operated with democratic or participatory principles in mind, their working methods and leadership did not necessarily conform to such values. At the same time, it is important to remember that appreciation of democratic and participatory values in these organizations in the form of conscious or explicit discourse does not necessarily translate into democratic, participatory practices. The study illustrated that the two communities (Guarari and Carmen Lyra) which had leaders who favored democratic and participatory values ended up reproducing organizational practices similar to those of the other communities, where such a discourse was absent.

As we will see, the objectives of the organization and the context in which such communities struggled for their interests determined the organizational forms and practices they chose. In the housing committees, 'effectiveness' was the fundamental objective and ultimately the one which shaped their organizational form. Since effectiveness was strongly determined by the conditions imposed by the socio-political context, this criterion of effectiveness often frustrated the potential of democratic and participatory practices in these communities.

One reason that democracy and participation didn't naturally develop is that such concerns didn't necessarily guarantee them greater chances of success. On the contrary, some organizations with authoritarian and centralist practices were more successful, in particular because of the role of the state in developing housing strategies. Simply put, the most effective way of acquiring a house was, as always, through patronage, contacts, and friendships with influential public officials and political party leaders. The same rules applied when it came to postponing an evacuation order, installing electricity and running water in an illegally-occupied lot, and negotiating lot boundaries or the size of the houses to be built. Of the communities studied, all but Carmen Lyra could trace their achievements to some friendship or political contact. Having such contacts was important in the selection of leaders.

Given the role of government officials and politicians, their support for particular housing organizations served as an important instrument of struggle. The names that the communities chose for themselves is a reflection of this strategy. So we find communities like Oscar Felipe, which have adopted the names of public officials and politicians, as well as those appealing to religious beliefs, as in the case of El Nazareno. The effectiveness of this tactic is clearly seen in Oscar Felipe. On the day the families were transferred to the land where they would build their houses, the community was visited by the Minister of Housing, an entourage of politicians from the incumbent PLN, and a cluster of public officials who committed themselves to helping their cause. Three days later, the community was visited by President Oscar Arias, who donated large sums of money to the community. The government also donated food to assist families during the first two weeks of settlement, and the presidential palace contributed 25 tents and construction materials.

The limitations placed on the communities by government patronage were also apparent. When the Oscar Felipe community established ties with a group of militants from a communist party which had been supporting the community in improving its internal organization, the organization's political patrons 'recommended' to its leader (who interpreted the recommendation as a threat) that all ties be severed with the group in question. The relation between the state and the Oscar Felipe community stands in sharp contrast to the lack of attention received by the Guarari and Carmen Lyra communities. Guarari's origins are traceable to the housing committees created in 1982 by the leftist COPAN. In spite of the force of their mobilization efforts, including the marches and mass protests between 1980 and 1986, this community was systematically ignored by the government. In addition to their political orientation – or rather because of it – COPAN leaders who were in charge of the administration of the committee lacked the requisite political contacts with government officials or party leaders. Only when COPAN decided to use pacifist methods, such as the hunger strikes organized by its local leaders in 1984, did the government agree to negotiate with them, although it later reneged on promises made during negotiations. In the meantime, despite the activism and combativeness of those families involved in its committees, upon seeing the lack of results many shifted loyalty to committees offering greater opportunities.

In order to prevent what seemed to be the end of COPAN, its top officials seized the opportunities opened by the 1986 electoral campaign to negotiate with Arias and the PLN. In return for promising electoral support for Arias, COPAN demanded that the Arias government meet their housing demands once in power. Immediately after the Arias government took office, COPAN declared itself 'non-communist' and devoted itself to nurturing the corresponding political contacts. That strategy proved fruitful and members were incorporated into the government's plan to build 80,000 houses; COPAN received vast sums of money to administer house construction projects as assigned by the government.

The case of Carmen Lyra is similar, albeit with a different ending. The community was headed by a well-known communist leader from the Vanguardia Popular who had few political contacts with state officials or influential politicians and consequently lacked the necessary mark of approval. This community's ties with the communist-affiliated ANAVI was not of much help in establishing or nurturing political contacts. When, after three years of futile efforts, the Carmen Lyra housing committee finally invaded a plot of state property, they were violently carried away by police. The scenario repeated itself when, on two occasions, they occupied a city park. To leave the church where they had taken refuge after one of these instances, the communist deputy from the Vanguardia Popular had to bargain for the suspension of the imprisonment orders made against the members of the organization. The Minister of Housing ardently opposed negotiating with this organization, which in his view was a 'rebellious group.' Even the priest at this church denied assistance, branding them 'communists' who were of 'no help to the church.' Finally, however, the struggle gained momentum as its cause reached beyond the demands of the housing committees and became the struggle of all the people in the area, at which point the government finally decided to meet the demands of the committee. This was one of the few cases where a committee's achievements were not the direct result of political contacts or patronage (following or interspersed with collective action and mobilization), but rather exclusively of collective action and struggle. Whatever their importance, political contacts alone were not enough. In El Nazareno and Oscar Felipe, regardless of political ties and contacts, the community had to rely on other forms of struggle, including land invasions, protests and street blockades, as means of exerting pressure.

Democracy and the Satisfaction of Needs

In the communities we studied we found a combination of two phenomena: first, the reproduction of representative democracy in the form of delegated power; second, the exercise of direct democracy, expressed through the right to revoke the powers of those leaders to whom decision-making had been delegated. Within the housing committees, reproduction of Costa Rican representative democracy allows participation in the selection of leaders. But it also means in practice that leaders gradually gain autonomy from the collective will; administration and decision-making are concentrated in the hands of a few. At the same time, however, grassroots members have maintained great sanctioning powers. Just as they have the power to elect their leaders, they also have the power to replace them. Impeachment of leaders has occurred because the organization saw no concrete results for a long time and saw the leader as ineffective; when the leader was suspected (or known to be) involved in some form of corruption; when the membership feels the leader has appropriated too many rights or abused power (although both practices are partly tolerated and considered part of the privileges of the job); and, finally, when the leader is not representing or adequately defining group interests and letting external interests (e.g. those of political parties, leaders from outside the community, or public institutions and officials) take precedence.

In short, people trustfully delegate power to the leader, but if their interests in obtaining housing are threatened, they may resort to direct democracy. This control over leaders is possible in small organizations where there is physical proximity, little bureaucracy, and a simple organizational structure. The simplicity of the organizations allows members to act spontaneously if they feel their interests to be threatened. In the Oscar Felipe community, when the leader refused to resign after having been accused of stealing money, people organized a 'silent march' in front of his home for several days, sometimes even throwing rocks at his house, until he resigned. Nevertheless, the removal of a particular leader, even when done democratically, causes tremendous conflict in these communities. Loyalties are divided and feelings are deeply hurt. By and large, these leaders retire completely from the work of the organization, as was the case in El Nazareno, where the leader set up his house at the margins of the settlement, removed from other houses, and who, today, has no contact with the community.

While the election and impeachment of representatives are seen as sacred democratic rights, many leaders stay on for years. In Carmen Lyra, the leader who initiated the organization was still in power after seven years. In El Nazareno, the Housing Minister chose someone he trusted to initiate, organize and lead the community's building project. This person, however, was soon endorsed by the majority of the community and was officially designated leader since she had successfully advanced the projects. Meanwhile, leaders officially elected to the job months earlier failed to win the support of the members, were bypassed in the management of the community and relegated to playing a secondary role during construction.

The upshot is organizations in which much of the work and decision-making power is delegated to a few. Joint or majority decision-making is mainly exercised through the election of leaders or in the adoption of key decisions such as land invasions or organizing a march or a blockade. These are decisions the leader cannot assume unilaterally as they require the consensus and participation of the majority to be carried out successfully. Still, given the local and grassroots nature of the housing committees, the exercise of direct democracy is also possible and is manifested in sanctioning powers over elected leaders who have failed to represent the majority's interests. In this sense, democracy in these organizations is closely associated with the satisfaction of common needs and the concrete benefits to be derived from it. According to this definition, acting democratically means being true to the interests of the community at large.

Of the communities we studied, only Guarari was an exception to these norms. This community is completely under the control of COPAN's leadership. These leaders assume all decision-making responsibilities, including the designation of grassroots leaders. The great power and control they exercise as a result of their close links with the state has impeded the community from adopting more democratic forms of organization. This explains why, when one speaks with community members, the words 'democracy' and 'participation' are recurrent, and the main reason why an opposition group within the community formed an alternative organization called 'La Nueva Guarari.'

Democracy, Participation and Leadership

The work and leadership methods, the decision-making processes, and the particular shape and forms that participation and democracy take make us think of these organizations as 'collective spaces for the supply of services.' The services consist in managing and obtaining housing; leaders grant the service and families consume them, and when a leader does not perform adequately, another is found. Petitioning for housing requires a great deal of know-how and personal skill. The leader must know or learn which institutions to apply to, the requirements of each, who its officials are, who makes the decisions, how they are made, how the institutions operate, the most effective forms of pressure to utilize with each, who the best contacts are in each, and how to negotiate with government officials and politicians. This set of abilities can turn into a profession in and of itself, in the service of the community. After serving her own community, one of the leaders from El Nazareno was sought by another housing organization as a consultant on institutional negotiations.

Under these circumstances, the opinions of the leaders often become directives and play a decisive role in defining issues and shaping the orientation of the organization. Whether or not this role means that the leader will accept responsibility for developing democratic and participatory practices depends on the specific community and organization. We found that a leader's actions and options are conditioned by the aspirations and expectations of the group as well as by the broader socio-political context. We repeatedly saw that the attitudes, ideals and aspirations of members play as important a role as the individuality and convictions of the leader. Even though the leaders may put a personal stamp on the organization, they can not impose their personal preferences over those of the group and people they represent. In order to maintain their leadership role, leaders must, at least to some extent, respond to the conceptions and expectations of the community they represent.

A power struggle between two leaders in El Nazareno, and the debate that ensued over the role and appropriate forms of leadership, is a useful way to illustrate the problems and dilemmas that confront leaders who try to promote democracy and participation. In 1987, almost a year after the invasion, it became clear that an eviction order would be suspended. The community's permanent occupation of the land was assured and Elias Muñoz, the organization's elected president, proceeded to co-ordinate the work of the community by delegating as many of the tasks as possible and encouraging broad participation in community activities. In addition to the traditional work groups (a general assembly, board of directors, and treasury board), he nominated 15 working committees to organize and carry out specific tasks ranging from cleaning and maintenance to youth activities and sports events. At the time, each committee had between 10 and 15 members: in all, about 150 people were actively participating in the management and work of the organization. Each committee had a co-ordinator.

Several months later, Elias decided to grant greater power to committee co-ordinators and proposed that the board of directors be replaced by a central committee composed of the co-ordinators of each of the 15 work committees and led by a general co-ordinator. This immediately ignited a clash between a member of the board of directors, Carlos Corrales, and Elias, the intended general co-ordinator. For Elias, this initiative was part of his philosophy of delegating responsibilities and integrating a larger group of people in the decision-making process. His notion of the role of a leader was that the leader should become a co-ordinator of activities and orient others in doing their jobs. Carlos, on the contrary, believed that the role of the leader was to centralize control in one or a few leaders so that the organization could become a consolidated, effective, and belligerent fighting group. In spite of his efforts to democratize the leadership and encourage greater participation, Elias was never able to abandon his fear of losing his own power. For this reason, he had insisted that all committee co-ordinators ultimately answer to the general co-ordinator (himself); he always remained concerned that the membership 'might organize a coup d'état' to oust the leader, as he told us in an interview in 1990. In the end, the same democratic and participatory practices he promoted cost him his position as leader.

It is undeniable that behind closed doors the two leaders waged a secret war for control over the organization. Elias attempted to surround himself with those co-ordinators he had promoted in the hope that they would help him consolidate his central power in the organization. However, it is also true that as long as he was leader, he did delegate part of the work and even ceded some of his powers. The delegation of duties and decisions was, in particular, handed over to those responsible for the working committees. Work was also carried out in a more democratic manner, which contributed to a great sense of communal participation, the extent of which was felt in the community long afterwards. Thus, whereas in the other three communities one finds only one or two leaders, in El Nazareno it is possible to identify seven or eight leaders formed through the experiences provided by Elias. Nevertheless, for Elias, democracy and participation were not very positive experiences; when he recalls the episode he warns that 'if you create horns, they'll pluck your eyes out.' Perhaps the most interesting thing about the whole experience is that, today, the members of the community interpret Elias's efforts as passivity and lacking a leader's involvement in matters of importance in the community. It is also worth exploring Carlos Corrales' position regarding the need for a more centralized organization. This other leader strongly associates institutional strength with centralization rather than with democracy and participation. His arguments were based on the fact that, in the case of El Nazareno, the organization drew together many people who did not really know one another before joining the organization. According to Carlos, strong, centralized leadership was required to give the organization some cohesion. The same thing seems to have happened in the other communities with respect to the construction of housing. There were so many people working and trying to accomplish a very complex set of tasks that, unless decisions were centralized, nothing could get done.

Elias's conceptions about the appropriate role and forms of leadership are not common among other community leaders in the housing committees. Just as democratic and participatory practices are not an objective for the organization as a whole, neither are they for its leaders. In these organizations, being a leader means exercising power, having the prestige and the opportunity to satisfy personal goals that one could never expect to realize otherwise. The power of being indispensable, having the support and friendship of public officials and political leaders, being a recipient of favors from political parties and the source of admiration for the community are these leaders' personal aspirations. For example, Oscar Aguilar, the leader of the Carmen Lyra community, was elected as a local representative to the municipal government of Turrialba and had a world of opportunities opened to him as a result, and recognition of his efforts as 'the' leader of this housing organization. (For a candidate representing a party as tiny as the communist Vanguardia Popular, this represented a major political breakthrough and a level of recognition and support whether he was re-elected or not.) In spite of the ideals or good intentions of a leader, they are almost always captive to their own need and desire for power and prestige.

The power struggles and conflicts that erupt in the organizations are the cause of a growing loss of legitimacy and credibility among leaders who are perceived as pursuing personal interests as opposed to those of the community. Members of all the communities referred to these conflicts as one of the principal factors discouraging greater participation. Does it make a difference if we are dealing with leaders with leftist orientations? In Carmen Lyra and Guarari, where both leaders are known leftists, there were few differences in the democratic or participatory practices used within the organization. In spite of COPAN's rhetoric emphasizing new forms of organization and community relations, in practice this has not translated into working methods or leadership practices which might achieve such an objective. Actually, it is possible to claim that out of the four communities studied it was in Guarari where we observed the most centralized, vertical and undemocratic forms of work and leadership. These habits, furthermore, had caused a divisive split within the community and violent conflicts against COPAN's top leaders. For COPAN, the traditional notion persisted of needing a vanguard to think on behalf of the membership. Centralization is regarded as a principle method of maintaining cohesion and organizational strength.

In Carmen Lyra, from the time the committee was formed in 1982 to this day, the community has had only one leader, Oscar Aguilar, who, as noted, is a member of the communist Vanguardia Popular and its housing front, ANAVI. While ANAVI has developed forms of struggle other than the clientelistic behavior pervasive in government and in the relations between politicians and other housing fronts, it hasn't created alternative mechanisms to make their organization notably different. The organizational dynamic involved in satisfying immediate needs and providing concrete results by the most effective means available overshadowed all efforts at internal restructuring. Moreover, the personal aspirations of the leader, who at one point even toyed with the idea of running as a deputy in the Legislative Assembly, got in the way.

The main difference we detected between those housing committees with leftist connections and those without them was that the former had more independent relations *vis-à-vis* the national and local state and mainstream political parties. In Oscar Felipe and El Nazareno, the organization was more vulnerable to the influence and control of government and politicians, while Guarari and Carmen Lyra were able to develop more autonomous relations with the state through their leaders, and therefore maintain community interests at the forefront. For instance, the two latter communities settled themselves on lands which offered much better living conditions than those made available to Oscar Felipe and El Nazareno. COPAN managed to maintain direct control over the Guarari housing project by having government funds geared towards the development of the housing project allocated directly to them. Guarari and Carmen Lyra negotiated with government to have power to administer the socio-economic surveys of their members and to decide on the classification of beneficiaries and the assignment of lots. In El Nazareno and Oscar Felipe, on the other hand, these tasks were exclusively left in the hands of a government official permanently stationed in the community, who, on occasion, substituted and displaced the organization's system of local administration.

Final Reflections

The achievement of the housing committees has been significant. The pressure exerted by the collective struggle forced the Costa Rican government to formulate and implement housing policies which, for the first time, took into consideration the needs and economic possibilities of low-income families. As part of its new policies, the state modified the profitability criteria and guidelines for the recovery of financial resources which had prevented state institutions from investing in poor sectors in the past and helps to account for the dramatic housing deficit among poor Costa Ricans. This achievement is even more significant once we take into consideration that state investment in housing for low-income families took place during a period of budgetary restraint and cuts in public spending resulting from the structural adjustment programme implemented in Costa Rica from 1985.

Likewise, the electoral victory which resulted from Arias's promise to construct 80,000 houses in response to popular demand cleared a path which other politicians would follow in the future – that is, 'the option for the poor.' Nowadays it is difficult to find a politician who does not advocate social justice, speak of the struggle against poverty, or make promises which soon become popular demands. On the other hand, although clientelistic political relations with state officials and political leaders are crucial in shaping the organizational and fighting practices of the housing committees, clientelism also presupposes the existence of general access to state institutions and political organisms, and, even more importantly, to public funds by organizers, thereby contributing to the democratization of public expenditures. Through their clientelistic relations and the contacts and friendships of their leaders, the housing organizations shortened the distance from traditional politics without having to abandon their position in civil society.

This compression of political distance may very well be an expression of the democratization of politics, even if, paradoxically, it usually remained within a clientelist framework. The leader of one community – who at 35 years old could barely read or write – described how her friendship with a deputy, who had lent her a desk, typewriter, paper supplies and his office phone in the Legislative Assembly, enabled her to get the work done for her housing committee. Nevertheless, it is obvious that popular discontent did not lead to a questioning of the established social, political or economic order. Not only was the system capable of confronting the crisis and containing the conflict but, without much resistance, it converted the crisis into the process of neo-liberal change and structural adjustment policies that had such terrible consequences for the living conditions of the popular sectors. As of 1986, the belligerence of the housing committees was turned into support for and co-ordination with state action.

The revolutionary fervor generated in Central America by the triumph of the Sandinistas and advancements in the revolutionary processes in El Salvador and Guatemala during the late 1970s and early 1980s created both hope and expectation among progressive sectors in the region that profound social changes would take place in Central America. Today, more than ten years later, the situation is quite different. The revolutionary path seems exhausted and at a dead end, something recognized by most of the region's revolutionary fronts, which have turned to political negotiation as a means of achieving change.

In this context, the struggle for improved living conditions makes all the more sense. In so far as the housing organizations represent a fight by the majority for more dignified conditions, these committees are both democratic organizations and bearers of participatory and democratic values. The process of the housing struggle leaves us with a series of experiences which we must not forget: the palpable importance of self-worth, pride, confidence in one's own abilities, and consciousness of the power of collective action as a tool for influencing policy. The struggle was a success because of the creation of a shared common history, the formation of leaders within popular sectors with limited resources, and possibilities for political activism and the application of such techniques in fighting other causes. The lessons still shape the possibility of reproducing the valuable experience of team-work and of undertaking tasks that enrich the quality of life in the community, including organizing day care services, youth groups, cultural and sports events.

Given that we are dealing with a contradictory process, full of tensions between the individual and the collective will, it is difficult to say what implications these experiences will have in the long term. The balance of attention often tends to tip in favor of individual needs and actions, and only when there is no other way forward do people seem to rely on collective action. And even within the collective experience, so many problems remain: distrust and skepticism expressed towards the organization, problems of money, corruption, abuse of personal interests and privileges, power clashes and arbitrary decision-making. Some community members even argued that it would be best if the government assumed control over the organization. The possibility of expanding on these experiences depends on their continuity. Their longevity, unfortunately, is threatened by the fact that these organizations are often dissolved once they reach their housing objectives. Although the memory of the experience remains, the practice gained from it fades with time. Undoubtedly, though, the struggle for housing constitutes an important collective experience, which will remain in the memories of those who participated in the process as a means of learning and expanding on the democratic possibilities available in Costa Rican society.

Notes

1. Two levels of analysis were used in the study. At the micro-level, the study looked at the internal organization of the Committees for the Struggle for Housing, with special emphasis on different forms and levels of participation, of democratic practices and management models. At another level, the study explored the national and socio-political context in which the struggle for housing evolved. For the latter level, the investigation concentrated on identifying those factors that determined the organizational practices of the housing committees as well as the impact of the housing struggle on the political system.

CEPAS would like to express its gratitude to the communities that participated in the study and that by doing so have helped to forge a better understanding of the needs, aspirations and challenges facing their communities.

We would also like to thank Marisol Granados for her collaboration during the field work, as well as Michael Kaufman and Sheila Knight-Lira from the Centre for Research on Latin America and the Caribbean (CERLAC) for the ongoing support they provided through their co-ordination efforts.

Naturally, we also extend our thanks to the International Development Research Council (IDRC) in Ottawa, Canada. This research would not have been possible without their financial support and encouragement.

2. See Rafael Guido and Oscar Fernández, 'El Juicio al Sujeto: Un Análisis de los Movimientos Sociales en América Latina,' in *Cuadernos de Ciências Sociales*, No. 25, (Mexico: FLACSO, 1989); Ruth Cardoso, 'Popular Movements in the Context of the Consolidation of Democracy,' Working Paper No. 20, University of Notre Dame, March 1989; Tilman Evers, *Identidad: el Lado Oculto de los Nuevos Movimientos Sociales* (Brazil: Materiales para el Debate Contemporâneo, 1984), and Eduardo Canel's chapter in this volume.

3. Norberto Bobbio, *El Futuro de la Democracia* (Mexico: Fondo de Cultura Económica, 1986), p. 33.

4. The bulk of field research in these communities (including preparatory work) took place between March 1990 and June 1991, although follow-up workshops were held at later dates. From an initial list of ten possible communities, these four were selected on the basis of several criteria: to include communities which emerged out of collective struggle and which demonstrated high levels of organization; communities which were in the intermediate or final phase of construction of their permanent housing and infrastructure; one community which had ties with COPAN and another with ANAVI – both leftist housing fronts which, according to their leaders, advocate democratic and participatory practices as one of their main organizational objectives; two communities which did not have permanent links with a housing front. In addition to observation, we conducted 68 partly structured interviews around these issues, surveying current and former leaders as well as grassroots members in four communities which emerged from collective struggle, and held ongoing discussions with various community members.

5. The formation of COPAN signalled a change in OST tactics from developing a political party to building a mass organization. The goal wasn't electoral, but to struggle day to day with the people. As part of this change, the OST was dissolved.

6. Bobbio, *El Futuro de la Democracia*, p. 42.

7. It was not possible to obtain data for La Guarari since COPAN, and not the state, controls this information and guards it jealously as a result of the conflicts that have erupted in the community in relation to the assignment of completed houses.

3

Participation and Development in Cuban Municipalities

*Haroldo Dilla Alfonso
with Gerardo González Núñez*

In the early 1970s, Cuban political leaders announced their intention to begin what they called a 'process of institutionalization' of the state and the political system at large, which was to include a sub-system of local government. At that time, Cuban researchers and others researching Cuba began to interpret the likely contents of a new, more democratic system.[1] Leaving aside the often unimaginative interpretations of some Cuban academics, which are less useful than official political interpretations, we would like to dwell briefly on various reactions among North American Cubanologists.

Although for some, such as Horowitz, institutionalization and the creation of local government was simply 'Stalinist, de-politicizing bureaucratic integration,'[2] other interpretations chose to avoid such indictments and instead focused on a more objective diagnosis, but often with a liberal theoretical approach, which left little room for analytical flexibility. These include Jorge Domínguez and his classic, *Cuba: Order and Revolution*. For Domínguez, the issue was simply a formalization of the political system and the transfer of the pattern of authority from charismatic to legal and rational considerations. This was to be complemented by regular political consultation at the local level as introduced by a 'consultative oligarchy' interested only in perfecting minor details of the decision-making process.[3] Meanwhile, for C. Mesa Lago, institutionalization was 'noted for central control, dogmatism, administrative-bureaucratic features and limited participation, in the Soviet mold.'[4] In this interpretation, the new municipal governments had only a very subordinate role to play. Archibald Ritter, however, recognized the implications of this process for the broadening of popular participation, even if within the framework of central planning and a one-party system, both factors affecting decentralization of power and the construction of participatory democracy. These views were shared in essence by Rhode Pearl Rabking.[5] Efforts in a different direction were undertaken by William Leogrande and Max Azicri on the issue of determining to what extent traditional patterns of participation were affected and renewed, especially *vis-à-vis* the creation of local government bodies. According to Leogrande, this was a new phase in Cuba's revolution, one noted for moving beyond the precepts of direct democracy and for recognizing that more than mobilizations in support of the government would be necessary for the construction of socialism.[6]

Naturally, between these usually critical and often pessimistic assessments of the democratic potential of institutionalization and of local government on the one hand and the more successful components of this decentralizing experiment on the other, there exists a chasm which can only be explained by the strong ideological bent permeating this debate. It is also to be explained by the absence of adequate field research in the municipalities themselves. As no theoretical production is ideologically chaste, it would be disingenuous to believe that this chapter will itself escape from a defined ideological proposition. Yet we have tried to avoid traditional approaches that ignore many of the realities of Cuba in favor of one particular paradigm. This essay attempts to analyze an aspect of the Cuban political system whose creation and dynamics have constituted a considerable step forward in democratizing the Cuban state and society. At the same time, the workings of this new system evinces sufficient weaknesses as to lead to the conclusion that we are not in the presence of the best of all possible worlds. The underlying theoretical proposition is that Cuba's democratic and participatory maturity will only be possible within a socialist framework, so that democracy and socialism appear in a direct and inseparable relationship, whereby the latter draws from the former not just its goals for human realization but, in more pragmatic terms, the very fundamentals of its own ability to govern. This is perhaps one of the most distinct lessons to be learned from the Eastern European experience.

In this article we develop some ideas about the sub-system of municipal government in Cuba. First, we give a brief description of the history and formal design of this system, as well as presenting the design of the research project. Then we analyze the participatory dimension of local government, especially in terms of decision-making. We return to some of the institutional peculiarities, including their horizontal and vertical relations. Finally, we examine possibilities for the development of Cuban municipalities in relation to the entire political system of which they are a part.

The Original Design of Local Government in Cuba

Municipalities in Cuba have a long history. Throughout the Spanish colonial period and especially during the pre-revolution republican stage, municipalities were significant players in political life, increasing legitimacy through the extension of political patronage. However, their role in regard to regional development or in the implementation of participatory structures was much more limited, chiefly because of the prevalence of undue centralization, a perennial lack of resources, and the corruption of local political elites.

With the onset of revolutionary changes in 1959, the system of municipalities was replaced by institutions with limited administrative powers, including the Juntas de Coordinación y Inspección (Co-ordination and Inspection Boards, JUCEI) and after 1965 by the Poderes Locales (Local Powers). The latter were administrative councils with stable local hierarchies and prerogatives delegated by central bodies, which, at the same time, were intended to play a role as mediators in the electoral process. Although JUCEI's and the Poderes Locales may be considered as the institutional forerunners of the present municipal system, the more relevant antecedent was a strong structure of community participation centered on neighborhood-based political and mass organizations. Examples of this were the Comités de Defensa de la Revolución (Committees for the Defense of the Revolution, CDRs) and the Federación de Mujeres Cubanas (Cuban Women's Federation, FMC).

The community became an arena for vigorous participation in support of the new system, for mobilization of human and material resources, for popular confrontation of counter-revolution, and also for political socialization. At the same time, particularly where the FMC was concerned, organizations became vehicles for sector representation and application of differentiated policies intended to encourage advancement of specific social groups. The 1976 creation of the Organos Locales del Poder Popular (Local Bodies of People's Power, OLPP), the first municipal system in revolutionary Cuba, was part of the 'process of institutionalization,' a project intended to modernize and democratize the political and administrative system in the country. A decision of this nature raised at least three difficult issues for its designers:

- First, they faced the challenge of creating an institutional and legal framework capable of providing local governments not just with delegated administrative powers, but with the ability to govern their respective territorial jurisdictions. At the same time they needed to keep in mind such facts as a centrally planned economy and the predominance of public property.

- Second, this had to be done in a sufficiently democratic manner, not just because of a need to maintain the high degree of popular involvement for which previous stages were noted. There was also a desire to strengthen participation patterns qualitatively by broadening the scope of such processes as leadership selection, public oversight, and popular control over local public administration.
- Third, the process entailed breaking away from political and administrative methods and styles that were deeply rooted in the public apparatus and the citizenry, and their substitution by a new political culture.

In short, the new system was based on the need for a local representative institution, the Municipal Assembly (Asamblea Municipal), made up of delegates elected by the constituencies through direct and secret balloting. An Assembly had the power to elect, oversee and recall both executive (Executive Committees) and administrative agencies, as well as their representatives to the provincial assemblies and to the National Assembly, the foremost state bodies. Considering that citizens, as voters, had the power not only to elect but also to recall their delegates to municipal assemblies, the system amounted to a chain of successive subordinations in which delegation of sovereignty was conditional while its effects transcended the purely local arena. Voters' recall rights were complemented by the obligation of those elected to be accountable to constituents and to submit to their scrutiny.

This participatory system contained an interesting combination of direct democracy and the use of representation as granted by election. In general, it attempted to provide citizens with the ability to choose the local leadership, express claims, oversee and evaluate local policy and its results, and become involved in projects of community benefit. Thus, although administrative bodies were subject to the authority of representatives, they had the prerogatives and resources deemed indispensable for the practice of government. Above all, the intent was to transfer to the new institutions the control of a wide range of services and economic activities hitherto run by the central government or through delegation of authority. Generally, these activities concerned the provision of basic social services (health, education, social security, employment) or such economic services as repairs, restaurants, cafeterias, building construction and maintenance, and so on. Only in very few cases were these activities related directly to production, which continued to function under provincial or central government control.

The task of planning the transfer of administrative powers raised two immediate issues. The first was how to harmonize adequate degrees of local autonomy within a centrally planned economy, so as to avoid atomization, resource waste and uneven regional development. The solution was felt to be found in the so-called 'double subordination' method, which gave central bodies methodological control of locally subordinated activities such as factories (here referred to as locally controlled). Methodological control referred to control over prices, salaries and consumption norms. Meanwhile local governments were given responsibility for administrative control. The second issue had to do with making municipal government actions compatible with the sum of the territorial economy, which included nationally subordinated corporations (*grandes industrias* or *industrias nacionales*, here referred to as national corporations). A set of norms was enacted to prescribe limited jurisdiction of local government over national concerns. This was variously referred to in official documents as a relationship of 'control,' 'assistance,' or simply of 'support.'

As expected, although a single institutional and legal model was established, later development of the system was affected by conscious and *de facto* changes made nationally that affected each local reality. This makes any general assessment difficult, unless it takes into account the fact that significant heterogeneity exists. At any rate, 15 years after first implementation, both the positive and the negative traits of the sub-system of municipal government can be seen – as well as the fact that many of the solutions advanced by the original design have become part of the problem.

Research Procedure and Setting

The previous description implicitly states the two main objectives of this research – that is, the evaluation of municipalities – as: (a) a focus of popular participation in leadership selection, decision-making and implementation of community projects, and (b) government bodies with decision-making, implementation and coactive prerogatives within their respective jurisdictions. For purposes of research it was not difficult to identify the fundamental institutional components of the municipal sphere: citizens, divided at times by their gender, generational, occupational and other distinctions; community-based social and political organizations, including the Communist Party; community representatives (delegates); municipal assemblies and subsidiary bodies; the Municipal Assembly Executive Committee; local administrative bodies; national and provincial institutions located in the territory.

Each of these subjects was studied between 1989 and 1991 through a variety of methods, including interviews, surveys, observation and discussion groups, and by a comprehensive documentary review. In some cases, subjects proved to be highly complex, to the extent that insights became possible only through the interaction of various research tools at intervals during the project. In-depth, specific research was required by certain situations through the course of the investigation, and this was accomplished by designing specific studies.

Given the lack of previous studies and of a reliable statistical foundation, we decided to select a group of four municipalities presenting traits sufficiently diverse to allow us to obtain a variety of observations which could then be compared. We considered twelve possibilities and selected four of them by combining two basic variables: population size and degree of socio-economic development. First, we wanted a municipality located in the capital, so we chose Centro Habana, which most acutely showed the issues inherent to urban congestion and overpopulation. Second, we wanted a municipality with a well-defined historical background and considerable population and geographic dimensions, so we selected Bayamo, in the east of the island. Finally, we picked Chambas and Santa Cruz del Norte, in the center and western parts of the island, respectively, both small municipalities (population under 40,000) with dissimilar degrees of development.

Proposing to research the municipal sphere in the absence of other considerations implied the danger of ending up with a study of the problems of public policy and administration which ignored the community dimension. Although Cuban municipalities are in effect political-legal communities, from a social and historical perspective they actually represent a multiplicity of communities – a logical result for institutions existing within a political and administrative arrangement barely two decades old. Townships and communities with varying degrees of development and cultural textures coexist within each municipality, occasionally showing so strong a sense of community that they collide with their neighbors. Consequently, although an understanding of the municipality as a whole was considered of major importance for analysis of decision-making, it was not enough for understanding citizen involvement and community dynamics, whose pace and traits were subject to numerous variables, some extending well beyond the merely political.

Thus, the study focused on the main urban center in each selected municipality, which in all cases both possessed a more pronounced urban profile and was the seat of municipal government. Within each district, between five and seven constituencies were chosen to represent two different variables: the type of leadership and socio-economic characteristics. In these constituencies the political community is an extension of the ordinary relationships of daily life, and it was here that we measured both the political conduct of citizens and the process of participation.

Centro Habana

Centro Habana is a focal point for commerce, where the complexities of life in a large city are easily observable. Although this municipality was created from the merger of five different *barrios*, these were sufficiently interrelated in history to avoid considering the resulting municipality an artificial creation. It would be an exaggeration to say that Centro Habana is a marginal or slum area. Highly efficient health, educational and social security services are available, and unemployment is not a significant phenomenon. Cultural life is intense and an important part of the population is well educated. Nevertheless, one of its more noticeable features is the decrepitude of the housing and the attendant social consequences that may be expected.

We must bear in mind that this municipality, with an area of only 3.5 sq km, is home to over 164,000 persons living in overcrowded conditions in tenements and rooming houses, where it is not uncommon to find scores of people sharing a single bathroom. Most buildings were erected more than 50 years ago and, practically in every case, have never been repaired, so that partial or complete collapses do not constitute spectacular news. Although delinquent behavior is not common in comparison with other large Latin American cities (Cuban figures are low in this respect), the rate is up, and local government and community organizations are responding with preventive policies and integration programmes. An interesting detail is that these policies and programmes are based on recovery of the cultural traditions of the *barrios* and implementation of community self-development programmes. However, the availability of resources has proved to be insufficient for adequate implementation of these programmes.

Of all municipalities selected for study, it was here that conflict and dissatisfaction indicators were highest, and where local government held the least legitimacy. Of course, this is determined by the inability of local leaders to adopt initiatives in a district located in the center of the capital, housing national institutions outside their control, and burdened by difficult problems caused not just by its own population, but also by the large crowds circulating daily through the commercial areas and using the services run by local government.

Bayamo

Bayamo, in the eastern zone of the country, has many characteristics in common with Centro Habana, but also notable differences. Among the former, we can mention population size – it has 187,000 inhabitants, two-thirds of them in urban centers. There is also nearly perfect overlapping of the legal municipality with the historical community. This is possibly the most salient trait of Bayamo, a city boasting long-lasting and distinct culture and traditions considered their own by all citizens. Being a *bayamés* is a condition which gives residents great pride, a fact recalled to every visitor by the numerous monuments and historical plaques in the city's streets. However, unlike Centro Habana, Bayamo constitutes a highly integrated political and socio-economic system where municipal government discharges its duties with great effectiveness, despite being a provincial government seat and home to numerous national corporations not subordinated to local administration. This fact does not preclude conflict among the different actors in the municipal arena; conflict, in fact, springs up with the spontaneity and frankness that characterize residents. But there is always greater room for the construction and management of consensus.

Probably the most significant issues faced by municipal government are unemployment and the status of women. Bayamo is a paradigm of the prevalence in Cuban culture of discriminatory patriarchal patterns, which are expressed with particular intensity in the eastern part of the country. Although female participation in the workforce is only slightly under the national average, this has not brought about sufficient changes in daily life. Although women have discharged their duties well in municipal and other government posts, only 12 per cent of elected delegates are women (compared to the 17 per cent national average). Strikingly, it is usual for women here to decline nomination publicly on the grounds of spousal prohibition. Even when true elsewhere, this would be considered at least inelegant in other regions of the country.

The unemployed here amount to some 14,000, mostly young people, a fact considered one of the most urgent challenges for local government. Their plight is the result of both high birth rates and significant migration from nearby mountainous areas, a situation only recently relieved by implementation of special regional development plans. Migration has led to a proliferation of slum belts around the city, in some of which community development projects with a strong self-management component are now being implemented.

Santa Cruz del Norte

The Municipality of Santa Cruz del Norte has 40,000 inhabitants, two-thirds settled into 12 urban communities. The largest of these is Santa Cruz, with 9,000 inhabitants. This is a quiet, beautiful coastal town whose inhabitants are interrelated by strong primary ties and where it is possible to locate anyone by simply asking a passer-by. Nothing here resembles the noisy agitation and the insoluble troubles of large cities. Every problem appears to have a solution and it strikes an outsider that Santa Cruz seems like an ideal place to live.

However, Santa Cruz does have its problems, some of which stem precisely from what is considered the source of its prosperity: rapid industrialization. Of course, industrialization has had some favourable aspects (including greater quantity and quality of human and material resources and an increased ability to attain effective social and economic integration) as well as negative ones (including environmental pollution and the massive influx of a labor force from the capital).

This has resulted in a peculiar dichotomy: nearly 20 per cent of the inhabitants are new arrivals, who, according to one local leader, 'have their feet in Santa Cruz and their head in Havana.' *Santacruceños* normally regard them as intruders, while the newcomers disdain what they consider the 'uncouth manner' of the local population. Although the conflict is usually resolved through mutual indifference, it has been a relevant factor in decision-making and has affected participation in various parts of the locality.

Chambas

Chambas, in the center of the island, is a municipality whose population features are very similar to those of Santa Cruz, but with more agricultural activity and rural population. The 8,000 inhabitants of Chambas, the capital, are interrelated by primary links that are probably stronger than those in Santa Cruz. Despite evident development of social services and significant economic investment throughout the jurisdiction, Chambas has changed little in the past two decades and there are no visible signs of dramatic change coming soon. It is not as prosperous as Santa Cruz, but there is no sign of the hardship observed in Centro Habana. We dubbed Chambas 'the municipality of consensus,' where everyone seems to agree with almost everything. This appears to be strongly related to the surprising vigor of the local leadership, where women play a decisive role, and to the weight of local traditions, which are more accepting of authority. Daily life in Chambas is permeated by a sense of sincere hospitality, for which our team was profoundly grateful.

From both a political and a socio-historical point of view, Chambas is the weakest of the four municipalities selected for study. The coincidence between legal and historical municipality is almost non-existent, and, save for the resolve of political leaders, there are no centripetal forces such as those present in Santa Cruz. The jurisdiction is divided into various regions with well-defined centers, usually revolving around large sugar concerns with weak interrelationships. It is not surprising that local leaders have had to make an effort to avoid what they call 'localism,' and thus many a local government initiative must be directed towards solving or preventing such conflict. This municipality has seriously suffered the consequences of the centralizing tendencies of the provincial government. Resulting cuts in the size of its administrative apparatus have impaired management abilities and the capacity to respond to population demands.

In conclusion, the municipalities selected were diverse enough to allow for comparison and generalizations that may be considered valid for the entire national spectrum.

The Selection of Leadership: Electoral Process, Conduct and Results[7]

Local Electoral Committees are responsible for organizing municipal elections, held every two-and-a-half years. These committees are chaired by a local leader of the Communist Party and are composed of representatives of various social and mass organizations, as well as by citizens with experience in organizing this type of activity. Committees have several duties, notably organization, mobilization of resources, and guaranteeing strict observance of the existing legal framework. In general, the process can be divided into two stages. Voters grouped by constituency elect delegates to Municipal Assemblies. Delegates then elect the executive of the municipal government, in addition to municipal representatives to the provincial and national levels. Let us first focus on the initial voting process, which we can divide into three phases.

The first may be considered the 'nomination phase,' and it takes place through a series of neighborhood meetings where residents decide who from their community is best qualified for nomination. This is followed by open, direct voting on all proposed candidates, until those deemed most adequate are selected as candidates. Each delegate position must have more than one candidate, to a limit of eight. In the communities we observed, slightly more than half of registered voters took part in these meetings, which attracted anything from several dozen to several hundred people, depending on the size of the constituency. Women and seniors are the most frequent active participants, not just in debate, but also in preparing the meeting place, generally a school, small auditorium or other public building, or simply outdoors. Although there is a ritual for conducting these gatherings, they are also noted for a climate of informal debate enlivened by the presence of neighborhood children, for whom these meetings present an excellent recreational opportunity.

In accordance with a basic rule of municipal electoral procedure, no organization may submit candidates or publicly support them. This is intended to guarantee free expression of voter preference and avoid possible external interference.[8] Nominations are usually put forward by individuals, or informally by a group of individuals. Once the round of nomination meetings is concluded, the second phase begins. The primary objective of this phase is to provide information on the background of the various candidates, so that voters may select the one they consider most adequate to represent community interests in the local government. The information procedure is rather laconic, limited to posting biographies and photographs of the candidates nominated by each constituency. As in the preceding phase, political campaigning and other acts on behalf of candidates are not allowed. Finally, secret and direct voting takes place. All citizens over 16 years old and in full exercise of their political rights (that is, excluding those in jail and those who are mentally impaired) may vote. Voter turnout is very high, always higher than 95 per cent, although this number falls in runoffs. According to our observations, most voters approach the voting booth with very definite ideas as to the candidate of their choice. As a result, few ballots are spoiled or remain unused.[9] Although polls are open until 6 p.m., most voters cast their ballot during the morning hours. In many places voting constitutes an opportunity for social interaction, during which neighbors chat and generally linger for a long time. It is common to see extended families in attendance.

In more than one sense, this political process constitutes a vital moment in the political life of the nation. Technically, it is the starting point for the constitution of all state delegate bodies, since municipal assemblies receive a mandate to elect both provincial and national assemblies. Seen from another perspective, voting for municipal assemblies provides the single direct electoral exercise Cubans enjoy within the realm of the state, and is therefore an experiment of great relevance for democracy-building and the creation of a culture of political participation.

Above all, since they take place within a single-party system, the experience of Cuban municipal elections may hold an interest that transcends the purely national setting. Its participatory qualities may perhaps be a significant indication of the actual possibilities for the development of participatory democracy within such a political context, including as an alternative to competitive, multi-party systems with their many limitations.

Of course, the participatory quality of any election is directly linked to the climate of freedom in which it takes place, including the ability of citizens to exercise their right to nomination, to select alternatives and to vote without coercive external interference. The empirical evidence we gathered indicates that local Cuban elections take place in a climate of sufficient freedom to gain legitimacy by the citizenry. This is not to deny, of course, the incidence of compulsive factors such as a sense of civic duty or political or ideological commitment. None of the individuals we interviewed who had made or discussed nomination proposals said that external forces interfered with the free choice of nominees or with the process of voting.[10]

Such a contention no doubt raises an eyebrow or two. After all, more than 70 per cent of elected delegates are members of the Communist Party (PCC) or the Young Communist Union (UJC), although membership of these organizations accounts for just 17 per cent of the electorate. For an important group of Cubanologists, this is perceived as over-representation of the *militancia* (the term used in Cuba for PCC and UJC members) resulting from an Orwellian manipulation of the system for the purpose of ensuring political loyalty in municipal bodies. From an opposite standpoint, this fact is narrowly interpreted as explicit indication of popular support for the PCC, and therefore a definite act of identification with the political and ideological values it represents. Although these assumptions appear to be antithetical, they have more than one point in common, notably the assumption that the vote is consciously cast in favor of a militant, voluntarily or not.

Reality, however, seems to lie elsewhere – and not exactly midway between the extremes. The electoral behavior of the communities studied, and consequently the orientation of the vote, seem to have more points in common with ethical considerations than with political-ideological paradigms. When asked which qualities they considered most important in a delegate, most of those surveyed referred to such moral considerations as honesty, solidarity toward neighbors, human sensibility, and so on. Political and ideological qualities were mentioned in second place, with concerns about the administrative and managerial abilities of the candidates ranked only in third place. Fewer than 10 per cent made references to membership of the Communist Party or the Young Communist Union as a desirable quality, although of ten candidates in the five constituencies studied, nine were members of the PCC or UJC. A significant number could not remember whether candidates were militants or not.

Of course, this argument does not pretend to dismiss the weight of political-ideological considerations upon voting patterns, or feign unawareness of the implications inherent in such results, at least in reference to its incidence on the legitimacy of the leading role of the Communist Party within Cuban society. The point we wish to make is that, rather than static readings from either side of the issue, the Cuban community phenomenon as a scenario for participation necessitates interpretations that take political and ideological factors into consideration, but that do not turn them into the sole consideration. Such an analysis ought to be able to integrate other dimensions, including the sense of community belonging, the strength of local leadership, and the peculiarities of the new civil society. This civil society is crystallizing after 30 years of revolutionary life into a collection of political values, norms and conducts that have become part of the national fabric, however diverse its gender, cultural, generational and existential texture.[11] Yet, even if we consider that a climate of freedom is necessary for a genuinely participatory electoral process, we have to recognize that this alone is not sufficient. All elections imply a certain transfer of power (in fact, they are only a chapter in the circulation of political power), so that their participatory qualities cannot be reduced to what the liberal paradigm pretends elections to be. In fact, democratic grading of the vote is directly related to its force as a conscious act of conditional delegation of sovereignty. This consideration was probably in the minds of the designers of the Cuban municipal electoral scheme. Compulsory norms were included in this respect, notably accountability before the community and recall rights, which will be discussed later on.

However, the system lacks the mechanisms needed to go beyond purely individual action and turn the electoral process into a sphere for citizen interaction and accord, and strengthen local leadership. The paradox of this restriction is that the critical factors are precisely those originally conceived to guarantee free exercise of the will of the citizenry. This statement may be illustrated by analyzing the way in which the circulation of information during elections was conceived. As we mentioned, in order to ensure equal opportunity for all candidates nominated by the citizenry, election rules ban campaigning or publicity on the candidates' behalf. The biography method described earlier is used instead. This is so low-key that it is not a major vehicle for communication. According to our study in Santa Cruz, for example, only 9 per cent of the population thought it was an effective information system, and fewer than one-third had read candidate biographies before voting. The poor dissemination of biographies shifts the circulation of information to primary links among neighbors, conceivably with such unwanted results as the transmission of conservative and traditional stereotypes. Moreover, the biography-based information system, which is intended to guarantee equal opportunity for all candidates, in practice achieves the opposite result. It penalizes such groups as women and youth, whose accomplishments in public or work life are usually more limited than those of male adults.

This is arguably the greatest weakness of the municipal electoral system. It is hard to understate the virtues of a leadership selection process that has managed to avoid demagoguery, mercantilization of the vote and fragmentation of the populace around patterns of loyalty to a party or political boss. Yet, it must be admitted that the focus on moral values and political conduct as the primary criteria for political leadership has been overemphasized and has created a serious obstacle to the emergence of dynamic, representative leaders who are capable of facing the challenge of power.

Although some of these unwanted results will be analyzed later in more detail, we would like to mention one of them: the under-representation of women. Eighty-four per cent of elected delegates are male, most over 30 years old. If we bear in mind that this is the result of a direct and essentially free election, we can only conclude that old patterns of discrimination, which assign to women certain obligations, including those attendant to their role as mothers, and thus limit availability of spare time for public service, are very much alive and are expressed during the electoral process through the casting of votes in favor of men. The inherent paradox is that women are generally recognized as the most efficient community activists, while the most successful delegates are those who ask for the co-operation of women.[12]

The degree to which this might negatively influence the quality of local policies is a debatable issue. Community representatives receive their mandate from society as a whole and not from a specific gender, generation or other such sector, so that sociological under-representation should not automatically be construed as under-representation of interests. There is no doubt that community representatives try to do their job with great dosages of social sensibility and spirit of sacrifice. Yet, it is not unreasonable to believe that the good intentions of an elected representative are not sufficient for the conduct of a public office requiring an understanding of the complex needs of sectors whose daily lives, motivations and wants they do not fully share.

We must recognize that considerable progress has been achieved since 1976, when the sub-system of local government was first established, including nearly doubling the number of women in local elected posts. Yet, these achievements have been slow in coming, and stronger positive action is necessary. This ought to include substantial reform of the election advertising and information methods prescribed by the system, as well as more dynamic and autonomous organization of individual groups, perhaps in the style of the Federación de Mujeres Cubanas. Although it may appear irrelevant to promote actions that sacrifice the effectiveness of popular representation in favor of sector representation, it does not seem likely that Cuban society will be able to reach higher levels of equality and renewal if reforms are left to the natural course of time.

Participation and Decision-making

In addition to elections, popular participation in Cuba's sub-system of municipal government takes place at various moments of the decision-making process – from expressing demands to defining the issues to evaluating the decisions made. This is done by means as varied as neighborhoods meetings, involvement in social projects and participation in accountability and oversight bodies, including committees, people's inspections, and so on. Community-based social and political organizations have a significant role to play in most of these participatory activities, notably CDRs, the community mobilization agent *par excellence*, as well as the FMC and other more informal, yet locally influential, organizations such as neighborhood and school councils, senior citizens' associations and youth clubs.[13]

Participation of residents and delegates varies considerably from one municipality to the next, and from one type of activity to another. In fact, although group members surveyed generally said they do not have enough time to conduct their inspection and oversight duties, most agreed it was a useful job from which they derived great satisfaction. In Centro Habana, however, the extent of dissatisfaction was much greater, given the complexities facing municipal decision-making there as well as reduced municipal encouragement of this type of work, which is conducted on a wholly voluntary basis. The type of activity, on the other hand, appears to have a direct bearing on the degree of satisfaction, which tends to be greater in the case of municipal policies that are well focused, have more central support and enjoy better resources, such as health and education.

Of the various types of participatory activities in the municipal arena, arguably the most relevant are the accountability meetings (Reuniones de Rendición de Cuentas, RRC – sometimes translated as Meetings to Render Accounts). These were conceived as a venue for information exchange between government and community; that is, for expression of demands by the population and explanation by the government of the scope or limitations of its work. They also provide an occasion for collective discussion of local issues and possible solutions. Meetings take place every six months and are chaired by the local constituency delegate. Government and administrative officials are usually in attendance, especially when deemed necessary or whenever the community requests their presence.

Although 50–60 per cent of constituents usually turn out (anywhere from 100 to 2,000 attending), audiences often dwindle as the meetings carry on. Meetings begin with reports from government officials and delegates. The heart and soul of the meetings, though, is the debate and discussion that follows. This period allows the expression of new demands and discussion of the most relevant issues facing the community. The length of RRCs varies considerably, depending on the complexity of the topics debated, the number of accumulated issues, and the skill of delegates leading the meeting, but they usually last 50–60 minutes. Those most closely connected to the community and its issues – that is, women and senior citizens – are often the most active participants.

To what extent RRCs satisfy the objectives for which they were created is a relative question. First, as in other community processes, this largely depends on the type of community and population, and on the ability of local leaders to mobilize resources and effect a satisfactory outcome. It is therefore not surprising that the most dynamic meetings take place in small communities and not in large urban centers, particularly in the capital, where the sense of community is weaker and the accumulated issues are more numerous and harder to resolve. And, as might be expected, some objectives are achieved with greater effectiveness than others.

Let us first consider RRCs as a mechanism for the formulation of demands. Through interviews with delegates and community members, and through our own attendance at meetings, we observed that meetings seemed to enjoy legitimacy as instruments for conveying claims and for providing feedback to government. Although there are other avenues for expressing demands (directly to local or national officials or by meeting privately with delegates), 68 per cent of the 6,571 demands submitted in the four selected municipalities between October 1989 and April 1990 were presented at RRCs. If we consider the existence of demands limited to family or personal issues, which people may prefer to discuss in a more private setting, this figure may be as high as 85 per cent.

The RRCs provide an opportunity for debate and agreement on everyday issues facing people and their community, for the expression and transmission of demands, and for effective transmission of information from the community to both local and national government. Local governments are aware that they cannot afford to ignore the outcome of these meetings – a fact well known by citizens and their representatives.

There are, nevertheless, weaknesses in the role and functioning of the RRCs. The converse flow of information from government to community is more limited due to the excessive formality of the information provided in reports, making it somewhat inaccessible and sometimes boring to the ordinary citizen. This limits the ability of citizens to exercise their oversight rights over public activity. Nor have the RRCs become powerful centers for collective action and accord. RRCs are an occasion for community interaction which is somehow isolated from other forms of interaction and organization. There is practically no previous accord among smaller organizations such as neighborhood, women's or youth groups, which might facilitate collective construction of demands. This explains why demands made at RRCs are generally presented in an individual manner, even when they pertain to collective interests. Of more than 6,000 demands studied in the four selected municipalities, only 6 per cent showed some degree of prior group agreement. The only chance to surmount the individual nature of demands seems to occur during meetings, and to a great extent this hinges on delegate ability and leadership. Although it is not impossible to find outstanding community leaders who rally constituents together, obtain support from local officials, and launch self-managed projects without immediate recourse to government authorities, these are the exception. Needless to say, this creates a demand overload for municipal authorities. An inevitable consequence is the regrettable underuse of the population's participation potential. Arguably, the imbalance between its successes as a conduit for raising and addressing demands and the weaker results of the accountability and accord functions may be a reflection of one of the greatest shortcomings of the community process: a paternalistic relation between the government, on one side, and the community and citizens, on the other. Not only does this work to the detriment of the stated objectives, but, from a strategic perspective, it is also detrimental to the establishment of a society where collective action and social self-management are meant to prevail.

The Institutional Hierarchies of Municipal Government

In any complex social setting, Cuban municipalities included, participation cannot be limited to direct citizen involvement – hence the need for indirect participation through representation. It is therefore useful to analyze institutional relations and the place occupied by representative bodies in the Cuban municipal system. According to the Constitution and its regulations, delegate assemblies are the highest state authority in each municipality. Designers of the People's Power system granted assemblies a number of electoral, oversight and recall prerogatives in relation to the remaining municipal institutions, including executive committees and the administrative apparatus. Although Municipal Assemblies are required to meet only for one or two days twice a year, they actually do so much more frequently. We noted that local governments complement their scant legislative timetable with informal meetings attended by all or most delegates, so that in fact they do meet to discuss community issues and make decisions practically every month. The agenda for these meetings is set by the respective Executive Committee and submitted to the consideration of delegates, who may modify it. They rarely do so, at least formally, and prefer to introduce issues for discussion during the course of the debate. Only in exceptional cases do the upper structures, either provincial or national, order the inclusion of some point of interest to them.

We observed that Municipal Assembly meetings are noted for lengthy, well-attended debate, particularly when topics related to everyday community life are discussed. Great efforts are made here toward building and organizing consensus on contentious issues. Unpopular pronouncements are seldom greeted by signs of disapproval, while delegates will applaud a point well made. Treatment is respectful and chairpersons use a democratic style in conducting these meetings.

Apart from meetings, Municipal Assemblies have other means of action. Permanent Work Commissions (Comisiones Permanentes de Trabajo) are perhaps the most relevant. As mentioned, these are specialized groups of delegates and ordinary citizens charged with supervising and evaluating various economic and social activities in the municipality. Work Commisions meet periodically to analyze the evolution of production, economic and social services or other such topics of interest, either at their own initiative or at the behest of the Assembly or Executive Committee. Subsequently, they prepare reports and make recommendations which become mandatory practices for all local state agencies, once they have been approved by the Municipal Assembly. To a great extent, commission work helps to compensate for the rather short time set aside for plenary Assembly meetings.

However, our analysis of the potential of these commissions indicates that they are vastly under-utilized, whether because of the shortcomings of the municipal system itself or because of the manner in which the various components of local government relate to each other. As noted, commissions were created to strengthen the accountability of representative institutions, notably Assemblies. In practice, however, commissions tend to be subordinated to Executive Committees (in fact, members define them as the right hand of Executive Committees), and their appearance at Assemblies is perceived as simply the last step in securing approval for a job which has already been evaluated by the EC.

If we keep in mind that in actual practice the relationship between Executive Committees and administrative authorities is closer than desirable for maintaining the independent performance of either, then it is not surprising to conclude that democratic control over municipal bureaucracies is limited. The same reasons explain why commission reports and recommendations are often not duly taken into account by decision-making bodies even though they have been formally adopted.[14]

An objective assessment of Municipal Assemblies indicates that they are important for discussion and decision-making in relation to the issues facing localities, and function well as a means of representing the interests of the population. If we bear in mind that no sustained historical experience of representative institutions exists in Cuba, then we ought to consider Municipal Assemblies as a remarkable step forward in building democracy, particularly at the local level. Yet it would be unrealistic to state that Municipal Assemblies have become actual centers of government power. In everyday life, different variables have impeded fulfillment of this role, even independently of the political will of local authorities.

A primary factor is the composition of Assemblies. As noted, they are composed of delegates elected through direct and secret balloting – by voters for whom criteria of efficiency or expertise are secondary and subordinated to ethical and political considerations. The composition of Assemblies reflects this fact. Although delegates are usually noted for a deep sense of their duty to represent voters, their governmental vocation is less satisfactory. As a result, the more sophisticated acts of governing – for example, discussion of a territorial Economic Plan, the earning ability of large enterprises, or election of the judiciary – are incomprehensible or at least not a major concern to them. Social and other issues which directly affect the community are thus debated more extensively during Assembly sessions. This also explains why delegates openly prefer informal meetings with a flexible agenda, generally focusing on discussion of the issues facing them in daily life.

This situation has been made worse by other circumstances, including high Municipal Assembly turnover following elections (about 50 per cent) and the short duration of their mandate (two-and-a-half years). This means that each term in government becomes a period of apprenticeship and training, which is then interrupted precisely when it begins to mature.

A third factor which limits the role of Municipal Assemblies as an actual locus of government power is the role of the Executive Committee. As mentioned, the EC represents the Assembly between sessions, which legally makes it a permanent body. A repository of the highest state power, its nature is twofold: administrative–executive, as well as representative. In order to meet the first requirement, professional members of the Executive Committee take on control and oversight duties for various social and economic activities within the municipality. They thereby enter into a direct relationship with specific sectors of the administrative apparatus in the jurisdiction, whether locally subordinated or not. However, in order to guarantee its representative nature and strict subordination to Municipal Assemblies, the designers of the system made the status of delegate a condition for EC membership. The intention was

that attainment of this high government office would have to be indirectly supported by popular vote.

Election of the Executive Committee is the last stage of the municipal
electoral process and consists of submission of a list of candidates to the
Assembly. The list may be modified and is always 25 per cent higher than
the number of posts being contested. It is presented by the municipal
electoral committee, which is chaired by the Communist Party and composed of social and mass organizations. These do everything in their
power to propose persons of sufficient prestige and competence to attract the delegate vote and guarantee at least a modicum of success for
the EC. Delegates then hold a secret ballot to elect Executive Committee
members from this list. Those elected then meet behind closed doors
and elect the three top positions: president, vice-president and secretary.

The method has enough controls to make a satisfactory grade on a
democratic scale. Yet the fact is that the process generally results in a
hybrid that fails to meet either the representative nature or the functional
requisites fully. This method, in fact, transfers a greater quota of power
than was intended to local administrative bodies, the most stable institutions, which therefore become the ones most capable of providing
continuity to local policy.

Several alternative formulas might be discussed, and probably none
would be completely accepted. But if we want to attain a democratic and
efficient institutionality, municipal governments must develop a more
precise definition of their function and structure in order to create a
more open and participatory electoral system than that now in place. The
issue of Municipal Assemblies actually becoming the top state body in
each jurisdiction is not exhausted by discussion of their relationship with
other municipal institutions. This is directly linked to what is in Cuba the
sensitive issue of the real ability of municipal governments actually to
govern, rather than just manage functions delegated by the central
authority.

The Ability to Govern

Evaluation of the actual governing abilities of local government comes to
a positive first conclusion. Comparison of the current situation with that
before 1976 shows that a great decentralizing of Cuba's public administration apparatus has been achieved. Whatever its current shortcomings,
to which we will refer shortly, local government is able to influence
development of territorial economic plans and local budgets, adopt policies
and initiatives that exert considerable local influence, and act as a point
of mediation for nationwide development projects. This is very significant

in a country where, just two decades ago, everything was directed in a centralized manner through subordinate institutions enjoying almost no decision-making role.

As noted, various administrative levels may coexist within municipal jurisdictions, including those under provincial and national control. This makes for a fairly complex mosaic, whose impact on the functional exercise of local government is worthy of note. A graphic example is the case of one of the medium-sized municipalities selected for study, where a total of 15 locally controlled bodies existed, including six corporations (housing construction, cafeterias and restaurants, retail, services, etc.), in addition to a similar number of agencies providing government-subsidized social services, including the education, health, finance, social security and employment directorates. Next are dozens of provincially controlled agencies in this municipality. Although their scope extends beyond the purely municipal sphere, they also offer services at this level, where they organize in the form of *establecimientos*. Grouped in this category are small producers of construction materials, food plants and small hotels. Lastly, territories are also home to corporations whose impact is national in scope and which operate under national control. In the case of the selected municipality, there are about a dozen such corporations, including power plants and agro-industrial complexes.

Given the complexity and asymmetry of the administrative powers dispersed throughout the jurisdiction, there is a conflict *vis-à-vis* the ability of municipal institutions to govern.

Establecimientos are created from the elimination of municipal corporations, or simply because it is deemed unrealistic to create a new concern and its attendant bureaucracy for small-scale activities. Municipalities exert or try to exert an influence upon *establecimientos*, but since current regulations establish that these are not decision-making areas, the impact municipalities can have, while greater than is the case with national corporations, is always limited – even when dealing with units that produce essential goods or services.

A national corporation generally has material and human resources as large as or greater than those of a municipality, especially if we speak about localities of moderate size. Municipal government can exert only limited influence upon them. This relationship, officially designated as 'co-operation' or 'assistance,' takes place through such specialized municipal bodies as the finance, labor, social security and statistics departments. Municipalities receive certain indirect benefits from revenues.

In practice, however, the relationship between municipalities and national corporations is richer and more fruitful than originally intended. National corporations can hardly do without the services offered by municipalities, which provide essential supplies and the labor force. Also, their significant local impact means that they are affected by municipal needs. These relationships are spontaneously expressed in the transfer of human and material resources toward municipalities for social service activities, as well as in the use of secondary production capacity in meeting local needs.

Many an example could be cited of corporation–municipality relationships with a positive impact upon the community. The fact that these relationships are fundamentally spontaneous – for the law allows for only modest municipal input – makes the real ability to govern depend on such variables as the bargaining skills of local authorities or the goodwill of corporate directors. Obviously, these conditions are not necessarily present and are quite fragile. All this is connected to a key issue of Cuban economic organization, which reaches well beyond the municipal arena: the ability of corporations to make autonomous decisions within their field.

Another area of conflict is the power of local governments to exert real control over activities officially defined as locally controlled; that is, those directly linked to everyday needs – health, education, food distribution, construction of housing and community buildings, cultural and sports services, and so on. According to the original design, these activities are to be conducted under the 'double subordination' concept, which grants administrative control to municipal government; this must operate on the basis of 'methodological indications' developed by the central government and supervised by provincial government counterparts.

The principle of double subordination is not faulty in itself. It is meant to offer technical supervision to decentralized bodies in order to avoid wasting of resources and services of inferior quality. It is also meant to provide practical training for new local authorities *vis-à-vis* their prerogatives and function. In practice, the initial concept left little room for local initiative, which was understandable in a context of the creation of new institutions. Fifteen years later, however, at a time when municipal bodies have attained sufficient proficiency, methodological subordination prerogatives seem excessive. In some regions, they have reinforced the centralizing tendencies of provincial governments, which often exceed original premises and dispense altogether with municipal prerogatives in favor of supposed administrative efficiency.

Thus the ability of local governments to govern and not just administer, and in so doing retain sufficient decision-making and coactive authority, has been rather modest. They have generally wound up in charge of those tasks more directly linked to everyday life and to the demands of the population, yet have insufficient resources available for an effective response. In addition, their ability to mobilize human and material resources at the local level is hampered by 'methodologies' handed down from the top and by centralizing provincial governments. As a result, only a very imaginative performance can save local leaders and institutions from the loss of legitimacy that results from being unable to make decisions.

Contrary to what may be presumed, the role of Communist Party Municipal Committees is significant in protecting and consolidating the authority of local governments. This is so not just because of the great political weight of the PCC, but for the more concrete reason that it is the only local institution whose jurisdiction extends to the entire economic and decision-making system in the territory, powerful national corporations included. This is probably why 77 per cent of delegates polled expressed satisfaction about the Party role in local government, although only one-third considered that the Party was involved in this type of activity.

Perspectives

The sub-system of local government examined here is not a mere institutional formality. On the contrary, even taking into account the limitations imposed by insufficient material and human resources and other hurdles noted here, Cuban municipalities have become effective mechanisms for local development and for meeting the everyday needs of the population, either through local initiative or as an arena for national plans. No less important is their role as a stage in the process of building democracy.

However, 15 years after implementation, the sub-system of local government shows sufficient shortcomings to lead to the conclusion that reorganization and revitalization have become primary tasks. This has been officially recognized, and has been placed on the agenda for improvement of the Cuban political system. Consensus about the need for renewal, of course, does not imply consensus as to where and how to renew. This makes the topic a bone of contention at administrative, political and academic levels.

A primary component of renewal is participation. Even considering its undoubted achievements, Cuba's municipal participation system has been hampered by excessive formality and bureaucracy, so that the final result falls short of what was wanted and planned in the original design. The system has consequently produced an unwanted result in encouraging a rather paternalistic, top-down relationship between local government and the community, all in a fundamentally parochial surrounding. Sustained community self-government experiences are few, while the differential appeals of participation remain stark. The meager performance of representative institutions *vis-à-vis* their prerogatives as top state authorities in their respective territories is also a negative factor. Naturally, rectifying such shortcomings will unavoidably require specific action designed to de-formalize and revitalize participation, in addition to the specific institutional adjustments we have noted through the course of this chapter.

Rather than restating the argument, we would prefer to frame our conclusions within what might be termed a series of substantial systemic modifications, without which the constraints faced by community and local bodies, in terms of both participation and decision-making, may be difficult to surmount. In the final analysis, community bodies and local governments are just segments of a larger society and political system, and the former share with the latter not just their virtues, but also their limitations, which set the modalities and the pace.

A substantial primary principle is the need to advance more pluralistic political styles, which will eventually encourage greater vigor and autonomy on the part of civil society. From a logical point of view, the issue seems simple enough: every society is diverse – class, gender, generational differences exist, and so democratic public activity can be expressed only through pluralism. Politically, the issue is much more complex because, among other reasons, of the rejection professed by most Marxists for the very concept of pluralism, and also because of the limited use made of it by the liberal academy, which tends to limit the concept of democracy to institutional arrangements.

In the case of the Cuban revolution, this is also strongly conditioned by history. Although there have been different policies aimed towards certain sectors (such as women), it is also true that unity around the concept of 'the people,' rather than emphasis on diversity, has been seen as the best guarantor of the revolution's agenda. Although three decades later unity is still vital, we ought to acknowledge that unwanted results have been produced in the process, mostly through unrealistic desires for unanimity and through holding a falsely monolithic paradigm of society as a measure of political success.

From this perspective, encouraging pluralism does not signify its reduction to the multi-party paradigm or elevate the latter to the status of a national historical goal. Various concrete theoretical and historical reasons lead us to believe that a multi-party system would have a counter-productive effect on furthering democratization and participation in Cuban society, and that in fact it would degrade many of the virtues of Cuban public activity in the heat of the political market-place. So far as local government is concerned, the point may very well be moot, since in many multi-party systems the dynamics of local activity exist outside party competition.

The opening of a space for socialist pluralism implies, above all, greater autonomy for political organizations participating in civil society, whose role cannot be reduced to that of a worn conveyor belt moving only one way – from the top down. This also implies reformulating the method of representation in state bodies. Finally, it implies recognizing conflict as a stage in building and guiding consensus, with the resolution of conflict proceeding through broader and more systematic public debate, both within and outside the Communist Party, whose political leadership role is in need of substantial democratization and anti-bureaucratic change. In the final analysis, within a single-party system, society will be only as democratic as the Party manages to be.

A second scenario of renewal deals with the status of municipal bodies as a segment of the public administration system that ought to have sufficient power to become fully responsible for its assigned governmental duties (i.e. decision-making, implementation and coaction) within its territorial jurisdiction. In other words, there must be changes in the balance between centralization and decentralization. This contradictory relationship (referred to in official documents as 'the achievement of an adequate balance between centralization and decentralization') is now of widespread importance, not just in reference to municipal issues.

The proven success of municipal government in meeting social needs wherever there is sufficient room for local planning, decision-making and deployment of human and financial resources is perhaps the most eloquent argument to be made in favor of greater political and administrative decentralization in Cuba. Only real proximity to power on the part of actual citizens in an autonomous, dynamic society will move beyond narrow mobilization and implementation objectives and towards popular participation that encourages initiative, greater oversight powers and effective control over public activities.

Far be it for us to suggest that the full answer to the numerous obstacles faced by the Cuban socialist project lies in the workings of local structures, or, from a systemic perspective, in the construction of a more participatory, pluralistic and decentralized system. Almost by definition, none of these proposals is a panacea, and the issues faced by Cuban society are, at any rate, extremely varied and diverse. What we wish to note is that no global solution can do without the democratic and participation goals explained here, and that, rather than economic effectiveness or technocratic efficiency, the main guarantee of socialist continuity will be its ability to move towards its historic goal of building a structure of human achievement without precedent in history. Such a goal, and the process of achieving it, is not an abstraction but an imperative of daily life.

Appendix: Methodology

Selection of municipalities and communities

One of the most acute methodological issues was selection of the municipalities where research would take place. We dispensed with the possibility of selecting a representative sample, since no previous studies existed and no reliable statistical basis could be obtained. We decided to choose a group of municipalities which presented sufficiently diverse characteristics to provide a variety of data that could then be compared. We analyzed a group of twelve possible candidates, and selected four of them on the basis of three basic criteria: population size, spatial relationship to central or provincial bodies, degree of coincidence between the legal and historical municipalities.

When selection was completed, we conducted a comprehensive statistical review of the economic, social and political-administrative organization in each locality. This allowed identification of both the basic issues and the main subjects present in each. Statistical analysis included a review of demands submitted during a six-month period and the type of response given by local government.

After identifying the principal subjects of our research, we used a set of instruments adapted to each situation. In general, we avoided quantitative measurement and emphasized the use of more intensive instruments to allow the active participation of subjects. Case studies were conducted on particular problems and issues. Initiatives undertaken in connection with each municipality were as follows:

1. *Ordinary citizens* A series of (non-participant) observations were conducted at the most relevant direct participation events, including neighborhood meetings, community projects, elections (one municipality only), etc. Various discussion groups were created. These functioned as workshops of great effectiveness, particularly where women's groups were concerned.

2. *Delegates* A closed survey directed at 170 delegates was conducted. Some 151 responded. Delegates were also targeted for observation in places where they participated as community leaders or local government representatives. Lastly, we formed discussion groups in which 24 delegates participated.

3. *Municipal Assemblies and Executive Committees* We made observations at regular and special meetings, reviewed all available documentation, and conducted semi- and non-standard interviews. Several rounds of discussion with presidents and vice-presidents of local governments were held. Discussion groups were also formed with delegates and ordinary citizens who sat in Work Commissions.

4. *Administrative Apparatus* We conducted a number of interviews with administrators in local government, subordinated concerns, and national corporations in the jurisdiction.

5. *Non-governmental political and social organizations* Interviews were conducted with leaders in the Communist Party, the Federation of Cuban Women, Committees for the Defense of the Revolution, labor unions, the Young Communist Union, and other groups represented in the community.

We also designed three case studies in order to establish the peculiarities of a locality in greater detail:

A. A study of elections in Santa Cruz del Norte, for which researchers stayed three months in the community. As elections take place simultaneously throughout the country, this could not be used elsewhere as it would have necessitated the deployment of specialized personnel we did not have. Methods used included observation, interviews, surveys, and a review of the documentation.

B. An analysis of administrative relationships between provinces and municipalities, on the basis of acknowledging the strong centralizing tendencies of provinces. This study was conducted in the province of Ciego de Avila and in the municipality of Chambas, where the relationship has been more strained. It included a documentary review, observations and interviews.

C. A study of the October 1990 creation of Popular Councils in Centro Habana. Councils are construed as an intermediate level between the municipality and the population. Pueblo Nuevo and Cayo Hueso Councils were selected, and several rounds of interviews and observations were conducted. The conclusions of case studies B and C are to be found in Haroldo Dilla and Gerardo González, *Participación y desarrollo en los municipios cubanos* (forthcoming).

Finally, as a contribution to the restructuring process taking place in the sub-system of municipal government, a number of measures were adopted to ensure rapid and systematic circulation of the data collected.

Notes

1. This study was funded with the generous support of the International Development Research Centre in Ottawa. This kind of study always involves a large number of assistants and a strong support network. In addition to the authors, several researchers took part in different stages of the project, including Armando Fernández (who helped develop the original design and worked through the first stage of the project), Aurelio Alonso (who led the project for a time), Ilya Villar,

Alfredo Prieto and Elina Peraza. Ana Teresa Vincentelli and Darlene Molina deserve special mention. Aurelio Martínez, Humberto Piñeiro, Ibis Pachot, Sonia Pérez, Barbara Erice and Luis Méndez assisted us in different ways. We thank Juan Valdés Paz for his timely criticism, Magaly Pineda for her suggestions, Chris Smart for his encouragement, as well as Michael Kaufman and other members of our regional network for their support. Above all, we want to express our gratitude for the support and hospitality shown by the people and local authorities in our research regions and by the National Assembly of People's Power.

2.   Irving Horowitz, 'Institutionalization as Integration: The Cuban Revolution at Age Twenty,' *Cuban Studies* (July 1977).

3.   Jorge Domínguez, *Cuba: Order and Revolution* (Cambridge, MA: Harvard University Press, 1978).

4.   C. Mesa Lago, *Cuba in the 1970s. Pragmatism and Institutionalization* (Albuquerque: University of New Mexico Press, 1978).

5.   A. Ritter, 'The Bodies of People's Power and the Community Party: The Nature of Cuban Democracy,' and R.P. Rabking, 'Cuban Political Structures: Vanguard Party and athe Mases,' both in S. Halebsky and J. Kirk, eds., *Twenty-five Years of Revolution* (New York: Praeger, 1985).

6.   W. Leogrande, *Modes of Political Participation in Revolutionary Cuba* (Pennsylvania: University of Pennsylvania Press, 1977); and M. Azicri, 'The Institutionalization of the Cuban State,' *Journal of Interamerican Studies and World Affairs*, vol. 22, no. 3, 1980.

7.   The empirical foundation of this section is to be found in a case study conducted in Santa Cruz del Norte in March–May 1989, later published as a working paper: H. Dilla and A. Fernández, 'Las Elecciones Municipales en Cuba: Un Estudio de Caso,' *Caribe Contemporaneo*, no. 23.

8.   This assertion deserves a brief explanation. Certainly this rule was an attempt to keep Cuban elections away from either the then-Eastern European model or the liberal-democratic model. On the one hand, the issue was how to avoid the typical formalism prevailing in the Eastern European electoral system, with its single candidates with Party support. On the other hand, the proposed scheme rejected some competitive patterns implicit in the liberal-democratic model of an electoral market, such as campaigns, individual promotion, etc. The intention was to give the project a touch of originality, assigning a leading role to the popular component.

9.   No Cuba-wide figures are available on the number of blank or spoiled ballots. Nevertheless, our own count in five Santa Cruz polling stations showed low numbers, close to 4 per cent spoiled and 3 per cent blank.

10.   This is borne out in our survey answered by 151 delegates. Only 10 per cent said they had received some suggestion to accept the nomination, while 6 per cent said they were always or frequently told how to vote. Most of these were from Centro Habana, where conflict seemed to be more acute. The sources of these suggestions are varied, and appear to be generally motivated by a desire to secure a capable Executive body (for reasons we will explain later) or consensus on a particularly difficult topic.

11.   R. Fernández and H. Dilla, 'Cultura política y participación popular en Cuba,' *Cuadernos de Nuestra América*, vol. III (July–December 1990).

12.   The percentage of female delegates changes considerably from one munici-

pality to the next. Centro Habana showed the highest figure (21 per cent) followed by Santa Cruz (17 per cent, similar to the national average.) However, in Chambas and Bayamo, the two more traditional areas in our study, the figure was closer to 12 per cent. At the same time, both the assembly president and secretary in Chambas were women. These posts stood first and third in the local hierarchy, and local opinion was positive about their role.

13. A successful example of citizen involvement in oversight activities is Working Groups (Comisiones de Trabajo), which assist Municipal Assemblies by reporting on the status of social services or economic activity in the jurisdiction. Although the structure of Working Groups may vary from one municipality to another, they are usually chaired by a delegate and made up of delegates and ordinary citizens appointed on the basis of expertise or experience in the area to be supervised. Estimates indicate that some 20,000 citizens are permanently or occasionally involved nationwide. Usually, these committees link up with networks of volunteer 'people's supervisors' involved in the same field.

Our research looked at a total of nine such committees (two per municipality, three in Centro Habana) involving a total of 122 individuals, 52 per cent of whom were not delegates, but rather local residents with some degree of experience in the type of activity they supervised. For example, the Food Services Committee (this includes municipally owned cafeteria and restaurant services) in one municipality had eleven members, with nine as active participants. Three of these were delegates, including the chair, while the rest were there because of their food services expertise, including two pensioners who had worked in restaurants and cafeterias for more than 30 years.

Although only one-third of committee members are female, they tend to be predominant in committees supervising social service areas such as health and education, where the presence of women is traditionally significant. The presence of seniors and pensioners is also significant, as they possess the necessary experience and have more time to spare.

14. Eighty-three per cent of delegates surveyed thought the work of committees to be serious and efficient, yet only 23 per cent believed their recommendations and resolutions were taken sufficiently into account. The latter figure is higher in Chambas, Bayamo and Santa Cruz, and lower in Centro Habana. Nevertheless, over half of those asked expressed great satisfaction with the work of their committees, even if they thought their influence limited.

4

Popular Organizations in the Dominican Republic: The Search for Space and Identity

César Pérez

This chapter is a summary of the principal findings of research into the popular organizations that led a massive community-based protest movement, local and national, in the Dominican Republic between 1986 and 1990. It attempts to show how contemporary Dominican political culture, forged since the 1960s, shaped the organizational structure of the protest movement, the way it conceived action, and the manner in which it related to political life. Some of the most active groups in the protest movement, those which have had the most influence and impact on the political system, are broadly described. Special emphasis is placed on Neighborhood Councils, the type of organization most commonly found in poor districts; a case study of one particular council shows some of the possibilities, prospects, and limitations of this type of organization, which is gaining considerable importance in the Dominican Republic.

The methodology employed in the study entailed combining several different quantitative and qualitative approaches, including surveys, various forms of interview, participant observation and workshops, as well as a review of primary documents and the daily press. We were able to participate directly in several congresses and task forces in at least three of the groups under study.[1]

Some Background on the Organizations

A wide variety of popular organizations exists in poor Dominican neighborhoods and shanty towns. Although many of the most relevant groups were formed during the early 1980s, others, including the Neighborhood Rights Defense Committee (Comité para la Defensa de los Derechos Barriales, COPADEBA) and many of the Christian Base Communities, have existed since the 1970s.

The predecessors of these groups were the Cultural Clubs, social action groups that operated in neighborhoods and parishes throughout the country. The Clubs reached their height during the 1960s, following the death of dictator Rafael Trujillo, who, during his rule from 1930 to 1961, had repressed all cultural, social, and political organizations of an oppositional nature. The Clubs, especially those in urban areas, were the first organizations to be joined by large groups of Dominican youth who sought new political, cultural, and ideological orientations during the post-dictatorship period of the 1960s.

The events of that decade had a strong impact on Dominican society. The 1960s witnessed the transition from 31 years of dictatorship to more democratic forms of government, although this process was interrupted by the US military invasion of 1965, which prevented a broad spectrum of progressive political forces from taking control of the country.[2] This profoundly disruptive period created a climate that tended to politicize all action by cultural, religious, professional, and labor organizations. As the predominant tendency in Dominican society was to look to these organizations as political and ideological reference points, the Cultural Clubs became the focus of significant power struggles among the various political and ideological currents prevalent in Dominican society at the time. Perhaps most significantly for our own analysis, this political emphasis was expressed in the propensity to link action immediately to an overall political line, without working towards raising local issues in a way that would involve the population in solving its own problems.

Although largely subordinated to the logic of centrist and left-wing political parties, and under the effects of the heavy repression that characterized this period, the Clubs played a very important role in organizing protests and social and political struggles during the 12-year right-wing Reformist Party government of Joaquín Balaguer between 1966 and 1978.

In 1978, the centrist Revolutionary Dominican Party (PRD) won the elections, opening up a new political situation. The PRD managed to win over several groups that had been important agents of social change, in particular the Clubs and labor unions, with their base among the poor and marginal sectors, and turned them into loyal supporters of the system and the government. The unity of the opposition was broken. Because of the fragmentation of the opposition and because of a pact with the ruling economic sector, which had been important for the PRD's accession to power, during the party's two terms (1978–86) government policies ignored popular demands and repression of protest was frequent.

A turning point in popular mobilization began to occur in 1983 with government cut-backs on social spending as part of an agreement with the International Monetary Fund (IMF). This intensified the economic and political crisis and increased social inequality and spatial segregation, which in turn rekindled organizational efforts in the neighborhoods. The popular sector began to raise certain demands, this time without help from the large parties in the system. The tendency to raise demands outside a party framework was significantly furthered by the crisis in the left (the traditional, strong standard-bearer of protest in the country). It was also furthered by the hesitancy of other opposition parties, including the center-left Dominican Liberation Party (PLD) headed by former President Juan Bosch, which lacked a tradition of mobilization and ties to the popular sectors. Such a situation heightened the inclination for grievances to be channeled independently of the parties rather than through them, as had happened in previous decades, and eventually to replace party loyalty by developing new means of struggle.

The result was to stimulate the creation of popular organizations which had different attitudes from those of earlier years. By the early 1980s several new efforts at organization had cropped up in the neighborhoods. These were encouraged by youth in Christian Base Communities, ex-activists and members of left-wing organizations, and members of the PRD rank and file who favored formation of Neighborhood Councils to raise specific demands.

The Eruption of Neighborhood Protest and the Emergence of Neighborhood Councils

Massive protests by slum dwellers and neighborhood and community organizations began during the first term in office (1978–82) of the centrist Revolutionary Dominican Party (PRD). Protest appeared in a moment of transition from a repressive regime to a government that would allow room for more democratic forms of participation. This factor was especially important in the subsequent growth of these organizations.

The new regime declared an amnesty and released all the political prisoners of the former Balaguer government. As part of a policy of induced demand, more currency was printed, public sector employment was doubled, and domestic market incentives were provided. These measures led to renewed expectations of social participation and to the channeling of popular grievances within the framework of the regime, which was perceived to be the opposite of its predecessor. One example was a reactivation of the labor movement following a Labor Department resolution recognizing the right to unionize – between 1978 and 1982, 384 new unions were registered with the department.

During this period, the City Council of the central part of Santo Domingo (Ayuntamiento del Distrito Nacional) promoted the creation of Neighborhood Councils (Juntas de Vecinos) as grassroots organizations intended to help implement and promote social programmes and other City Council-sponsored activities. These Neighborhood Councils were able to involve many neighborhood residents in such local improvement initiatives as solid-waste disposal, construction of parks and recreational facilities, erection of street signs, tree planting, organization of crime watch groups, construction of sports installations, and other community activities conducted with municipal government assistance and with the self-management and self-help of the residents.

Although in many ways a positive and novel development, Neighborhood Councils were also perceived as client organizations allied to the governing party, whose internal wrangling and power struggles for control of executive, legislative and municipal office in the next electoral term they mirrored. The Councils were in fact consumed and weakened by party politics – that is, they were manipulated by the PRD – which eventually prevented them from fulfilling their assigned role. In the mid-1980s, however, this resulted in a breakdown in relations with the PRD, which led most of them to continue to function autonomously. Some maintained weak ties with City Hall, but the majority gradually acquired a clear autonomy.

Economic Reorganization and Social Protest

Owing to a variety of internal and external factors, toward the beginning of the 1980s it became clear that the import-substitution model in vogue for the preceding two decades had broken down. The government responded by reversing and reshaping its economic and social policies, changes soon evident in drastic monetary and fiscal spending restrictions, increased unemployment, inflation, loss of buying power, and in a return to government, police, and private sector intolerance. The new rules of the game excluded the poor, who responded with major protest movements. These were led especially by labor, and to a lesser degree by nascent neighborhood or community groups in such municipalities as Bayaguana, Salcedo and Cotuí.

In general, these initial neighborhood protest rallies were in solidarity with labor grievances; later on, they took up such consumer issues as demanding price cuts for food and medicine. As the organizations grew, specific local and territorial demands were incorporated, including improvement of streets and sidewalks, power and water supply, construction of sewers and drains, and complaints about police brutality.

Community and territorial movements in South and Central America were part of the struggle against military dictatorships or their remnants. In the Dominican Republic, however, most movements emerged under governments that were more tolerant of political rights. As a result, actions didn't have to be as restrained or limited to civil rights, but often became focused on broader economic issues. Also, a variety of social and political actors, including labor and professional organizations, took part in these neighborhood movements and organizations. Their initial calls to action were spontaneous and without co-ordination between one zone and another.

The most violent national protests, which included rock-throwing, tire-burning, firebombing, and looting, took place in April 1984, reaching their peak between April 23 and 25. Such protests, which focused on salaries, inflation, and the cost of living, continued throughout the 1980s and included five national shutdowns or strikes. Following these incidents, the need for and possibility of co-ordinating a movement at the local, zone, territorial and national levels were posed. The protest had been put down in a virtual bloodbath; according to press reports, more than 100 people were killed by army bullets.

In social and popular imagery, the April 1984 street uprising became a symbol of revolt which deepened the tendency of Dominican political culture and practice to politicize social issues. To left-wing organizations, whatever legitimacy the state and the traditional parties had ever had was lost in these events. They regarded their aftermath as an auspicious moment to bring about the breakdown of the system through the work of neighborhood organizations, and set out to push this understanding within the protest movement. This led the Dominican Left Front (FID, comprising several small left-wing parties) to call for 'forming Popular Struggle Committees the length and breadth of the country, for all the exploited to join the mobilization, from the bottom up, and to co-ordinate all sectors that make up the power base and the popular forces that can defeat official intolerance and the power of the dominant minority.'[3]

The Communist Workers' Party (PCT – Partido Comunista del Trabajo, a pro-Albanian organization), which did not belong to the FID, also called for the formation of Popular Struggle Committees, because 'they are the conveyor belts between the party and the masses, and in them the close union of the party and the people will become effective.'

The labor movement, weakened by division into numerous federations, low worker affiliation and the massive layoffs caused by harsh fiscal policy, also regarded the territorial and community stage as a place to organize for advancing class grievances, something that was becoming increasingly harder to do on the shop floor.

The Neighborhood Organizations[4]

The first of the neighborhood organizations to emerge was the Neighborhood Rights Defense Committee (COPADEBA – Comité para la Defensa de los Derechos Barriales), which in 1979 brought together clubs, Neighborhood Councils and, in particular, Christian Base Communities from several northern Santo Domingo neighborhoods. Initially, there was strong influence from supporters of the PRD, an influence that would undermine its work and lead to significant changes later on, including a reduction of all party influence. COPADEBA's immediate goal was the defense of residents threatened with eviction from the land where they had built their homes. Although limited to neighborhoods in the Northern Zone, Sabana Perdida and the Alcarrizos – two communities on the outskirts of Santo Domingo – COPADEBA was a well-structured, consolidated organization.

During the protests of 1984, neighborhood dwellers from various political backgrounds reformed Popular Struggle Committees (CLP – Comités de Lucha Popular), which had a presence that was geographically broader than COPADEBA.[5] The CLPs served as vehicles for a vast outpouring of protest and demands among the poor, and sprang up rapidly and spontaneously across the country. However, they were also the form of neighborhood and territorial organization to which the different components of the left laid claim. This had a number of negative effects, including their fragmentation relative to that of the left, which led to their eventual demise, the victims of ideological and tactical differences within the Marxist groups.

The Popular Unity Council (CUP – Consejo de Unidad Popular) was founded in May and June 1984 from these fragments. This organization did not emerge from the grievances of specific neighborhoods (such as a demand for parkland or for empty land to be used for housing). Rather, it came into existence out of the political or tactical debates that its members had with the CLPs. Specifically, while it was interested in organizing and building popular protest within the neighborhoods where protest was occurring, CUP's political and ideological view was that neighborhood demands needed to be linked to demands for political reform of the state. The main political force in initiating the CUP was the Communist Workers' Party (PCT, the pro-Albanian party mentioned above), although many CUP militants were not PCT members. CUP remained one of the leading neighborhood organizations and was headed by Virtudez Alvarez, a woman who has achieved national renown for her leadership, something recognized even by the President of the Republic.

Somewhat later, in 1985, the Broad Front for Popular Struggle (FALPO – Frente Amplio de Lucha Popular) was founded to co-ordinate the CLPs, as well as the Housewives' Committees, the Student Movement and the class-based labor movement. Although not a neighborhood organization *per se*, it served as a co-ordinating body between such organizations and other groups. FALPO had neither the institutional structure nor the clout of COPADEBA or CUP, but in several towns and cities its grassroots organizations have strong local influence.

The last of the organizations with national scope was the Popular Organizations' Collective (Colectivo de Organizaciones Populares). Formed in 1989, it defines itself as a co-ordinating body where popular groups can converge to organize specific protest activities. Initially, the Colectivo included COPADEBA, FALPO, the CUP, several labor and professional organizations, and local, municipal and provincial organizations. This gave it the capacity for mass mobilization, and its principal leader gained national standing. However, in the period that followed, the Colectivo adopted the positions of the most radicalized sectors of the left. This, combined with several failed calls for a national strike, led its most important member groups to walk out.

All these organizations had their heyday between the mid-1980s and the early 1990s. There also existed other community organizations with varying degrees of local influence in various cities, but no others achieved the national or territorial prominence of those described here. Many of these smaller groups occasionally worked with each other both locally and nationally. In addition, there have been several community research and action centers, and certain NGOs which work in a limited but systematic way with the people.

In Search of 'The Subject'

Increased media access was one element that significantly affected the emergence and the ultimately political nature of the neighborhood and community movement. Coverage by the huge number of new local and national publications, television channels and radio outlets spread the debate and brought demands for new democratic participation opportunities to a wider segment of the population.

Through these media, community leaders gained access to a permanent and rapid means of communicating with the rank and file and with the population at large. Although this enormously increased their potential ability to mobilize people, the sudden attention also had the effect of confusing some leaders, who for a time overestimated their actual capacity to bring about changes in the system.

The numerous broad-minded media also facilitated the spread of ideas and concepts being discussed in Europe and South America about urban territorial movements. As leaders and activists in community organizations became aware of them, many began to see their organizations as the building blocks of a larger movement, one capable of channeling social demands to the point of becoming an alternative to the existing political system. They were similarly influenced by a number of social sectors and political activists who had formed popular education centers for social action.

As the movement became more politically oriented, it was generally believed that it would lead to a confrontation with the state, which could force concessions in the way the country was run, and could eventually be the spark of a broader social revolution. Step by step, measures were taken in the neighborhood and community organizations toward political action that sought to replace the left-wing parties, which were not playing a major role in the co-ordination of protest actions during these years, 1984–91, partly because of a lack of capacity to do so, partly because of a lack of will. At the same time, the cost to the popular organizations of playing this role, was, ironically, a diminution in the opportunity to shape an identity of their own. They weren't particularly clear about their objectives; they tended to believe that their actions would stimulate the development of a new revolutionary subject which would lead to the fall of the government. They were trying to voice local demands and link up with local struggles, but these demands (and presumably their solutions) were always put into the context of national politics; that is, they were subordinated to national demands. The struggle was conceived as progressing hierarchically from local mobilization to marches, to work stoppages, and to national strikes. Although these strikes were held along territorial rather than labor-related lines, they did put forward both local and territorial grievances.

This logic prevailed above all because the mass of the population generally tends to develop a common-sense view of its actions, which almost always comes from the political traditions of the social and political sectors influencing them. However, the political tradition and practice of Dominican parties obscured the possibility of making a connection between local and larger issues. Distinction between the demands of each of the social sectors for purposes other than action was not made, and thus preservation of their identity and that of their movement was made more difficult.

These popular organizations were the foundation of a broad urban movement which was at times the main focus of social and political struggle in the Dominican Republic. The movement is significant because it became a disruptive element in the political system. Their importance lay in their capacity to mobilize the population in a struggle for demands aimed at the state. The truth is that these struggles did not obtain tangible results; nevertheless neighborhood, regional and national strikes and protests had an impact on politicians as well as on the business sector, which demanded, on several occasions, that the government listen to the popular concerns. The actions of COPADEBA, for example in 1992, stopped a massive eviction of residents in La Ciénaga *barrio* in the capital, where the government wanted to build a tourist complex. As a result of this type of work, and in particular the role of national strikes in Dominican politics in recent years, these organizations have played a significant role. And yet, the lack of well-defined internal organizational structures and institutional mechanisms made the actions of the urban movement reactive and short-lived. This eventually rendered it incapable of decisively confronting the system, and even jeopardized its continuation.

The popular organizations that first emerged around local problems were led by a combination of militants and ex-militants of left-wing parties and Catholic militants influenced by the theories of liberation theology. Their ideas of action were very much a product of the left, with its stress on the party as the historical vehicle of change, its millenarian stance, and so forth. Their conceptions led them to politicize each action in the sense of casting demands at the level of national politics. This, in turn, impeded the development of community-based organization focused on concrete problems, and of a solid consciousness of local problems and how they might be solved. Focused action, based on the mobilization of communities around concrete objectives, would have been a more successful way of actually forcing the government to help find solutions to problems and to bring tangible results.

Rather than taking such an approach, the popular organizations tended to focus on the plane of national political and economic policy without reference to the immediate needs of a community, or at least to matters that could be conceived of as obtainable goals of struggle. Because local matters and actions were quickly taken beyond the community before struggles and consciousness of the struggle could mature, and because of organizational weaknesses, the protests in these years had an episodic character.

A Case Study of the Máximo Gómez Neighborhood Council

At the same time as these movements were developing, the Neighborhood Councils continued to evolve. Despite their origins as a government effort, these smaller and less dramatic organizations were dedicated to fighting for local issues in a way that put them in a special relationship with the population.

Although recourse to negotiation with the government has not attained the rank and permanence that would be desirable, given the level and frequency of territorial grievances, community organizations have developed a logic of negotiation with sectors of the system and the state. This process is sometimes mediated by government bodies, most often by the institutions of civil society. None has yet been capable, however, of creating permanent mechanisms for maintaining dialogue.

Among community organizations in the country, Neighborhood Councils have been noted for a tendency to foster a more permanent and stable relationship of dialogue and negotiation with the Government. There are two reasons for the permanence of this relationship: first, their actual creation was directly encouraged by local governments; second, they were the least ideological of all community organizations, perhaps because left-wing and liberation theology activists considered them to be pro-government and tended to keep their distance. As noted, they were founded on the initiative of municipal authorities during the 1978–82 presidential term. However, only a few were actually controlled and manipulated by the Revolutionary Dominican Party when it was in power. Their gestation, formation and development was fairly spontaneous and free of political-ideological manipulation from any party. By definition and objectives, Neighborhood Councils have remained local in scope. Their protests and grievances are specific and well within the framework of neighborhood issues, which makes them an acceptable form of organization even in middle- and upper-income areas.

The Máximo Gómez Neighborhood Council is a good example for study. The neighborhood, where some 1,200 families live, is one of many housing developments built by private developers for working-class and middle-income families on urban land made more valuable by the government through construction of wide thoroughfares.

But the middle-income moniker is deceptive. Neglect by the National District City Government and the Public Works, Public Health and Police Departments deprived Máximo Gómez of refuse collection, street signs, and the ability to stop a ravine running through the community from being used as a waste dump and contaminated by a nearby meat-packing plant. The neighborhood had neither green areas nor facilities for sports or recreation. Residents requiring medical care had to travel several kilometers to reach a private medical center. Of all the services Máximo Gómez did not have, the most urgently needed were refuse collection and running water. Although water mains were installed in the area, they were not connected to the supply network. Refuse was never picked up because the neighborhood was too out of the way. Although residents publicized their grievances, there was never an official response, and so each family found its own way round these problems. At first, one group of 30 neighbors pooled their money to pay for garbage collection and kept a watch to prevent others from throwing their garbage into their dump. But this solution was limited and temporary, and the garbage dump kept filling up.

However, the fact that they had joined together had an effect. It created friendships, solidarity, and a growing awareness of the neighborhood as the place in which the most important moments and activities of life took place: home, entertainment, rest, study, and, more and more often, productive work, as a consequence of the expanding informal labor market. Three months after neighborhood leaders Juan Ureña and Carmen Payano first put forward the idea, the Committee for a Máximo Gómez Neighborhood Council was formed. The Council was formally installed in May 1986.

Over the next six years, five different Boards of Directors were elected, and three males and two females served as President. Article 4 of its by-laws defines its objectives: 'Through the collective integration of area residents, to organize and implement development programmes in co-ordination with public and private institutions, in order to encourage and improve living conditions for all residents [of the neighborhood].' The Council identified ten basic problems requiring solution: inadequate water supply; biological and chemical contamination by the Torito Dominicano meat-packing plant; broken and unpaved streets; faulty housing construction; cracked walls, leaky roofs; numerous garbage dumps throughout the neighborhood; lack of home collection of garbage; collapse of one of the neighborhood access streets; no sports facilities; lack of green areas; recurrent crime.

Once constituted, the Council established formal relations with City Hall and sought recognition as a non-governmental organization. It also launched a programme to fight to solve all of these issues, beginning with access to running water. Five months later, in October 1986, the Council organized a vigil and picket line outside the People's Savings and Loan Association, the private banking institution which had made the real-estate investment. Five hundred residents took part. This pressure forced the bank management to agree to talk to a commission and start negotiations, which culminated in the bank's agreeing to solve the construction problems and pave the unfinished streets. The bank also issued a cheque to the Santo Domingo Water and Sewage Corporation (CAASD) for 25,000 pesos, which covered the cost of linking the neighborhood to the water distribution network. With responsibility for the water issue now in the hands of the CAASD, the struggle took on another dimension. Now the fight was against a government institution.

The vigils and the picket line were transferred from the bank to the CAASD office. However, there was no response. The Council then organized a series of marches and night-time rallies around the neighborhood for 15 consecutive days. On the last day, pickets – mainly women, but also some men and children – blocked traffic on Avenida Principal, which links the entire area with downtown Santo Domingo. It was a Monday morning during rush hour, when thousands of people were commuting to work. With traffic stopped and emotions running high, a Colonel from the National Police (who was heading the detachment assigned to keep order) volunteered to mediate between the Council and the CAASD. The Colonel contacted the CAASD Director and asked him to meet the Neighborhood Council. Thanks to his intervention, the protest remained peaceful; dialogue and negotiations began between the Neighborhood Council and the Director of the Water and Sewage Corporation. Eventually the water problem at Máximo Gómez was solved.

The Máximo Gómez Neighborhood Council also carried out a lengthy battle against pollution of the ravine by the Torito Dominicano meat-packing plant. This was a three-way fight involving Torito, the Public Health Department and the Environmental Cleanup Commission. As a result of pressure by the Neighborhood Council, Torito Dominicano was forced to sign four agreements in which it made a commitment to find a solution to the problem. Subsequently, since both the company and the Public Health Department failed to honor these agreements, the Neighborhood Council went to the Environmental Cleanup Commission. The Commission, originally created by presidential decree, was headed by Pedro Candelier, an army colonel with a reputation for being resolute in fulfilling his orders.

At the request of the Neighborhood Council, Col. Candelier shut down the packing plant until the company built the installations needed to stop contamination of the ravine. Although the plant could not be kept closed until all work was completed, the Council did manage to force Torito to follow through and put an end to contamination. According to a local activist, this was the result of more than five years of fighting for the right to a healthy environment.[6]

The Máximo Gómez Neighborhood Council has been at its most persistent, however, in its relationship with City Hall, a relationship described by community leader Juan Ureña as one of confrontation, dialogue and negotiation. He explains that the confrontational component consists of organizing demonstrations, vigils and picket lines, and getting the news media to speak, for example, of the need for city garbage collection to prevent the proliferation of garbage dumps on every corner. Dialogue, for its part, involves attending City Council meetings to explain the problems and submit demands and petitions. Negotiation is the whole process, including discussions to influence city employees with whom the Council has a close relationship.

In 1990, at the time of new Council elections, the outgoing officers' report summarized the following achievements: eradication of all garbage dumps in the neighborhood; regular garbage collection by City Hall; construction of a retaining wall to prevent a street from caving in; construction by residents of a volleyball and basketball court with assistance from City Hall; installation of traffic signals and street signs; installation of running water; reclamation of vacant green areas; construction of tanks and filters by Torito Dominicano to stop contamination of the ravine running through the neighborhood.

In addition, the Council sponsored numerous recreational activities, games, ceremonies and artistic events. These, according to former Council President Carmen Payano, help integrate families into the defense of their neighborhood and the preservation of its identity. The Máximo Gómez Neighborhood Council holds a Cultural Week on the anniversary of Máximo Gómez's birth. (Gómez was a Dominican hero who fought with Jose Martí in the War of Cuban Independence.) During Cultural Week, there are block parties, student parades, sports tournaments, family marathons, and other activities. At other times of the year, the Council organizes a Corn Fair, an Arepa Festival, Christmas parties and a *Kermesse*. Although these activities get both young people and adults involved in the Council, most regular participants are adults. Only one of the nine current officers is under 30. Carmen Payano points out that young people are in a very special situation. Although they are not part of the Council's structure, and not particularly interested in the actual Council, they participate in assemblies, in the rallies and protests, and in all the self-help and self-management activities promoted by the Council.

The participation of women is striking. Women are the most enthusiastic about the work, arrive first and in greater numbers for protest rallies, and are the first to show up for meetings and neighborhood assemblies (which attract 100 or more people.) This may explain why in a previous election an all-female Board was elected. Gender representation evened out in the last elections, however, and the current Board is made up of five women and four men. All positions are voluntary and without remuneration; members can be re-elected for more than one term. In addition, there are commissions which have responsibility for particular problems or issues.

Does the Neighborhood Council truly represent the interests and grievances of the people in the neighborhood? The current Board of

Directors claims that the Council is a recognized neighborhood force, which has real authority to make important decisions about local issues. For example, if someone wants to set up a sidewalk stand, he or she requests authorization from the Council. Whenever someone has a dispute with the Real Estate Bank over housing, he or she goes to the Neighborhood Council first; if someone breaks the rules of neighborly life, those affected report the misconduct to the Council and ask that the offender be reprimanded for violating the Neighborhood Social Code.

Carmen Payano says that this works because the Neighborhood Council does not make decisions without the consent of residents at General Meetings, in home visits made by the Board of Directors, and in opinion polls. However, well-known leader Miguel Uribe thinks that the Council's strength is only relative. Government and municipal authorities make many decisions affecting the neighborhood without the slightest consideration for the Council, sometimes as if it did not even exist. In any case, the Máximo Gómez Neighborhood Council is an example of what a community organization can mean and accomplish for a neighborhood. According to Juan Ureña, everything has been possible because the Council has a stable core of active participants, has become a consolidated organization, follows up on plans, defines clear and attainable objectives from the start, is not involved in the ideological struggles of political parties, provides honest management of resources obtained, and has permanent ties with the community. Part of its success lies in its political independence. The Máximo Gómez Council has turned down offers from the city council for modest financial help that it has extended to some Neighborhood Councils. The rationale is that the Council has been able to sustain permanent activity precisely because of its financial independence from the local government. The Council also eschews party politics as potentially manipulative. Although two of its main leaders are members of political parties, they function at arm's length from their organizations. The Council does believe, however, that councils should transcend the limits of purely local struggles and should even try to forge electoral pacts with political parties if it helps in the fight to solve their problems.

New Neighborhood Councils with broader agendas are being created all the time in other communities – in all, some 50 or 60 have been set up. Most manage to get off the ground and attain a certain degree of recognition in their home areas. But they have their limitations: they may be reluctant to engage in political action, they may not be overly certain as to their objectives, and they may have few tangible achievements. But to the urban population of Santo Domingo they remain the chief reference point for raising local issues.

This is borne out by a survey we conducted in the three Santo Domingo neighborhoods which were the main focus of the 1984 protest rallies – Capotillo, Simón Bolívar and Las Cañitas, with a total population of 115,000. In the survey, while 65 per cent of the population said that they knew about the Neighborhood Councils, only 27 per cent knew the major popular organizations mentioned in the first part of this chapter. There is a perception in these communities that by joining together, residents can solve problems on their own. When asked about the best way to confront neighborhood issues, 59 per cent said it was by uniting the people in the neighborhood, 37 per cent said with government help, and only 6 per cent said with the help of the political parties. Again, this shows the degree of distrust that exists toward these organizations. This survey also demonstrates the crisis of legitimacy facing parties, as well as the suspicion of mediation between the people and the government: only slightly more than one-third believe that such mediation can lead to the solving of community problems.

Other data indicate that people in these areas are mainly concerned with immediate issues (as opposed to the desire to change the government, which some organizations had felt would be their ultimate concern). And so, for example, 74 per cent of those surveyed saw garbage and the high cost of living as their main problems, while 68 per cent also emphasized concern about crime. About 40 per cent considered housing their principal problem – which perhaps isn't surprising since the other 60 per cent owned their houses in these areas (although they do not own the lots on which they are built). This concern with immediate problems helps explain the tendency to organize around fairly concrete questions and the lack of interest in the larger issues advanced by popular organizations linked to projects which are national in scope.

Conclusions

It is indicative of their limitations that the larger national popular organizations which had the greatest influence in Dominican politics since the period between 1984 and the early 1990s ended up facing a marked loss of influence and diminished growth and objective achievement prospects. Between 1991 and the mid-1990s, the number of their activities, their influence, and their impact all diminished. Many of the tasks they undertook remain unfinished, and efforts to complete others produced mediocre results. This is not only the conclusion of this research but also the assessment presented by the head of the Popular Organizations Colectivo in a report to the ninth General Assembly in February 1992.

It now seems evident that it will be impossible for these organizations to achieve their objective of articulating an alternative to the crisis facing Dominican society. These organizations have stuck with their tendency to orient their actions towards violent confrontation with the state, which makes it impossible to articulate local demands in a way that would allow effective negotiation. Even more importantly, this orientation tends to prevent community members from actually organizing to find solutions to their problems as opposed to focusing all attention on the state. Change in this approach is unlikely until, or unless, the political parties of the left working within the Colectivo and other organizations change their own orientation.

It is equally evident that more focused local organizations, unencumbered by the messianic vision of more ideological and political popular organizations, are now emerging to continue the fight for social change. Neighborhood Councils, such as the one in Máximo Gómez, stand out among these new forms of social organization. Although this particular experience is different in many ways from other local efforts, our observations indicate that these councils have acquired greater prominence in organizing and promoting popular protest.

This makes it clear that the leaders of the groups that led the recurrent protests between 1984 and 1990 were unable to interpret correctly the demands of the Dominican people in general, and those of the urban poor in the capital and the city of Santiago in particular. A review of the grievances raised in the last few years shows them to be quite varied, with local demands for improved living conditions thrown together with others of a political or wage-related nature. In general, however, most demands of the popular organizations, as opposed to those of the neighborhood councils, dealt with the fight for civil rights and consolidation of democratic gains made in the political arena, which, it was thought, would lead to the replacement of the current government and state by an alternative power. What the groups did not understand was that popular demands weren't yet focused on a change in government or state, but rather on redressing wretched living conditions.

Some of the factors behind the sometimes violent protests included the lack of opportunities for democratic political participation, as well as an awareness of the right of access to the material goods the system offers but seldom delivers. The ever-more apparent debility of the institutions in Dominican society impedes the participation of popular social forces, and has even taken away traditional representation in the formal mechanisms of the system. Disenfranchisement is compounded by the fact that Dominican political parties have become almost exclusively electoral machines, which come alive only every four years, at election time. This creates a political vacuum which is occasionally filled by local protest movements. This, in turn, politicizes these movements and lines them up against the state, even when their position is merely defensive or even supportive. Demands of a political nature have certainly been made by the population, including calls for a change in economic policy and abrogation of the agreements made with the IMF, which crop up in the grievance list of every national strike. The mass of the population has never, however, called for changes in the system or the state.

The leaders and activists in the national organizations studied and whom we interviewed, as well as many leaders in left-wing groups, see the protests and the neighborhood movement as the setting in which a new social subject will emerge, a subject capable of making much-needed economic and political transformations. This wishful and, it seems to me, rather flawed interpretation of the role that Dominican popular organizations can and should play has been a determining factor in bringing about the current state of paralysis in which they find themselves. Such, too, is the criticism by a leader of the Máximo Gómez Neighborhood Council who suggested to us that the positions taken by popular organizations have not contributed to the battles fought by Neighborhood Councils to solve local problems. Simply put, the national popular organizations have not adequately understood the struggle of the neighborhood councils and the struggles at the neighborhood level.

Finally, we have noted the weakening of the larger organizations such as the Popular Unity Council (CUP), the Broad Front for Popular Struggle (FALPO), the Popular Organizations Colectivo, and the Neighborhood Rights Defense Committee (COPADEBA). This is due primarily to the fact that these groups used work stoppages and national strikes as almost their sole form of struggle, and neglected the fight for local issues, including mobilizing people to solve their own problems. Organizational weakness severely hampers the chances of creating an identity as a community movement and makes it harder for leaders and groups to maintain links with the grassroots. This is probably why current trends in the protest movement point to greater difficulty in organizing and maintaining links with the masses.

Most importantly, however, the struggle of the members of the Dominican neighborhood and community movement reflects the need to entrench respect for their rights as citizens. It also reflects their desire for social integration on the basis of awareness of these rights and of the need to phase out the old forms of participation and representation that focus more or less exclusively on labor unions and political parties.

The legacy of these struggles in Dominican society is strong. Although poorly channeled at present, they helped make the political class aware of the need to take the people's grievances into account. Although the parties in which the political class is organized have not yet incorporated popular demands into their platforms, at least some are beginning to refer to the issues raised by the broad-based protest movement of the past six years. The fight has been continued by a variety of neighborhood organizations, which have taken up the legacy left by the struggles of the 1980s. The passing on of this torch is one of the most relevant factors in the deepening of democratization in Dominican society.

Notes

1. This study was financed by the Ford Foundation and was carried out with the assistance of José Leopoldo Artiles, research associate, and Pedro Hernández, research assistant.

2. The progressive forces were headed by the Revolutionary Dominican Party (PRD), a centrist, populist party and the leading coalition member, by the Social-Christian Revolutionary Party (PRSC), and by the pro-Cuba July 14 Revolutionary Movement.

3. FID manifesto, quoted in César Pérez and Leopoldo Artiles, *Movimientos Sociales Dominicanos* (Santo Domingo: Instituto Tecnológico de Santo Domingo, 1992), pp. 100–101.

4. This discussion of the various organizations is greatly abbreviated from our analysis in Pérez and Artiles, *Movimientos Sociales Dominicanos.*

5. The first CLP actually started a year earlier as committees in solidarity with union leaders fired by CODETEL, the telephone company. These committees got off the ground in a number of *barrios.*

6. Although the role of Colonel Pedro Candelier might seem unusual, it is not so unusual in the Dominican Republic to establish a working relationship between an individual in authority, some community organizations, and those they are in conflict with. This was successfully done in several parts of the country.

5

Popular Organizations and the Transition to Democracy in Haiti

Luc Smarth

The popular movement that was so evident in Haiti between the overthrow of the Duvalier regime on February 7, 1986 and the return from exile of popular leader Father Jean-Bertrand Aristide in October 1994 was felt at all levels of society, in all regions of the country, and in all aspects of national life. More than any other new factor – the role of the army being nothing new – it shook the very essence of the country as it took shape in an ongoing process inside the fragmented Haitian society.[1]

The precursor of what would become a vast movement for freedom of expression had begun by 1974. A group of journalists, mostly young, decided to break through the wall of silence imposed by the Duvalier dictatorship. Partly through a long stream of newspaper articles on social and economic conditions, but most importantly through radio, they helped shape a broad, solid current of critical opinion, which slowly gained support among virtually all sectors of the population.

This awakening of national consciousness, helped along by Jimmy Carter's term as US president, would later become a widespread cultural upheaval. Theater with clear social and political overtones and veiled yet persistent criticism of the dictatorial regime met with instant success. (From this struggle, a talented young writer and journalist named Evans Paul emerged as a leader. Later, as head of one of the most important Popular Organizations in the country, he played a significant role in the democratic struggle following the overthrow of Duvalier, and, in the general election of December 16, 1990, was elected mayor of Port-au-Prince with 85 per cent of the vote.)

Protest became more generalized and full-blown for a time in the late 1970s. Starting in 1978, the newly created Ligue Haitienne des Droits Humains added its voice to the fight for human rights. The following year, two Christian Democratic political parties were founded that were clearly in opposition to the dictatorship. Intellectuals were part of this cultural and social awakening, and denounced censorship of the press and theater; in 1979, twenty of them created the Association of Haitian Writers.

The wave of defiance which began to take shape in 1974 came to a brutal end in November 1980. Journalists, leading opposition politicians, and intellectuals who criticized the regime were arrested. Some were expelled from the country; others chose to go into exile. It was a hard blow to the nascent democratic movement.

But in the following year, Radio Soleil – which had started up in 1978 – resumed broadcasting. Its new place on the public scene was a turning point in the process of rebuilding the broad-based popular movement which would eventually break onto the political stage following the overthrow of the Duvalier dictatorship. This radio station, owned by the Catholic Church, gave new life to earlier efforts undertaken by a group of young, independent journalists, most notably through Radio Haiti Inter. It reinforced the defiantly democratic orientation of Haitian broadcasting, which was among the most combative and militant in the whole continent.

Broadcasting to the entire country in Créole, the language of the people, Radio Soleil played a leading role in the shaping of an anti-dictatorial, critical and progressive awareness. Dissemination of the social gospel of liberation theology fanned sentiments of justice, dignity, equality and solidarity. This helped surmount the ubiquitous fear of Duvalierism and turned the station into, as it called itself, 'the voice of the poor and the oppressed.' Its lead was soon followed by Radio Lumière – owned by the reform churches – Radio Métropole and others.

This was also the time when Christian Base Communities (CBCs – which first emerged in 1968) were consolidating their presence all over the country. Along with neighborhood organizations, they were the most direct forerunners of the Popular Organizations (POs) that came into existence after the fall of Duvalier. Since their inception, the CBCs played a basic role in shaping a critical and democratic consciousness and in sowing the seeds of hope, challenge, mutual aid and participation. (Into the early 1990s, the CBCs remained the most functional structure in the nation's democratic movement, but their presence in the years following the return of Father Aristide in October 1994 was greatly diminished.) In contrast with previous popular movements, the winds of freedom were now blowing not only in the cities but also in remote corners of the country. This led, in many places, to the organization of the peasantry, which was an important step in the development of democratic forces.

In May 1984, in the midst of a deepening economic crisis, the climate of collective reawakening led to renewed popular mobilization. Termed 'food riots' by some because food was taken from foreign relief depots, these events were both an expression and a symbol of the discontent of the poor. Crowded in slums by the tens of thousands, these people were rejecting both a way of life and a decomposing political regime. Within two years, many activists who led these mobilizations become militants and leaders of the POs.

Popular protest continued in 1985, the Year of Youth. With the support of the Catholic Church, a crowd 40,000 strong took to the streets to show its opposition to the government of Jean-Claude Duvalier. This opposition became more evident and wider in scope, and by July 1985 the country had become ungovernable. Besieged by internal and external pressures, Duvalier resorted to calling a referendum on the issue of his holding the presidency for life. Voter indifference was nearly complete.

The critical moment in the escalation of rebellion came on November 28, 1985. During a demonstration in Gonaïves, a town in the center of the country, the army murdered three schoolboys. The immediate effect of this triple crime was an upheaval throughout the entire country – except for the capital, which would only join the national uprising at the end – which lasted until the regime was overthrown on February 7, 1986.

It would be incorrect, then, to believe that the 29 years of the Duvalier regime caused political life to disappear. For the people of Haiti, those long years of dictatorship were a period of difficult, yet intelligent, apprenticeship. Their centuries-old wisdom and capacity for political and cultural resistance stood them in good stead in finding the most adequate forms of struggle and in patiently undermining the foundations of the Duvalier edifice. In the same movement, they were building up steam to conquer and create a new democracy.

The Emergence of Popular Organizations

As soon as Jean-Claude Duvalier fled the country, all social sectors came forward to exercise the right to participate in political and civil life. Organizations were created to formulate and fight for long-postponed grievances. Students, teachers, peasants, city laborers, journalists, lawyers, doctors, artists, street vendors, priests, soldiers, young people, women, shopkeepers, businessmen, all joined together in fighting for their rights and making their voices heard on the issues and decisions concerning the future of the nation.

Their efforts were helped along by the new political morale and strong determination instilled into society by liberation theology, the new press, independent militants and, to a certain extent, opposition political parties. Help also came from the emergence of democratic movements in many parts of the world (including Latin America), the existence of which broadcasters and some newspapers had taken care to publicize among young people.

Neighborhood Committees were a creation peculiar to the period immediately following Duvalier's overthrow. Although in incipient and informal existence since the last years of the Duvalier regime, on February 7, 1986 they literally sprang up overnight and had a massive presence in all working-class and in some middle-class areas of the capital, in all provinces and in parts of the countryside. Base Committee activities included street upkeep and such urban improvement initiatives as planting trees and painting colourful graffiti and murals with political and social content. They also enlisted government help in attending to such community issues as water and power supply, construction of schools and medical care centers, and organization of adult literacy campaigns.

In addition to community work, a further factor unifying Neighborhood Committee members was the fight against Tontons Macoutes and other diehards of the Duvalier regime – in fact, some committees distinguished themselves in monitoring and, in some cases, capturing and executing Tontons Macoutes. Thus, although formally apolitical (some members, in fact, sympathized with ideologies and candidates outside the 'popular camp'), Neighborhood Committees were actively involved in mass mobilization against neo-Duvalierist governments, to the extent that they later played a crucial role in the massive January 7, 1991 uprising, which thwarted a coup attempt led by Macoute leader Roger Lafontant. But they also played a role in the transformation of physical space and, for example, took on the enormous task of cleaning up the capital for the February 1991 inauguration of President Jean-Bertrand Aristide, considered a symbol of the popular struggle.

A factor of interest in analyzing the role of Neighborhood Committees was their sense of opportunity. An example of this concerns a hotel abandoned by its owner, a Duvalier follower, which was then taken over by young Committee members in that area. They cut off vehicle access to the area, then marched to the Ministry of Education and successfully demanded that the hotel be converted into a public school for the neighborhood. (Even after the coup of September 30, 1991, this secondary school still functioned and also hosted neighborhood dances and handicraft sales.)

The democracy-building process in Haiti benefited from the method of operation used by most Neighborhood Committees. They often had no leaders or steering committees of any sort; instead, members participated in one of several possible sub-committees (relating, for example, to culture, sports, maintenance, or finances) which had no chair, secretary or general co-ordinator. Weekly meetings, often held on Sundays, were chaired by a moderator chosen from among those in attendance.

Along with CBCs and current or former members of underground left-wing parties, Neighborhood Committees played an important role in building social and political awareness among the population, notably young people, after the fall of Duvalier. Dozens of youth groups sprang up in slum areas of the capital and provincial towns, with members constantly debating issues of national and international interest. Emerging from the intellectual freeze of a dictatorship started before they were born, they showed a tangible hunger for knowledge and an obsession with the need to organize the people.

These youth groups were the origin of the so-called Popular Organizations, which emerged throughout the country, especially in the capital and larger provincial towns, after the flight of Duvalier. From their inception, they defined themselves as spreading and defending the rights and claims of the popular classes, but as organizations with little similarity to traditional groups, which they dismissed as part of the existing political system. From their perspective, political parties, the left wing included, were incapable of standing for the rights of the majority: parties were seen as an outdated proposition which stood for patronage and sharing in the spoils of state power. As far as POs were concerned, the people could only count on their own autonomous forms of organization. They took on this mission, which also entailed the ideological education of the poor and oppressed.

The birth of POs was warmly welcomed in the neighborhoods. The reasons for this reception included a complex and subtle mix of emotional, cultural and historical factors directly connecting POs to the daily life of their communities. In spite of setbacks and the repression of young militants following the September coup, POs remained the most solid conveyor belt of the feelings of the people, and were regarded by most as the front line of anti-Macoute, anti-Duvalier fury. Moreover, though, POs symbolized repudiation of the values and practices embodied by the Haitian ruling class and political system. They constituted an obstacle to what had been, effectively, a political class – and here I refer not only to the traditional, backward-thinking group of politicians noted for manipulation, corruption, and violently excluding the country's majorities, but also to the new group of mostly foreign-trained politicians who fancied themselves as the torch-bearers of political modernity. These new politicians saw themselves as practitioners of *realpolitik*, and opposed any kind of populism or meaningful transfer of social and economic power. (The influence of these politicians was greatly diminished by the election of Aristide and, in December 1995, of his successor René Préval).[2]

Popular Organizations opposed concentration of power in the hands of those they saw as professional politicians. They ascribed much more value to 'the power of the street' and to popular participation in the country's social and political life. They were radically opposed to traditional, elitist practices that excluded or suppressed the will of the majority. Their chief mission, in their view, was to control the state and so, when possible, they applied pressure on its apparatuses to force it to act in the interest of the oppressed. Next to participation, they demanded social justice for the downtrodden and challenged the corruption that had permeated the exercise of political power since the inception of the Haitian state, corruption which had seeped through interpersonal relationships as well.

Consequently, the POs of this era of mobilization and change can be seen as part of the political current flowing through Latin America and much of the world which propounded an entirely new manner of practising politics based on the primacy of ethics. In Haiti, these currents were encouraged by the considerable influence of liberation theology upon a traditionally devout nation, by the complete suspicion of political leaders due to the existence of a 'political class' noted for retrograde ideological and cultural thinking, and by 29 years of repression under the Duvalier regime.

In other words, Haiti's POs came into existence because of a powerful historical need for political renewal, for the emergence of a new political subject. They were part of a process whereby the people evolved into a subject, rather than an object, of history. This explains the quick ascendancy of POs and their strong presence in different walks of Haitian life, in spite of being much debated and considered an enigmatic phenomenon.

The Popular Organizations remained something of a riddle to political observers. Although on the surface they gave the impression of playing no specific political or social role, they multiplied quickly throughout different social strata. POs were formed by students, youth, women, residents of a particular area, former soldiers, artists, street vendors, literacy workers and the unemployed. The 'OP-17' (the September 17, 1988 PO), for example, was formed by democratic soldiers who tried to overthrow the undemocratic government of General Henri Namphy. 'Veye-Yo' (We Must Be Vigilant) came into existence when the Church hierarchy attempted to expel Jean-Bertrand Aristide, leader of the rebellious youth, from the country, at which time groups of young people kept a round-the-clock watch on Aristide to prevent his expulsion from his parish. Several

POs were born on the morning of January 7, 1991 as the people mobilized *en masse* to stop a coup attempt by Duvalier zealot Roger Lafontant.

Liberal and conservative political parties continued to attack them as the enemies of democracy. Popular Organizations were seen as arrogant and intolerant; their inflammatory rhetoric exciting passions and their threats to use 'the necklace' (some Tontons Macoutes were executed by means of a burning tire around their necks) instilled terror in those who disagreed with their political ideas or attitudes. Although it was not used nearly as widely as the conservative press maintained, the popularity of this form of execution (known in street jargon as *Père Lebrun*, after a tire-shop owner) was a sign of their lack of any faith in the justice system.[3] In spite of this lack of support by some political parties, others (such as KONAKHOM, which has connections to the Socialist International) have gone out of their way to try to enlist the support of at least some POs.

Throughout Jean-Bertrand Aristide's first seven months in office, from February to September, 1991 – the government that was called *Lavalas*, or avalanche – Parliament waged a veritable war against the executive branch of the government. Its most serious criticism was leveled at the allegedly intimidating and intolerant behavior of POs toward the Chamber of Deputies (which along with the Chamber of Senators makes up the Haitian Parliament) and all 'true democrats.' Nevertheless, the Chamber of Deputies once publicly sang the praises of SAJ (Solidarity Among Youth), one of the most radical of these organizations, for its 'correct understanding of democracy,' and invited it to meet with Deputies, who were attempting to exploit differences between SAJ and President Aristide. The SAJ leadership, however, berated Deputies for being opportunists who wanted to capitalize on the political performance of the POs, and urged them to clean up the Chamber and throw the Macoutes out.

A common charge was that certain corrupt leaders had created POs for the sole purpose of lining their pockets, with no real concern for the organization or the country. The truth was different: most of these leaders were dedicated fighters who stood up to very brutal repression and were ready to give their lives.

In short, the least that may be said is that POs were an unusual creation, which aroused the curiosity and interest of social and political analysts. Their very existence constituted something of a mystery. How can one account for the fact that groups with such an apparently loose structure managed to maintain an active presence and become active participants on the social and political stage? Did they have common elements which would allow precise identification of a group as a PO? I will attempt to find answers to these and other related questions through an analysis of the internal life and structure of Popular Organizations.

Inside Popular Organizations

Save for certain exceptions, notably SAJ, which operated underground since the twilight of the Duvalier regime and surfaced in public in early January 1986, most Popular Organizations were born following the February 7, 1986 overthrow of Jean-Claude Duvalier. Arising in impoverished areas of the capital and provincial towns, and to a much more limited extent in the countryside, they were, at first, small groups of restless, politicized youths, often university students or pupils of popular education centers, who would meet to discuss the political situation and the future of democracy in the country.

Many of these youths came from the ranks of Neighborhood Committees and CBCs, and from the political parties or groups which had been working underground prior to Duvalier's overthrow. As they led political agitation against the regime, they evolved into experienced militants. Only a few had much ideological training, acquired mostly from reading, analysis of the militant print media, popular education, discussion of liberation theology with priests, and, in some cases, political training provided by revolutionary groups. In a country emerging from dictatorship, the sophistication of some of these youths on international issues was often surprising.

Their thirst for knowledge was remarkable. They would attend every meeting or debate of a social and political nature which mushroomed throughout the capital and some provincial towns after the flight of Duvalier, as well as popular education workshops. They would miss no opportunity to invite intellectuals to address their organizations, and followed with particular interest the upheavals in Eastern Europe and the Middle East. The day the Gulf War broke out, for example, many stayed up through the night, watching news reports on television and discussing events with friends and neighbors. They took pains to instill this thirst for knowledge in other youths and adopted the custom of administering a short quiz before starting the guest talks they secured for their groups – including questions on Haitian history, recent international events, chemistry, physics, or an article of interest in the current issue of *Le Monde Diplomatique*.

However, their sectarianism was also evident. Although their visceral hatred of the Macoutes was understandable, their outright rejection of anyone who disagreed with their propositions concerning the political struggle, as well as their exaggerated self-esteem and their contempt of those who differed, were disconcerting. They professed nearly blind faith in the idea of 'final victory,' thus excessively underrating the strength of those opposed to changing the political system. Nevertheless, they sometimes showed openness and political maturity, especially when an acute crisis required the unity of democratic forces. That happened, for example, in March 1987, when they joined a coalition of 56 political and civic organizations very dissimilar in their ideological orientation. In the general election of November 1987 they supported the Front National de Concertation (National Coalition Front) to form a united opposition to Duvalierism.

The self-importance and sectarianism of PO leaders did, however, seem somewhat understandable. In the first place, in the context of national politics, they enjoyed considerable success and prestige. Their substantial ability to identify with the oppressed, interpret their deepest hopes and understand the problems they faced in daily life, and their readiness to formulate, channel and support these aspirations – in short, their marked sensitivity to all things 'popular,' as well as their significant charisma – earned them a leading role in the process of democratic transition.

Meanwhile, political parties, supposedly leaders in the construction of democracy, were playing a practically marginal role in the Haitian democratic process during these years. This marginality was due to three factors: first of all, the country didn't have a tradition of political parties; as a result, most parties were still cutting their teeth, most had only a few members and were little more than a collection of leaders motivated by dreams of political and economic power. They had no real social base in the population, a problem linked for many of them to their ties with traditional interests. Second, they simply were not trusted either politically or morally. Such distrust stemmed from two centuries of betrayal by Haitian political leaders and was one of the reasons why religion and POs were having such a great political influence in the country. Third, the loss of influence of political parties and the growing impact of new social movements were part of a worldwide phenomenon with its own expression in Haiti.

Popular rejection of the political system and of the perversity of the political class was so obvious in Haiti that POs considered the slightest concession to the status quo or tolerance of traditional politics inadmissible, even immoral.

Forming Popular Organizations

In many cases, a PO came into existence as a small core, announcing its presence to the community, and then growing on that basis. Through press releases, residents became familiar with its acronym and political stance and such releases were an important vehicle for groups that seldom had resources to produce their own papers. These press releases served to attract new members, convey grievances, denounce police repression, attack government maneuvering to stave off demands for free elections, expose black marketeering, and fight price increases for basic staples. Press releases were used to state a position on topics ranging from proposals for a general strike or a demonstration against Tontons Macoutes or the government, to a response to national elections or a *coup d'état.*

As groups started to make their presence felt, they took steps to formalize their existence. Organizers found a regular meeting place – a school, someone's home, a training center, a church or a parish community center. It was through these initial encounters that political and ideological affinity was consolidated and the complex web of friendship and shared experience that supported the life of a PO was spun. 'Let the current run through,' as their leaders said. They then undertook writing their by-laws and statutes, usually a drawn-out process which produced by-laws that were never final or complete, with regulations added or repealed as circumstances dictated. This behavior was explained by one of the golden rules of POs: always learn from practice and experience.

This allegiance to the dictates of reality and the particular situation also helps explain how POs multiplied so rapidly after the fall of Duvalier. If deemed necessary by circumstances, it was not uncommon for some leaders to leave their organization, normally on friendly terms, in order to create new POs in other neighborhoods. At other times several small POs would band together to form a larger one. (We shouldn't discount the possibility of a leader's egotism playing a role in some of the splits and the tendency for new POs to be founded.)

This process of forming new organizations was particularly strong in relation to the PUCH (Unified Communist Party of Haiti). Dissatisfied members who thought the party was distancing itself from the masses often left the ranks and formed POs, spreading through working-class areas of the capital to train and organize young people. In the process they created close organizational links amongst the new groups.

Were there special circumstances motivating the creation of a PO? The elections of December 16, 1990 provided an example when groups were created 'to prepare for the elections,' as their new leaders said. Another particular moment of formation was the coup attempt by Tontons Macoutes leader Roger Lafontant – the fight against the Macoutes and other Duvalier supporters became a reason for the creation of new POs. However, these events appear as something of a pretext. While there was a desire to organize and a sense that a PO answered the need to struggle, the actual goals of a PO were usually much less well defined.

As noted, POs were formed by such diverse groups as street vendors, artisans, artists, women, youth, students, ex-soldiers, and peasants;

neighborhood and area POs also existed. While many of these POs included workers, especially young workers who might even dominate particular groups, there were no POs formed specifically by labor.

Popular Organizations originated in the hunger to organize felt by the people who, in however disorderly a way, suddenly stormed the political stage, and who together were determined to become fully fledged political actors. These people remained in search of organizational alternatives which fitted both their day-to-day and long-term hopes and aspirations, their cultural traditions and their desire – really, at the time, one could talk of their fever – to participate effectively in public life. All this was happening within a society that was in the process of breaking away from its archaic social and political past, starting on a difficult road to democracy.

The 'disenfranchised majorities' quickly realized that political parties were not up to these very difficult tasks. The leaders of the myriad political parties which emerged after the overthrow of Jean-Claude Duvalier on February 7, 1986 were too inept and timid when faced with the unknown. In those years, the eagerness of dozens of men to become President or otherwise gain admission to the corridors of power only kept them away from the masses.

Popular Organizations benefited from being the offspring of the people, sharing their joys, anxieties and wants. Although immature and searching for the way forward, they played a role in filling the organizational vacuum of the post-Duvalier years. As people said about POs, to paraphrase a widespread attitude, 'They may be ugly, but they are our own. The challenge now is to make them beautiful.'

Internal Structure

To understand POs better, let us delve deeper into their internal workings. As noted, most members and sympathizers come from working-class backgrounds, and although most were young, members over 40 were found in almost all groups. In some, notably those formed by street vendors, professionals or former soldiers, the average age was over 30. As a rule, there were no elderly members. While males tended to predominate, men and women coexisted in nearly all POs (although I was aware of one group composed exclusively of 15 young men).

Women's groups also existed which, in addition to the political and social role common to all POs, articulated and defended specific women's rights. For example, some women's groups were made up of street vendors, others of factory workers. But even the POs that organized specific groups of women played a more general role in challenging sexism in their communities.

Their organizational structure appeared rather undefined and amorphous, at least from the outside. But they actually took several more or less defined forms. Most operated within restricted geographical zones, but those POs that aspired to be national in scope (never fully attained in those years) had a pyramid-like structure. Local committees at the city and municipal level elected a steering committee, which sent a representative to the departmental level. Each departmental committee, in turn, sent a delegate to the national co-ordinating committee, which elected a general co-ordinator. Aiming to maintain a unified strategy, groups tended to favor centralized organizational structures and rigid discipline in order to combat what they saw as liberal tendencies and the propensity to division of the various component parts. That said, only three organizations actually fell within this category: KID (Unified Democratic Confederation), ANOP (National Alliance of POs), and APN (National Popular Assembly).

The most prevalent type of PO, those with a more limited geographical focus, steered clear of such structures, as they too closely resembled the centralized power which defined the Haitian political system. They felt the pyramidal arrangement tended to foment competition for positions of influence and to associate power closely with individuals, two features of the Haitian political class. Nearly all POs preferred to work through committees charged with specific tasks. Common committees included communications, education, public relations (also known as the contacts committee), finance, secretarial (which took notes, drafted documents, and ran off copies), and organization. Other groups had human rights, literacy, cultural, security, international relations and popular economics committees.

These committees normally had five to ten members, with each committee sending a representative to the top body, called the General Secretariat by some groups. There was usually no chairperson, secretary or co-ordinator of the committees of the PO as a whole. Representatives to the General Secretariat, which in some cases included women, in theory rotated every year or so.

The committee arrangement, then, could be an incentive to internal democracy. It encouraged teamwork, fostered a sense of responsibility in those assigned specific jobs (the usual practice called for committee chairs to submit a report at meetings), and, as they had to work together, improved communication between the top echelons and the rank and file.

A few organizations had a chairperson, deputy chairperson, general secretary, and adjunct general secretary. In these cases, the usual result was that the responsibilities for the entire organization were usually carried by one or two leaders who became political jacks of all trades. This, in the end, blocked the practice of internal democracy. According to our interviews carried out before the coup of September 1991, leadership elections were held every 12–18 months, although in some organizations still being formed, elections had not yet been held. It appeared that most leaders who had been active on the political stage since the flight of the Duvaliers had not yet been replaced.

Selection of new members was conducted in a democratic and solemn manner. New recruits needed two members of the organization to vouch for them. In the case of PO fronts (distinct from the national fronts mentioned above), acceptance of a new group officially needed the support of two member organizations. In practice, however, the process was sometimes less formal – the POs usually didn't have the organization or capacity to be so precise or to have such control over new members; nor, for that matter, were they usually particularly strict when it came to building the organization.

One of the component features of POs was the rather ethereal nature of their organizational and membership structures. Many organizations seemed to disappear into thin air at times of political ebb or police repression, only to come back later with much effervescence and determination. There were no membership rosters, and loose circles of supporters and sympathizers were an important part of the group. Few had offices, since most members were unemployed and had no money – the few that did were made up of craftspeople or students. Leaders did not get paid. None of the POs had a newsletter or any kind of internal information papers.

Another factor that contributed to their elusive nature was that there were many small POs which had only three or four members – perhaps half of the POs were this tiny. Their popularity depended on their one or two charismatic leaders and their rhetorical power and determination to fight. But even in the bigger POs, the personalities of a very few leaders could be decisive, although members continued to have a strong and active role. At the same time, this special role of the leadership was not so much a sign of the desire of these leaders to be stars as of the lack of an organizational tradition in the country and the fact that the POs were a new and emergent type of organization.

All in all, this flimsy nature tallied with the spontaneity of their daily practices, a fact seen in the haste with which mass demonstrations were organized and the dynamic manner in which the most appropriate means of action and communication were determined.

In the Haitian context, flimsiness was in no way the exclusive preserve of POs. The dozens of political parties that came into existence after February 7, 1986 did not possess a meaningful organizational structure, significant membership, or even a defined social base. (For a time, the Christian Democrat Party of Haiti was an exception, but they lost whatever popular support they had by supporting the September coup.) Several of the parties were just an empty shell for one or two presidential or cabinet hopefuls, who were often completely ignorant of politics and were incapable of getting even a modest mobilization of public opinion in their favor. This situation owed as much to the fragmentation of civil society and the absence of democratic traditions as to the ongoing search for new forms of political expression and social coexistence taking place within the process of democratic apprenticeship.

The Work of the Popular Organizations

I have commented on the presence of the POs on the political and social stage, yet just how and when did their presence become evident – exactly what did they do? Let us look at some common PO activities, chief among which was keeping Tontons Macoutes under watch. To protect the population, POs often exposed these thugs and turned them over to the community. When the Macoutes went on a rampage, POs deployed 'watch brigades' in various neighborhoods of the capital to thwart their attempts to sow terror.

Popular Organizations were skilled at marshalling and using many forms of communication, including word of mouth ('mouth radio'), typed or handwritten leaflets, and radio and television. Through these means they spoke of the need to control prices, fight black-marketeers and stop tax hikes affecting low-income earners. In 1987 they organized nationwide campaigns against taxes and called for taxpayers' revolts, although with little success. Members enjoyed the advantages of 'being out there' and blending in with the poor, who understood their language and trusted them because they identified with their ideals and their way of life. They would send out 'their people' to various parts of the community to pass on news, rumors, or calls to action. Most members seemed rather fearless about the possibility of repression and scoffed at danger. Although there might have been a bit of *machismo* in this stance, it was a way to tell people that they had defeated the fear that paralyzed people under Duvalier's regime.

In short, PO members made excellent political agitators, something in evidence during street rallies or whenever a general stoppage was called. The national mobilization called to stop the coup attempt of January 7, 1991, which tried to prevent the inauguration of President Jean-Bertrand Aristide (who was elected on December 16, 1990), illustrated their skills. Although all working-class and some middle-class sectors took part in affirming the democratic aspirations of the people, the leading role seemed to be played by POs.

As we heard in a number of interviews following these events, several PO leaders were able to move into action against Roger Lafontant simply because they were in the habit of going to bed late – a habit acquired while keeping an eye on Tontons Macoutes and coup-prone generals. When Lafontant appeared on national television at 2 a.m. to proclaim himself the new President, PO leaders immediately alerted colleagues in the provinces by telephone and issued a call for everyone to mobilize and block streets and roads. They immediately spread the word from door to door and asked for all available weapons to be assembled. People contributed rifles, revolvers, machetes and clubs; streets were blockaded by burning tires, and the billowing smoke alerted the rest of the population that mobilizations were occurring.

This was a frenzied night for the leaders of the POs. Throughout the entire country they helped or led people to erect barricades, which completely stopped all traffic in cities and on highways. They went into police stations to convince policemen to join them in the street. An impressive throng converged from all points on the National Palace, singing their resolve to 'get Lafontant out of there.' Along the way, they killed some Macoutes who tried to resist, and in some areas the homes of notorious Macoutes were ransacked.

On the morning of January 7, members of POs and Neighborhood Committees launched an assault against Macoute Headquarters in the Port-au-Prince suburb of Delmas. The attackers hauled out a security guard who stood watch at a shop owned by a wealthy merchant and commanded him to fire on the Macoute stronghold. They taunted the Macoutes and stoned the building, running quickly back into hiding. The Tontons Macoutes fired wildly, finding it difficult to hit their attackers. After shooting down three attackers, their ammunition ran out. The mob then overran the barracks and began hacking Macoutes to death with their machetes. Twenty-two were killed.

This offensive against the killers who protected the Duvalier dynasty expressed the pent-up rage of the people against a regime which had systematically denied them the right to life. They put their hearts into this attack, forgetting about their children, spurning death. 'On January 7,' said a proud and intense young leader of a PO, 'we went out to seal the victory of December 16 [when Aristide was elected president] with our own blood.'

Popular Organizations fought against more than Duvalierism and the Macoutes. They opposed all forces or institutions which, in their judgement, posed a threat to popular hegemony. They fought with Parliament because it tried to control an Executive which, despite occasional disagreement, they regarded as best placed to carry their dreams to fruition. Their skirmishes with Parliament also revealed their potential for intolerant and authoritarian behavior, since they did not accept opposition and did not always see dialogue as the means to solve differences. PO leaders, however, claimed that they actually prevented the burning of the Legislature at one point by those who wanted more dramatically to vent their irritation with certain members of Parliament.

The POs didn't function exclusively in a defensive mode – protecting the population against the Macoutes, fighting police repression, and denouncing the politics of exclusion. Some of their activities had a less defensive character and constituted a promotion of positive measures. For example, in the clean-up of the civil service and the construction of an efficient public administration undertaken by the Aristide government, while PO members played an important role along with militant civil servants in rooting out Macoutes and Duvalier diehards and in removing incompetent, dishonest or negligent public employees, they also considered it important to join the public service themselves as a way of exerting influence on the state apparatus, a consideration which dovetailed with the aspiration for decent employment among the hitherto disenfranchised.

Popular Organizations also participated in a commission of the Ministry of Commerce that was charged with controlling black-marketeering as part of the fight against rising costs. The Senate protested against this initiative and asked Prime Minister René Préval to appear before them to explain the role of the POs in his government.

They made attempts to build other alternatives. For example, in the populous Port-au-Prince neighborhood of Bel Air, the largest PO in the area (RADEB – the Rassemblement pour le Developpement du Bel Air) took over the moribund Centre Educatif du Bel Air. It appointed some of its members – including several technicians and a RADEB leader who was a trained engineer – to get this public technical school started again. In the context of a more general public service reorganization, talks began with government authorities to transfer the school formally to the community. RADEB was successful and the school was scheduled to reopen, but the coup on September 30, 1991 prevented completion of this plan.

Many POs took community improvement initiatives on their own. In addition to demanding that the state supply power, drinking water, and educational services, POs and local residents often carried out street paving work, literacy and Créole courses, sporting and cultural events, and concerts. (At least two POs were composed entirely of artists.) Some started Caisses Populaires (savings and loan funds) while others taught financial management courses to shopkeepers who wished to improve their business skills.

Some leaders went much further and aspired to seats in Parliament. In the parliamentary elections of June 1995, no PO members ran directly, although three senators with close working relations with the POs ran for the Organisation Politique Lavalas (OPL, the party of Aristide's supporters.) More dramatically, though, the new mayor of Port-au-Prince, Emmanuel Charlemagne, was a candidate for one of the POs and was elected with 45 per cent of the vote among many candidates. (His PO changed the first word of its name from Pouvwa Rasambleman des Oganizasyion to Pati, the créole word for party, in order to qualify to run in the elections.)

The financial straits of POs were often the most significant obstacle to the implementation of their stated goals. Most were financed entirely from membership dues, which were either voluntary or a portion of the member's income. Since most members were unemployed, and those who had jobs often earned a pittance, these groups had no financial muscle. Although a few received occasional contributions from foreign NGOs for specific projects (such as literacy programmes or street paving), most chose to be financially autonomous from foreign organizations. They chose this course to maintain ideological independence and to avoid corruption among leaders.

A few POs were created with the main purpose of attracting foreign donations, although this didn't mean their leaders were any less militant or committed to the popular cause. And in those cases where corruption might have occurred, although one can understand it in the light of the deplorable economic situation of certain leaders, it did have a deleterious ripple effect in stigmatizing other POs.

In spite of their economic weakness, the POs possessed important resources: the generosity of professionals who supported their fight, shared their ideals and often acted as volunteer advisers; and training centers and development education organizations, which often lent support for writing press releases and running off photocopies. Nevertheless, even those few POs with a modest bank account barely managed to tread water. Although it is a sign of organizational narrowness, this state of permanent destitution did not seem to worry the leaders of these organizations.

Their Gatherings

Until the temporarily successful coup of 1991, most POs held general membership meetings twice a month, although some held them as often as once a week; steering committees generally met once a week. General meetings were usually attended by anything from 15 to 60 core militants, plus sympathizers and the 'periphery' of the organization. Discussions centered on the political situation, planning for upcoming demonstrations, or issues such as participation in elections. There were discussions on a wide range of issues, from ethics in the public service to the nature of the state and the question of the IMF. (As for internal affairs, more delicate matters were usually dealt with by steering committees.)

The tone of these gatherings was democratic, with rank and file members being encouraged to participate actively and express their point of view with no restrictions. It was common for an ordinary member to be asked to speak at the next meeting on a certain topic or to ask him or her to chair that meeting. Given that one of their distinctive features was a strong 'grassrootism' which called for careful consideration of the views of the rank and file, this anti-vertical behavior among PO leaders was not surprising. This approach, in fact, explained certain criticisms before the coup to the effect that President Aristide did not find the time to visit and discuss political strategy with them and so, in their judgement, was drifting away from the grassroots. Popular Organizations, they claimed, could have informed him of the signals they were picking up from 'street power.' They also wished to voice their deep concern that he was surrounding himself with what they saw as bourgeois advisers. (When Aristide returned to Haiti, he met with the POs, but infrequently. At this point, he did not deal with them the same way as before, as a supposedly homogeneous group, but met the leaders who supported him and his policies. His successor, René Préval, has been even more distant.)

In short, our interviews gave us the sense that most PO leaders were aware of the need to establish egalitarian relationships between leadership and membership, and of the importance of practising full internal democracy. This observation also guided the fight against male chauvinism within these organizations, although everyone recognized that this objective was difficult and would take a long time to accomplish.

Conclusions

The feat of January 7, 1991, when the masses thwarted Lafontant's coup attempt, could not be repeated late on the night of September 29, 1991. This time the Armed Forces laid siege to all populous areas of Port-au-Prince and quickly took control of the capital and provincial towns. POs castigated President Aristide for failing to pass word of the impending coup, of which he first heard on the night of September 27, following his return from the United Nations. Had they been told, they say, they would have once again occupied the entire country and aborted the military assault.

It is not possible to guess the effects of such an uprising. Some say it would have halted the coup; others that it would have brought an even bloodier outcome. (Most observers estimate that between 3,000 and 5,000 people were murdered in the three years following the coup.) The fact remains that the coup, which was meant as preventive surgery with a broad range of economic, social, and political goals, lashed out most brutally at popular sectors, especially POs. The wretched and illiterate should never again dare to leave their ghetto; they should never again be allowed to challenge law and order and 'the decent people.' The coup leaders in effect said to them, 'What is the matter with you? In Haiti, you have always been considered as dogs and that is what you are.' Upper-class and comfortable middle-class individuals agreed that those filthy slums ought to have been cleaned out once and for all.

As surgery, the purpose of the onslaught against POs and the popular sector was to remove a vital organ from President Aristide's *Lavalas* government and from the progressive Haitian movement in general. The POs seemed to represent an obstacle and threat to a system of domination nearly two centuries old. The brutality of the offensive against the POs was evidence of their standing and their potential. They challenged the system and its repression, segregation, social injustice, bureaucracy, manipulation, intrigue, embezzlement, mediocrity and ignorance. They stood in the way of those individuals and institutions who propped up the old system – notably the Macoutes and Duvalier followers and the Armed Forces. Armed Forces members, particularly the most senior, had taken seriously the PO threats to use the necklace against them if they should attempt a *coup d'état*.

The represssion of the POs in the three years following the coup had a lasting effect on their activities: many leaders were killed, others went into hiding (which meant the groups had difficulty functioning); some leaders went abroad as boat people and never returned.

The Catholic Church hierarchy was – and remains – seriously weakened by the presence in its midst of the Base Communities, the comrades-in-arms of Popular Organizations. The Church had played a progressive role in the overthrow of Duvalier. But immediately after, the Church hierarchy opposed the popular movements; such opposition continued to the extent that it is widely believed that it played a part in the coup against Aristide. Only one bishop, Mgr Willy Romélus of Jérémie, Grand-Anse province, consistently showed a combative attitude in favor of change. Meanwhile, at the base of the church, there was a group of democratic, even revolutionary, priests, who saw Aristide as their leader and who remained committed to radical change. There was a division between the popular and official church, although the spokesmen for the latter maintained that there was, and always will be, only one church. Although the church hierarchy has still not regained its prestige, since Aristide's return there have been no outright conflicts between it and the popular church, as there had previously been.

Earlier, I alluded to the watchdog role of POs in the process of breaking down the old order and bringing into being a new Haiti. For example, the numerous political parties which sprang up after February 7, 1986, and which were subsequently called upon to join in the democratic struggle, aroused suspicion, animosity and even outright rejection among the POs. Until the coup of September 30, 1991, Parliament, brought back to life after a long dormancy under the Duvalier regime, suffered incessant harassment by POs, which considered it to be an enemy of the systemic transformations they sought. Popular Organizations played a leading role in the *Lavalas* government initiative to clean up, restructure and bring functionality and efficiency to the public service, a notorious stronghold of Duvalier supporters and a sanctuary for mediocrity, patronage and corruption. All in all, POs were extremely conscious of their role in the functioning of territorial communities – the foundation of local government and true seat of democratic power – which the *Lavalas* government unfortunately failed adequately to build. Perhaps more generously, I should say it had yet to build what were called 'territorial collectivities' or communities, something that was planned but not yet implemented at the time of the coup.

Since the restoration of constitutional government (signaled by Aristide's return in 1994), this issue of territorial communities has begun to be addressed. PO leaders and militants of the radical left have continued to push for the establishment of local structures as mechanisms of participatory democracy. OPL, the President's party, supports such measures. It is now written into the constitution. However, building such local structures won't be easy for several reasons: the Haitian state has no money, not even for elections (its national budget is similar to that of a small North American city); there are crucial matters that are taking precedence, such as negotiations with the international community for financial 'help,' the issue of privatization, and the whole problem of developing and adopting a national budget; finally, there is inadequate public awareness of the importance of local government – Haitians are used to a centralist, presidential political system.

The presence of the POs in the post-Duvalier transition was, as a whole, a positive factor. Yet was it true, as certain leaders asserted, that POs were the pillars of democracy? Such a viewpoint seems to be an exaggeration. First, as opposed to their internal conduct, their behavior on the political stage aroused doubt as to their adherence to democratic principles. For example, there was the necklacing threat against the 'enemies of democracy.' It is true this was used by all popular sectors and not just POs – widespread mistrust of the justice system, as well as the role of the threat in keeping the destructive power of the Macoutes and the Armed Forces in check were reasons. Nevertheless, did this not represent a threat to democracy as well? Such a question also applies to the pressure they exerted on Parliament in its dispute with the Executive. It is true that their rather vitriolic attacks against Parliamentarians were intended more to dissuade than to disrupt the role the Deputies were playing. Yet, is there a democratic tenet in whose name one can claim the right to step on democracy, even for the avowed purpose of defending it? This type of stance brings to mind the arrogance and sectarianism of vanguards who claimed the right to put everyone else in their place because they felt science and history were on their side. This approach by some POs mirrored the authoritarian practices of the ruling political, intellectual and financial elites. Such practices have existed throughout the history of Haiti and profoundly pervaded the political and civic culture of its people.

Second, legitimate reservations exist about the political productivity of POs. In other words, were they in fact able to act efficiently upon the political system and would they have eventually democratized it? Their spontaneity, amorphous nature and organizational weakness were obvious constraints to such productivity. What is more, this deficiency (which, we recall, was also their source of strength) represents a potential danger for the construction of democracy. Anyone may create 'his' PO and use it for his personal use or for political manipulation. This has been seen in a number of cases since the coup. Both before and just after Aristide's return, there was talk of establishing a mechanism to channel the energy of the POs in order to implement their democratic potential. But such talk has waned, and this possibility seems increasingly unrealistic.

Another shortcoming was the POs' limited institutional substance. Ultimately, democracy rests upon solid institutions. Yet POs received their strength from 'the street,' not from developing structures that institutionalized democratic norms or provided mechanisms of representation and delegation of the will of the masses. Statements like, 'in the next elections we will have representatives in Parliament' started to ring rather hollow, particularly since the POs regarded the institutions of the state and civil society with scorn.

The events of September 30, 1991 illustrated this. Parliament, derided and underrated by both POs and the Executive, played a leading role in the violent overthrow of President Aristide. The constitutional President was, after the coup, forced to negotiate with a deceitful Parliament, despite its transparently unconstitutional complicity in the coup.

Their understanding of the concept of power was another weaknesses of POs as regards the democracy-building process. Their concept of power was grounded in their strong 'basism': according to them, real power was not the power of institutions but the 'power of the streets,' which has to control the institutions of the state. They did not care too much about constructing political strategy and a programmatic platform. That position was shared in part by the first (pre-coup) *Lavalas* government and President Aristide. This probably contributed to the success of the coup.[4]

These limitations should not be used to minimize the significant contributions made by POs in the social and political era that began the day Jean-Claude Duvalier left for exile. To downplay or dismiss their role would be a mistake. Six years of transition to democracy brought forth new social actors who had, of necessity, to undergo a long and difficult learning process. Political parties, parliament, the executive branch, President Aristide and POs all suffered from being inexperienced, following almost two hundred years of authoritarian rule, and lacked sufficient tools to develop an adequate programme and strategy of change.

By the time their shortcomings and mistakes are finally rectified, a high price will have been paid; these actors themselves will undergo further change. The learning process has been made much more difficult by the generalized confusion that has characterized the entire post-Duvalier period. Before the coup, POs were clearly inspired by the principles of participatory democracy, which they saw as entailing a radical break from the entire system of domination *and* from all traditional forms of political engagement. On the other hand, a great part of the national democratic movement felt their goal was representative democracy, and for its achievement they needed to act with caution, be realistic, and avoid the confusion between speed and haste.

In the years since Aristide's return, Haitian politics has continued to evolve. For the majority of Haitians, the road to democracy seems to be getting clearer at the same time as they know that change will not be as easy as they thought. They have fewer illusions about the type of changes that will be possible in the near future. It is also now clearer that participatory democracy should not be opposed to representative democracy, contrary to what many POs still think.

After Aristide's return in October 1994 and the subsequent elections in June 1995 (parliamentary and municipal) and December 1995 (presidential), the POs played a less pronounced role. This diminished role is not surprising. The POs emerged at a time of popular mobilization with

a clear mandate to challenge the system. The beginning of the institutionalization of alternatives ushers in a moment, at least for the time
being, when the POs, at least as previously conceived, have less of a
political role to play.

However, this much is true: something unprecedented took place in
Haiti. The political process that unfolded there since 1986 – and that
remains, in spite of the tremendous obstacles – has historical implications which go well beyond the borders of this small country. The type
of democracy to be built in Haiti, although perhaps based on the lessons
and achievements of Western societies, will also be inspired by the history
and culture of Haiti, which are so different from those of democratic
countries. Of this culture and history – and the first successful slave
rebellion in history – the POs can claim to be a legitimate child. In this
sense, Popular Organizations stand as an original experience, the value of
which must not be underrated. At the very least, they have earned a
tribute for their audacity and courage. They had the honor of daring to
introduce utopian dreams into a society in which, as Max Weber said of
a different era, 'whoever goes into politics enters into a tactical pact with
the Satanic powers surrounding the powerful,' and where 'the genies or
demons of politics live in eternal strife with the god of love.'[5]

Notes

1. The bulk of field research was conducted during 1990, although work was
continued in subsequent years The research project was made possible by a grant
from the Ford Foundation. I would like to thank Lovely Chéry and Bethy Casty
for assisting me in the interviews.

Interviews were conducted in Port-au-Prince with leaders of various POs, the
Federation Nationale des Etudiants Haitiens (FENEH, National Organization of
Students), a trade union that worked closely with the POs, other neighborhood
and community organizations, and with Father Jean-Bertrand Aristide before he
ran for President.

2. One social democratic party, for example, was led by politically ambitious
intellectuals who had been living in Europe At first, this party had strong ties with
the French Socialist Party. Following Duvalier's exit they took government and
other positions and progressively moved to the right in the name of *realpolitik*. This
climaxed, after the coup, with a public claim of neutrality, which in effect meant
openly standing alongside the most repressive and conservative forces in the
country.

3. The 'necklace' was mainly used in the capital just after Duvalier's exit in
February 1986 – used by people in popular quarters and slums against those who
had spread terror for decades. The Catholic Church, which had played an important role in the overthrow of the regime, called on the people to cease its use. Since
then, it has been more uncommon: two Macoutes were killed immediately following

the aborted coup of Roger Lafontant, the main representative of Duvalierism, on January 7, 1991. It has been used several times as a warning to Macoutes – for example, at the time of the trial of Lafontant, and in August 1991, when there were threats to depose Aristide's Prime Minister, René Préval.

4. Following the return of Aristide, attempts were made to address these issues by building a real political party (the OPL – Organisation Politique Lavalas) and a political grouping composed of the OPL, the Pati Louvri Baryè (Créole for the party that will open doors), and the Mouvement Ouvrier Paysan. On the other hand, my own thinking on these issues continues to evolve. It sometimes appears to me that the articulation of a strategy and platform doesn't necessarily, in our context, mean that pressing problems will be solved. Faced with such daunting problems as the drastic situation of the economy, the almost complete absence of money, the problem of a public administration characterized by inefficiency and corruption, negotiations with international financial institutions, and huge pressures concerning privatization, it does seem that a government that does a good job as regards these problems (especially the issue of reconstructing a public administration largely free of the crippling problems of the past) would be taking a giant and decisive step forward. Having a well-articulated political strategy and programmatic platform might mean that these issues are all addressed in words. But such a strategy and platform does not necessarily guarantee the political capacity and economic resources to implement them.

5. Max Weber, *The Politician and the Scientist* (Mexico: Premia Editorial, 1981), p. 57.

6

The Hidden Politics of Neighborhood Organizations: Women and Local Participation in the Poblaciones of Chile

Veronica Schild

An important legacy of the authoritarian experience in Latin American countries is the proliferation of urban grassroots organizations.[1] Chile is no exception: for the last decade poor neighborhood self-help groups such as economic workshops, soup kitchens, cultural groups, and the like have multiplied in a context of economic and political repression. The primary objective of these organizations is to aid people in poor neighborhoods or *poblaciones*[2] in their struggle to survive. These self-help groups are not entirely new, for they have their roots in earlier neighborhood-based collective experiences.

What is new, however, is the leading role played by women in the neighborhood organizations. Indeed, women are the dominant force behind these organizations in the poblaciones of Chile's capital, Santiago, making up over 90 per cent of those participating in self-help groups. More important still, there is a new kind of solidarity and social identity evident in the groups, which, though only embryonic, does nevertheless raise interesting questions about the nature and potential of poor neighborhood organizations.

The phenomenon of neighborhood organizations has been studied primarily in terms of the problematic of social movements.[3] In Chile, as in other countries of the region, initial euphoria about the potential of urban collective action has given way to more subdued appraisals of the phenomenon. Some researchers have assumed that these organizations constitute a movement, a term they use descriptively.[4] Others have concluded that these initiatives do not constitute a movement after all.[5] With some exceptions, however, most studies have unnecessarily reified the phenomenon of urban grassroots organizing. They have conflated neighborhood with community, and have assumed a degree of homogeneity of conditions, both in terms of relations to forms of production and to authority structures, as well as of interests, which simply do not hold on closer scrutiny. Moreover, because these studies are gender-blind, they have also ignored the importance of women in urban grassroots organizing.

Poblaciones are neighborhoods without a unitary character or a single principle of collective action. For one thing, people's social relations are shaped not only by forms of power which are class-based but also by others such as gender. Gender relations, moreover, defined here as relations of unequal power based on sexual difference, have contributed in fundamental ways to shaping the heterogeneous character of poor neighborhoods and the forms of collective action found there. Thus, how women and men are differentially located in the home, neighborhood, and organizations needs to be accounted for to understand the complex nature and significance of these organizations. Why are women predominantly involved in neighborhood groups? What is the nature of these collective experiences from the point of view of the women involved? What are the possibilities and limitations of these collective efforts?[6]

In this chapter I will argue that neighborhood organizations are spaces in which women contest relations of power. In this sense these organizations are spaces for local-level participation or political learning. For women, to become involved in collective neighborhood activities means in the first place learning how to question the routines and norms that govern their everyday lives. It may also, by that token, mean developing new decision-making and activist capacities.

Gender and Local Participation

In *Participation and Democratic Theory*, Carole Pateman, relying on Almond and Verba's important study of the development of adult political competencies, argued that 'lower-level' participation, for example self-management in the workplace, has a positive impact on adult political socialization. Having access to decision-making power in an area directly relevant to people's lives predisposes them toward 'higher' forms of participation. By making decisions, and monitoring their own work, people acquire a sense of self-confidence, as well as of personal and political efficacy. Almond and Verba argued that 'the structure of authority at the workplace is probably the most significant – and salient – structure of that kind with which the *average man* finds himself in daily contact.' The question remains, however, as to what are the most significant structures of authority for people who are either self-employed, domestics or unpaid workers – as, for example, is the case with many adult women. What forms may participation and political socialization take in these cases? Although Pateman's argument focuses exclusively on the workplace, she recognizes that 'one person whom the opportunities for participation in industry would pass by is the full-time housewife.' And she suggests that the housewife 'might find opportunities to participate at the local government level.'[7]

Even for the adult woman who continues to be engaged in paid work, the home and the neighborhood, not the workplace, are primary. These settings have distinct structures of authority. In fact, the experiences of most adult women suggest that there are contexts where disempowerment results from relations of inequality that are not exclusively work-based. Thus gender, as well as race and other sources of unequal social relations, existing alongside unequal relations of production, either make possible or hinder personal and political effectiveness. In a more recent critique of Almond and Verba's study, Pateman argued that although their empirical findings show differential participation based on sex and class, these authors failed to problematize their findings. She suggested that to account for this unequal distribution of personal and political competencies we need to explore the crucial factor of socialization inside authority structures of everyday life.[8] Pateman and others have argued that neither a conception of what constitutes political competencies nor one of how these are developed, if both are ultimately based on the experiences of the workplace, offer a viable way of understanding how women's different political competencies and participation are shaped.

New research proposes a different definition of politics and of political socialization; it offers a fruitful way to understand hindrances to participation and the development of political competencies in sites other than the workplace. This research, influenced by the work of, among others, Habermas and Foucault, follows the so-called 'linguistic turn' in the social sciences and focuses on language as a site of domination and on politics as a discourse by which people establish common goals and 'determine who they are and who they shall become as social beings.'[9] The feminist implications of this recent work are important: it leads to an understanding of politics which includes struggles against limiting gender identities, and of political learning as acquiring, among other things, cultural resources to forge alternative identities.

In the following pages these definitions of power and politics will be employed to understand what occurs in neighborhood-based organizations, but before turning to the organizations, the national forces that have shaped life in the poblaciones will be described.

The Broader Context

The military coup of 1973 led by General Augusto Pinochet put an end to a process of increasing social and political mobilization which had been initiated in the early 1960s and had culminated with the socialist government of Salvador Allende. This social process, which involved industrial workers as well as many women and men from poblaciones and the countryside, was suppressed by the dictatorship with unusual brutality. Deprived of the support of the left-wing parties, of the politically significant trade unions, and of the government-sanctioned, neighborhood-based organizations, millions of people affected by massive unemployment and a sudden drop in their standard of living found themselves without a public voice. Thus, after years of depending on a government which had played a significant social role, working-class people and the poor were left to cope on their own with the devastating combined effects of the recessions and the economic policies pursued. Even by the late 1980s, in the midst of Chile's economic boom, 42 per cent of the population (5 million out of 12 million) could not meet their basic needs.[10] In short, the working class and the poor ultimately bore the brunt of the radical economic transformations brought about by the authoritarian regime, the so-called 'modernization' of Chile.[11]

Pobladoras (working-class homemakers) have been the hardest hit by the devastating economic transformations of the past two decades. Although the political context changed with the election of a civilian government in 1989, the economic situation of the poorest segments of Chilean society, and particularly of women, has not improved significantly. For these women, work possibilities, which were never very good but had been improving steadily during the 1960s and early 1970s, greatly deteriorated during the Pinochet years; consequently, open female unemployment increased sharply.[12] In addition, many worked in unstable, exploitative conditions without the right to unionize. In a labor market characterized by a strong gendered division of labor, women have typically worked in low-status, low-skilled, and low-wage occupations such as domestic and other service jobs, as well as artisanal and low-wage factory jobs (predominantly in the textile and food sectors). With age, women's participation in the labor force has traditionally tended to decline in formal employment and to increase in informal work. These trends in women's employment have become accentuated in the past 20 years.[13]

Increasingly, women constitute an important number of those employed in the new, dynamic sectors of the export economy. The work conditions in these sectors are highly unstable and exploitative.[14] Recognizing women's massive, and subordinate, presence in today's economy, critics of the present economic model refer to the 'feminization' of Chilean labor. Put differently, the restructuring of the labor process in that country increasingly also has a woman's face.[15]

Over the years women have learned new strategies to cope with the effects of these devastating economic changes. During the economic recessions of 1975, and particularly of 1982, for example, women in the urban areas who were expelled from the formal labor market did not retreat to their homes. Instead, these women, and many wives of unemployed workers who had not worked before, joined the informal sector in massive numbers.[16] These homemakers, in fact, compensated for a dwindling family income by undertaking paid work in addition to their domestic duties. And, in so doing, they acted as mediators or 'shock absorbers' of the economic crises in their families.[17] Since the physical survival of their children and husbands was often at stake, many pobladoras not only increased their work at home, producing those goods that the family could no longer afford to buy, but also accepted any remunerated activity whatsoever outside the home. Usually these precarious economic activities constituted an extension of the skills and activities women deploy in their domestic work and really amounted to 'strategies of survival' only. During the 1980s, neighborhood-based economic organizations, sponsored by the Catholic Church and by NGOs, offered pobladoras one possibility to supplement the family income. These organizations did not constitute a long-term viable economic alternative for women, however, and pobladoras knew it. Nevertheless, the groups offered women immediate help and a space for collective action.

Since the installation of the civilian government in 1989, many women have withdrawn from neighborhood organizations, possibly – in some cases at least – because they or their men found more adequate means of earning an income.[18] Indeed, neighborhood leaders and NGO workers interviewed recently suggest that at least some types of organizations are diminishing in numbers, although exact figures for this trend are not available.[19]

Life in the Población[20]

The organizing of poor neighborhoods is primarily, though not exclusively, an urban phenomenon, and it is especially prevalent in Santiago. Roughly 1,400,000 people, one-third of the capital's population, live in peripheral poor neighborhoods or poblaciones. A long-established población is a poor and very heterogeneous neighborhood – in terms of both its physical appearance and the kind of people who live in it. Historically, most recent poblaciones have originated from *campamentos* (shanty towns), which are typically the first outcome of an organized illegal land seizure; older poblaciones were the outcome of *callampas* or spontaneous land invasions. Also, a number of poblaciones were built by earlier governments, and some even by Pinochet's government.

An established población is a place characterized by deep cultural differences. Though people in the población identify themselves and their neighbors as pobladores, this generic definition hides complex strategies of differentiation in which factors like gender, place of origin, ethnicity, degree of schooling and work experience, as well as political experience, are deployed by women and men in the población to establish differences between themselves. Commitment to a particular party ideology has traditionally been a strong differentiating element among Chilean men, including poor and working-class men. For most women, party politics has never played this role. Indeed, during the authoritarian period anything sounding 'political' elicited suspicion, distrust and fear among these women (and also among a considerable number of men). Marta, a member of a women's group and a Church group in the Southern Población explains why people in the neighborhood were afraid of politics: 'This regime really keeps us in constant fear … we have seen the repression, that is, we have felt it, because either they take a neighbor away or a young man disappears.'

The passivity of people in the poblaciones in the 1980s, however, should not be equated with tacit support for the regime, nor, for that matter, with tacit identification with the left. In fact, although many of these people did not dare join in any collective activities, neither did they abandon their political commitment. Informal interviews reveal, for example, that the whole political spectrum was represented in the neighborhood, including the right-wing parties which emerged after the coup and were referred to as 'the civilian arm of the dictatorship.' Moreover, political ideas and commitments continued to divide the neighborhood as they had before the coup. Particularly in the case of men, political choice, even when not accompanied by activism, seemed to determine which people they would socialize with, whom they would tolerate, and whom they would simply distrust. Thus, the distinction 'us/them' was present within the población, as well as between pobladores and outsiders. This should make us aware that a populist collective identity such as 'the pobladores' is neither consistent nor coherent.

Social relations based on sexual differences are central in the articulation of neighborhood heterogeneity, defining the characteristics of appropriately male and female practices and discourses. Equally important are those relations based on differences *within* gender. Furthermore, the discourses of *machismo* and *marianismo*, which legitimate gender inequality on the assumed bases of biology and religion, are an important aspect of relations between the sexes throughout Chilean society, as indeed throughout Latin America. These discourses are deeply entrenched in the poblaciones. *Machismo* and *marianismo* are not merely dominant ideas which reflect the material subordination of the pobladora; rather, they are an effective cultural resource through which gender identities are constructed and maintained in everyday life. In other words, these discourses which determine what it is to be a man or a woman provide the framework whereby a power hierarchy is made possible in gender relations, both in the población and in the society at large. These legitimating discourses of sexual/gender inequality, together with other practices, discourses and institutions, make up the Chilean and Latin American 'sex/gender system.'[21] Thus the sex/gender system is present in the población, and indeed throughout society, as a kind of subtext buttressing all social practices: the work people may engage in; the forms their relations to authority structures may take; the responsibilities they may have to the community and to the immediate and extended family; as well as the collective activities they may engage in, and their access to a public voice and to decision-making power.

The Homemaker's Everyday Life

A young pobladora's expectations are shaped by the ideal of domesticity, which includes a view of family life that envisions the man as economic provider and the woman as homemaker and mother. For almost 30 years there has been a concerted effort on the part of the state, with the help of an army of middle-class women volunteers, to disseminate this ideal in the poblaciones. Thousands of women were trained, and continue to be trained today, in the tasks of responsible motherhood and competent homemaking through government-sanctioned Mothers' Centers. This attempt to 'domesticate' pobladoras has been central to the disciplining of the working class.[22] However, although social legislation with respect to wages, health, schooling, and social benefits made it possible in the past for some pobladoras to become full-time homemakers and for many to desire a domestic lifestyle, most still had to work to supplement the family income.

The ideal of domesticity promoted by the Mothers' Centers, which were tightly controlled by the authoritarian government, jars against the reality of increasing pauperization.[23] Most young pobladoras work outside the población, either in domestic and other service jobs or in a factory, before marrying and starting a family, and with few exceptions these young women still desire a full-time domestic lifestyle. However, most married pobladoras are forced to undertake paid work at one time or another to supplement the family income. Indeed, in the last ten years a great number of them have become the main income earners in their households while retaining their domestic duties. For most women this change in their economic role has not meant major changes in their everyday lives. These pobladoras' everyday lives are characterized by an endless work process, a series of repetitive, time-consuming, arduous routines crucial to the functioning of the family.

The material hardship faced by the pobladora is underscored by her subordinate position in the family. Accordingly, the predominant relationship between wives and husbands resembles a parental one, with the husband as authority figure. A clear illustration of this is the prevalence of the vocabulary of 'permission' in interactions between husband and wife. Obtaining permission to go out with friends, to join organizations, to seek paid work, or alternatively challenging imposed decisions, makes up an important part of the wife's interaction with her husband. In concrete terms, her subordinate position places the pobladora in a position where she is responsible for the material and psychological well-being of the family, but in most cases has no part in important decision-making. The actual domestic experiences of pobladoras vary according to their education, their income, their experiences outside the home, and their success in negotiating arrangements with other family members, including husbands, mothers and sisters. Ultimately, however, the responsibility for the household and children rests exclusively with them.

Today younger, more educated men and women struggle for equal relationships and against limiting gender identities. Nevertheless, these younger couples still have to contend with the judgement of family and neighbors, who are the keepers of traditional values – that is, 'respectability' and 'decency' – and of traditional domestic roles. Most women who are older or less educated must still grapple with husbands who limit and control them. As Mercedes, leader of a workshop on the north side of Santiago put it, 'ninety per cent of the women do not participate [in activities outside their homes, such as workshops], because of their men.'

For many women, challenging the authority of their husbands may even invite verbal or physical abuse.[24] As mentioned already, however, women in the poblaciones do not go along with their subordination passively. For most pobladoras their unequal condition entails maneuvering with greater or lesser degrees of success in a situation with very restricted possibilities for independent action. Moreover, the fact that many women join and stay in self-help groups is an indication of their resistance to their disempowered condition.

The economic hardship which pobladoras and their families have had to endure for the past two decades has clearly made the dream of being exclusively a homemaker and mother more unattainable than ever. Ironically, these difficult times have also brought about new opportunities: many women have found in these organizations a space where they have begun to question their subordinate role *vis-à-vis* their families and, in some cases, to challenge authority structures outside the home.

Women in the Organizations

Until 1983 the predominant kind of self-help group in the poblaciones were *comedores populares* (popular canteens) and *comedores infantiles* (children's canteens), opened by the Church with the volunteer work of pobladoras. However, by 1983 these early initiatives had been replaced by more permanent groups, *ollas comunes* (soup kitchens). After 1983 other permanent self-help groups flourished. These neighborhood groups have been classified into three general types, according to their explicit goals. Some generate income or services and goods for their members. Others act as pressure groups, demanding collective solutions to common problems such as unemployment, utility or mortgage debts. And still other groups promote cultural and educational activities. In the early 1990s, *ollas comunes* and other self-help groups that sought to address the problem of hunger seemed to be disappearing. This trend may very well be a reflection of the government's employment policies. Wages improved slightly for some sectors and unemployment steadily decreased after 1991, though as the Minister of the Economy himself recognized – and the leaders of the powerful Central Unica de Trabajadores, or CUT, reminded him – the quality of jobs had not improved.[25]

Of the three general types of organization, the groups where members take part in economic activities were dominant until very recently. In November 1982, for example, 495 economic type groups were counted in Greater Santiago. In March 1984 the number of these groups had increased to 702, and in July 1985 to 1,103. By 1986 there were 1,386 groups in Greater Santiago. In 1982 these organizations had reached 22,567 people, including members and beneficiaries, while in 1986 the number had increased to 190,239.[26]

Furthermore, according to some estimates, between 1986 and 1989 economic type groups doubled in number.[27] These groups became known as either 'popular economic groups' or 'groups for economic survival.' The exact number of economic type groups in existence today is not known, although as mentioned before it seems to be declining.

Economic type groups are distinguished according to the activities they engage in. In fact, two basic sub-types of these groups have been identified: consumer groups and handicraft workshops. The former produce goods and services for their members' own consumption. For example, there are family vegetable gardens, bulk purchasing groups, bakeries, and soup kitchens. There are also health workshops, housing and debt organizations, *sindicatos de trabajadores independientes* (unions of informal sector workers and unions of unemployed workers).

The handicraft workshops orient their production to the market, and are far more numerous and enduring. Of the 1,383 organizations registered in the 1986 survey, 415 were workshops. These absorb almost 90 per cent of people organized in economic type groups, most of whom are women. For example, in 1986 (the last date for which detailed information exists), of 364 groups, 344 had an exclusively female membership. Of a total of 6,483 people directly involved in these groups (as producers of goods), 6,412 were women.[28] Although today the overall number of organizations may be declining, there is no reason to suspect that this gendered pattern of involvement has changed. Women continue to be the majority of those engaged in the groups. Handicraft workshops have an average of 18 members, and a flexible meeting schedule. Activities include knitting, crafts, sewing, carpentry, electricity, hairdressing, printing and bookbinding, and repair and manufacture of shoes, toys, and textiles.

Pobladoras who decide to join a workshop have, more often than not, done so after having waged a battle at home for 'permission' to join. This constraint is probably the reason why most organizations operate during the hours when husbands are away. In the workshops women engage in activities which may not necessarily be those they desire, for much depends on the resources made available to them by the sponsoring agencies. The organizations are, therefore, not an outcome of the spontaneous decisions of women, though it may seem so at first sight. In periods of crisis, women desperate to find something for 'the pot' have got together and decided to start an organization. Typically, they make this decision because they know in advance, from neighbors, friends, and other women in the community, that the Church and other NGOs give them material support to get started. They also know that domestic type economic activities are supported, so they tend to set themselves up as knitting or sewing groups. At the same time, pobladoras are well aware that these activities are poorly paid and that, therefore, they are not equivalent to 'real' work. They are also aware that they do not always learn marketable skills in the workshops.[29]

The Church, through its social office or Vicariate, played a major role in the creation of these organized activities in the mid-1970s, and was for a long time their main supporter. In fact, the Church relied on its vast experience with pobladoras for its social work during the authoritarian period. Historically, the Church was engaged in programs to help poor women and their families, which subsequently became the basis for government efforts in the poblaciones in the early 1960s.[30] Considering itself as the protector of the family unit, the Church has traditionally sponsored activities designed to help women ease their families through periods of economic hardship. Thus women have opted for strategies to increase the family income in a context of limited alternatives.

Appealing to the government's commitment to repay the so-called social debt to the poor, the Church ceased to support neighborhood-based activities it began to consider to be beyond its jurisdiction.[31] Indeed, the dismantling in November 1992 of the Vicaria de Solidaridad, the office established after the coup by the Church to co-ordinate human rights and other forms of assistance to the poor, is a good indication of the institution's shifting priorities.

Typically, most women who join workshops plan to leave them as soon as the economic situation of their family improves. In today's changed political context poor and working-class families have experienced some, however minimal, economic improvement, and NGO personnel and government officials working with women share the perception that at least some women are indeed opting out of workshops. However, the continued importance of the workshops, and more specifically of women in them, was highlighted by the actions of the government itself. For example, the Ministry of the Economy promoted a program for 'micro-enterprises' whose aim was to help handicraft workshops become economically viable. In addition, the government granted funds to NGOs promoting work-related-skills development programs for women, in the context of its program for micro-enterprises.[32]

Economic type groups seem to be sufficiently significant to be the centerpiece of economic programs geared to low-income groups. This importance is also suggested by the promises made to organized women by candidates running for the municipal elections in June 1992. Invariably the candidates' appeals to organized women – regardless of what the nature of their particular organizations was – centered on promises to help them promote and sell the goods they produce.[33]

Whatever the present trend may be, what is certain is that a considerable number of those women engaged at one point or another in economic type groups have become committed to the organizations. For them, the appeal of the groups has ceased to be economic and has become social and political. The extra-economic appeal of these organizations is linked to the intangible aid women have received over the years from supporting institutions in the form of educational workshops on such topics as sexuality, family violence, parenting, the legal rights of women, and leadership training. Curiously, on the one hand, much has been said to date about material aid; that is, supplies and money that neighborhood groups receive, and about the long-term effects this form of aid may have on people's capacity to act autonomously.[34] On the other hand, very little has been said about the intangible aid that the organizations receive, and particularly about the long-term effects this form of aid may have on women. The political-educational function, which I argue is central, is related precisely to this aspect of the organizations.

Pobladoras who participate in educational workshops enter into a network which I would call 'symbolic' because it consists of an exchange in language, and because what they obtain through it are cultural resources. In other words, through this network women acquire new meaning-making resources with which to make sense of their world and their own place in it. Through this symbolic network, pobladoras come into contact with professionals, in the form of popular educators, social workers, lawyers, and psychologists. This in itself is not new: pobladoras have historically been in contact with such middle-class women, for example through the government-sanctioned Mothers' Centers. One could argue that the interactions between middle-class professionals and pobladoras are of questionable benefit to pobladoras because they are relations of unequal power: the former possess knowledge, while the latter simply receive it. While there is a tradition of middle-class women working for the poor, what is new today is that many of the professional women working for NGOs (many of whom lived in exile during most of the Pinochet years), with whom organized pobladoras come into contact, are on the left and are feminists. These women's political inclinations shape their relations with pobladoras and translate into a commitment to work with pobladoras as opposed to for them. For pobladora leaders this means that the terms of their relationship with these professionals are in principle open to challenge; this is expressed in their everyday speech as a demand to be recognized for their own worth and to be treated as equals.

Ironically, then, the feminist discourse, with its strong emphasis on equality and rights, not only encourages pobladoras to speak differently about themselves and their place in the world, but also encourages them to question their relations with middle-class feminists. Therefore the interaction between these two groups of women is not facilitated by shared experiences – class relations shape these women's lives differently – but by a discourse which makes it possible to question and challenge paternalism.

Thus the encounters between these pobladoras and middle-class feminists can be problematic; conflicts of needs, interests, and expectations continually arise. Their relations may at times be characterized as paternalism, underscored by subtle, or not so subtle, prejudice on the part of the middle-class women, and suspicion and frustration on the side of the pobladoras.

Some have suggested that the new economic role of pobladoras has led to changes in their domestic roles. Economic need, according to this view, forces women to come out of their homes and to start collaborating with others. Carrying out duties competently in spheres other than the home, and sharing similar experiences, allow women to question their personal situation in a wider context; this in turn leads them to become conscious of their class and sexual oppression, and to develop a sense of solidarity based on their common identity.[35] If this is a mechanical and partial account, it is because the mediating role of ideology is unrecognized. There is no such thing as a unitary sub-stratum of women's experience, which, once discovered, leads to a total identification or sense of 'sameness.' Instead, pobladoras experience gendered and class-defined everyday life differently and are able to speak to this through a combination of their own linguistic resources and those derived from their interactions with middle-class feminists. In other words, solidarity for these women is not the outcome of discovering an identical experience, or essence, which lies beyond language; it is rather a negotiation of differences and similarities *through* language.

Depending on their level of education, their degree of involvement in the organization, and especially their past organizational experience, the pobladoras will benefit in different ways from participating in the symbolic network through their organizations. Some, for instance, regard the organization primarily as a friendly meeting place where, as many put it, 'they can overcome their sense of isolation, and exchange personal experiences' as well as 'learn new things.' Most of these women tend to be either older or less educated, and have little or no previous organizational experience. For them the group is a first window to the 'outside.' Many of these women use their experience in the group to develop a sense of self-confidence and competence, a sense of personal autonomy. Maria, a member of a workshop in Renca, explains: 'We are a great number of women who, because of our living conditions, didn't have any possibility of education and have found this opportunity to acquire it … I don't believe that any of us could once again limit ourselves to the home … this is like a seed that has been sown and is germinating.'

Other women see themselves in what I would call a more active relation to the organization; they are the doers and movers and may have leading positions. These leaders learn to speak in terms of rights, which means not only confronting recalcitrant husbands but also other people in positions of authority with whom they are in regular contact, for example doctors, social workers, school teachers and, the professionals with whom they work. *Hacerse respetar* (to elicit respect from others) as well as *pelear por sus derechos* (to fight for one's rights), figure prominently in the speech of these organized women. Being in regular contact with middle-class professionals may be an important factor that contributes to the development of these women. As Mercedes, the leader of a workshop in Renca, explains:

> In the beginning we went to the Vicaria because of the concern over subsistence, because they helped us with food … now I go because of the courses they offer, and because I like the environment. In institutions like CEMA [the government-sanctioned umbrella organization that co-ordinates the activities of Mothers' Centers] they are distant and cold and everything comes to us as if by charity … as if they were saying poor women. It is not like here where we are all the same. Just because someone has a title doesn't make her better than someone who only knows how to clean pots.

The notion of feminism has, interestingly enough, become an important differentiating tool for many of these women; it allows them to distinguish between themselves and organized middle-class women. The label 'feminist' is one which these women flatly refuse – with very few exceptions – to appropriate for themselves. When asked about feminism, one typical response was: 'Feminists are extremists, just as machistas are. They want everything to be done their way, just as men want things done theirs,' said Eli, a member of a women's group in the Southern Población. Women who have a more subtle understanding of feminism reflect an awareness of class-based differences, which is expressed as a recognition of their limited possibilities compared with middle-class 'others.' To quote Eloisa, a member of a workshop on the West side of Santiago: 'I say I am not a feminist because they [middle-class feminists] speak a lot about liberation but we will always be conditioned by our children … if they lack food, we have to provide it for them.'

For many pobladoras the most important outcome of participating in the neighborhood groups is developing a new sense of self-confidence, of their 'own voice.' Furthermore, it would seem to be the case that, once developed, several factors contribute to strengthening this new sense of self-confidence. It is true that the authoritarian regime's propaganda promoted a very traditional view of women and that the Church reinforced this view. But the Church, through such activities as promoting collective work among women, has also set up conditions for women to question this view, and in some cases to openly challenge it. In addition, the main tool of government propaganda, National Television – which boasts of reaching just about the entire territory – may also have been the pobladora's greatest ally against traditional images, owing to its persistent presentation of images of apparently autonomous, competent women who wrestle with the tribulations of balancing career and family life.[36]

Some of the women in the organizations, usually those in leadership positions, develop the confidence to make decisions and to speak outside their organizations, and also develop a desire to expand their collective work. Indeed, frequently a gap is created between the expectations of regular members and leaders as a result of this difference, which may result in conflicts about leadership. When several members in an organization become active, they may redefine the goals of the group, giving primacy to the educational and political aspects. Others, however, tend to join different organizations, quite often in addition to their original group. A woman may, for example, belong to a church group, a workshop and a women's group simultaneously.

Certainly, this increased interest in simultaneous group activities was shared by most of the members of a women's group in the Southern población, for whom joining this organization was already an expression of their further commitment to this kind of work. Some, like Julia, who was the co-ordinator of the group, chose deliberately to concentrate their efforts in organizing women through women's groups. She and most of the other members of the group had finished high school, had worked until getting married (some in skilled jobs, others as maids or waitresses), and some had continued to work afterwards. Moreover, most came to the women's group with previous organizational experience acquired in a variety of settings, such as the girl scouts, catechism groups, Mothers' Centers, or workshops. For them, joining a women's group was the next logical organizational step. What they wanted out of the women's group was a chance to address common concerns, and, more importantly, to be able to set their own agendas and not, as Julia put it, to 'waste time in useless activities like embroidery and crocheting.'

This women's group did not recruit new members on the basis of political preferences. In fact, its approach was pluralistic: the two principal rules for recruitment were a commitment to show tolerance and respect for one another, and a willingness to work together. For this group, establishing the meeting time became a political statement. They deliberately chose 7 p.m. because, as they put it, 'they had a right to establish their own schedules and priorities.' As was to be expected, this choice of time became a major stumbling block in their recruiting efforts. For Julia and two others, Filomena and Maria, the commitment to a women's group has translated into a commitment to organize women in their población. Toward the end of 1988, these women, in co-ordination with middle-class professionals, had set up the local branch of an ambitious city-wide women's network, which was designed to help pobladoras find solutions to their problems, and they were busy making the presence of the network known to their neighbors.

Today this women's group in the Southern población continues to recruit women through a pluralistic approach, and to meet on a weekly basis, although many of the original members are no longer part of it. Some of those women have moved away from the población, while others continue organizing but in new settings. Julia and Filomena have, in the meantime, left the city-wide women's network they had joined in the late 1980s and have been recruited by a nationwide NGO committed to popular participation for social change. They continue, now as paid staff, to organize women from their población, as well as from adjacent poblaciones. Increasingly, however, these women's own commitments are at odds with the changing priorities of their employer. This NGO, and for that matter many NGOs working with poor people today, share the government's own conception of the role of popular participation for social change. This conception considers empowerment and participation in the context of a narrow economic definition of poverty, and poverty itself as a problem for which technical solutions can be found.[37] This shift, in a context where no substantial gains are perceived by many in the poblaciones, is experienced by Julia and Filomena as a betrayal of the organization's commitment to meaningful change. The struggle over organizing priorities and aims waged by Julia, for example, has led her to redefine the work of people like her as 'political.' In a recent interview she stated that, 'back in the 1980s when I joined the women's group and started organizing other women I saw our work as social. Today, however, I realize how naive I was; our work is political.'

Finally, it should be noted that in the course of acquiring a sense of personal and political efficacy, women who choose to participate in advocacy groups with men face the toughest challenge. For it is one thing to develop a capacity for decision-making and to acquire a public voice in a predominantly female context; it is quite another to carry these achievements into contexts where unequal gender relations have historically appropriated for men both the public voice (with its distinct political vocabulary) and the power of decision-making. One of the reasons why efforts to organize the various neighborhood groups into viable regional bodies have failed may be the difficulties women leaders encounter in these organizations. The leaderships of these regional or middle-level bodies tend to be party-affiliated men. Women leaders of neighborhood organizations often complain of the authoritarian leadership structure of such bodies, which in effect is a union or party leadership model. These women also complain of being effectively silenced and, therefore, of being marginalized from decision-making. These women often feel that the politically motivated leaders ignore the needs and wishes of the grassroots and impose their own logic on grassroots collective efforts. Feeling marginalized and angered, many lose interest in these middle-level organizations. Elsa, a member of a workshop on the West side of Santiago summarized the frustration of pobladoras with their treatment by male activists: 'Women are not taken into consideration when plans and decisions are made. These are men's things. But they sure are taken advantage of when it's time to go to a demonstration or to build barricades in the streets.'

Concluding Remarks

In many respects the phenomenon of self-help organizations in the poblaciones represents a new will among the poor in Chile, as elsewhere in Latin America, to cope in an active way with the severe economic and political situation first imposed by authoritarian regimes. A key characteristic of these organizations – that they are predominantly a female phenomenon in a context shaped by distinct gender-based power relations – is largely absent from studies of the phenomenon.

My field work in a población in Santiago gave me an opportunity to study how gender relations structure everyday life, and to examine the activities of organizations. While the findings of other observers (noted at the beginning of this chapter) provide interesting leads to understanding self-help organizations, for the most part they fail to pay attention to the vital role of women in these groups. Ignoring how gender relations structure both opportunities and hindrances to neighborhood-based forms of collective action, their work overlooks the political significance of the groups. Unless we problematize the massive presence of women in these organizations and consider how gender relations have shaped and continue to shape their possibilities for action, any reference to a gender-neutral popular movement is at best inconclusive and at worse distorted.

Contrary to the approach of these investigators, I found strong evidence for the fundamental role of gender relations as a constitutive factor in the functioning of the organizations as well as in their future potential. I realize that my conclusions are based on a limited study and that, therefore, they ought to be treated with caution. However, in the light of information from other researchers in this area, I would argue that the gender-specific political function of neighborhood organizing is not limited to Santiago, nor to urban areas. Moreover, my findings are corroborated in part by studies of poor neighborhood organizing in other Latin American cities.[38]

Neighborhood organizations in Santiago function as places for local-level participation for many women. Developing a sense of self-confidence and competence is the fundamental first step in a process of participatory learning. How successful these women are in appropriating for themselves a public voice and a share in decision-making in the broader political arena is another issue. It would be naive to think that pobladoras, suddenly armed with a distinct sense of personal and political efficacy, would easily manage to establish representative advocacy groups or join mixed groups *en masse* in order to struggle for change. The political arena, even at the local level of the población, remains male territory; pobladoras will most probably not be invited there, and will have to muscle their way in. In any case, the political effectiveness of Chilean women in general, let alone pobladoras, has traditionally been limited by prejudices which are deep-seated in Chilean political institutions and culture. However, given the outcome of the plebiscite of 1988, when an overwhelming number of women said 'No' to General Pinochet, it would be rather irresponsible for politicians to resort to the old truisms about women's political behavior.

The experience of pobladoras suggests at least the potential of their emergence as important social actors. Just how important pobladoras might be was intimated by the attention lavished on them by candidates during the municipal elections in June 1992. These, mostly male, candidates running for office as councillors, and indirectly for mayor, met with women's organizations during their campaigns. Assuming that these women's demands were primarily economic, the candidates promised them economic solutions such as spaces where they could sell their handicrafts. However, for the women this offer was not good enough. They had very clearly in mind something else, and invariably replied: 'what we want is a space of our own where we can choose what we do.'[39]

Notes

1. This chapter is an updated version of an article that appeared in *Reader II zu Problemi von Frauen in der Dritten Welt*, edited by Renate Rott (Saarbrucken, Fort Lauderdale: Breitenbach, 1992); in *N/S Canadian Journal of Latin American and Caribbean Studies*, 30 (Spring 1991); and as a CERLAC Working Paper for the Community Power Project (1990). It is based on research conducted during two visits to Chile (September–October 1991, and May–June 1992). Funding for this research was provided by a SSHRC post-doctoral fellowship (1991–93).

2. Because they are used throughout, the Spanish words 'poblaciones' (referring to *barrios* or popular, working-class neighborhoods) and 'pobladoras' (the

working-class women living in these areas) are not italicized.

3. The work of Alain Touraine in the sociology of social movements has shaped the debate in Latin America. For a regional overview which reflects this influence, see *Los movimientos sociales ante la crisis*, edited by Fernando Calderón (Buenos Aires: UNU, CLACSO, IISUNAM, 1986).

4. For example, Clarisa Hardy and Luis Razeto, 'Los nuevos actores y practicas populares: Desafíos a la concertación,' *Materiales para Discusión*, No. 47 (Santiago: Centro de Estudios del Desarrollo, 1984); Luis Razeto et al., *Las organizaciones económicas populares*, revised edn (Santiago: Programa de Economía del Trabajo, 1985); Teresa Valdes, 'El movimiento de pobladores 1973–1985. La recomposición de las solidaridades sociales,' in *Descentralización del estado: Movimiento social y gestión local*, edited by Jordi Borja (Santiago: FLACSO, 1987); and Clarisa Hardy, *Organizarse para vivir. Pobreza urbana y organización popular* (Santiago: Programa de Economía del Trabajo, 1987).

5. For example, Eugenio Tironi, 'Marginalidad, Movimientos Sociales y Democracia,' *Proposiciones*, 14 (Santiago: SUR, 1987); Guillermo Campero, *Entre la sobrevivencia y la acción política: Las organizaciones de pobladores* (Santiago: 1986).

6. Also see Chapter 7 in this volume.

7. See Carole Pateman, *Participation and Democratic Theory* (Cambridge: Cambridge University Press, 1970), pp. 49 (emphasis added) and 109.

8. Carole Pateman, 'The Civic Culture: A Philosophic Critique,' in *The Disorder of Women* (Stanford, CA: Stanford University Press, 1989), p. 157.

9. Samuel Bowles and Herbert Gintis, *Democracy and Capitalism* (New York: Basic Books, 1986), p. 150.

10. Michael S. Serrill, 'Pinochet's Fruitful Economy,' *Time*, April 24, 1989.

11. The neo-liberal policies pursued by the Pinochet government with varying degrees of orthodoxy in its restructuring of the economy have made of Chile a model of economic success hailed throughout the region. At the same time, the reversion in Chile's social development to the levels of the 1930s is conveniently overlooked. To be sure, the high concentration of income and wealth that has occurred in the last twenty years has allowed a few Chileans to enter into the 'modern' world promised by Pinochet and his neo-liberal acolytes; on the other hand, there is no denying that the majority of the population is engaged in a struggle to maintain an already low standard of living. One thing is clear about the Aylwin government: although it has committed itself to repaying the so-called social debt, it does so while fostering the model which generated this debt in the first place and perpetuates it.

12. For the statistics of this trend, see Dagmar Raczinsky and Claudia Serrano, *Vivir la pobreza: Testimonios con mujeres* (Santiago: CIEPLAN/PISPAL, 1985), p. 53.

13. The book *Mundo de Mujer*, edited by Centro de Estudios de la Mujer (Santiago: Centro de Estudios de la Mujer, 1988) details the characteristics of women's employment in Chile.

14. For a description of women's work in the fruit growing sector, and attempts by women to organize to struggle for better conditions, see Gonzalo Fallabella, 'Reestructuración y respuesta sindical La experiencia en Santa María, madre de la fruta Chilena,' paper presented at the XVII International Congress of the Latin American Studies Association, LASA, Los Angeles, September 24–27, 1992.

15. See, for example, Fernando Ignacio Leiva, 'La apertura y los trabajadores:

La otra cara del modelo chileno,' *Boletín sobre libre comercio y respuestas populares en América Latina y el Caribe*, Vol. 1, No. 2 (September 1992). In addition, see Jaime Ruiz-Tagle, 'Desafíos del sindicalismo chileno frente a la flexibilización del mercado del trabajo,' paper presented at the XVII International Congress of the Latin American Studies Association, LASA, Los Angeles, September 24–27, 1992.

16. For the statistics, see H. Cheyre and E. Ogrodnik, 'El programa de empleo mínimo. Análisis de una encuesta,' *Revista de Economía*, No. 7 (Santiago: Universidad de Chile, 1982); Jaime Bustamante, 'Algunos antecedentes estadísticos sobre las O.E.P. según catastro de 1985,' in Razeto et al., *Las Organizaciones económicas populares*; and Mariana Schkolnik and Berta Teitelboim, *Pobreza y desempleo en poblaciones: La otra cara del modelo neoliberal* (Santiago: Programa de Economía del Trabajo, 1988).

17. I borrow the apt term 'shock absorbers' from Nona Glazer, whose study of homemakers during the 1970s recession in the USA suggests that women's mediating behavior is a widespread phenomenon. See Nona Glazer, 'Everyone Needs Three Hands: Doing Unpaid and Paid Work,' in Sarah Fenstermaker Berk, ed., *Women and Household Labor* (Beverly Hills, CA: Sage, 1980).

18. There are no statistics to show this conclusively. However, the increased availability of jobs, and increments in incomes experienced by poor Chileans, do suggest that those women involved in income-generating activities would in effect find it unnecessary to continue participating in economic groups. This was suggested to me in discussions with members of the newly installed Women's Bureau, Servicio Nacional de la Mujer, or SERNAM, during a visit to Chile in September 1991.

19. Interviews were conducted during two separate visits to Chile, in September–October 1991, and in May–June 1992. According to those interviewed, the organizations which aimed directly at helping pobladores stave off hunger, such as soup kitchens, buying co-operatives, and vegetable gardens, all but disappeared. This may very well be linked to the slight improvements in incomes and also to greater efforts on the part of the government to create jobs. In fact, government figures put the official unemployment figure in Chile in January 1993 at an all time low, 4 per cent. Researchers from PET (Programa de Economía del Trabajo) criticized the official figures, however. In a study conducted in 1991, they challenged the INE (National Institute of Statistics) measurements of unemployment. INE's figures measure only open unemployment, and do not include forms of subemployment rampant today. Clearly, these critics argue, overlooking exploitative, precarious and underpaid forms of employment masks the real extent of unemployment in Chile (see *Mensaje*, 405, December 1991, p. 489). These concerns were echoed by labor leaders. They warned the government about its optimism *vis-à-vis* falling unemployment. The quality of work available to people has not improved, they said; indeed, it continues to deteriorate.

20. This examination of everyday life and participation in neighborhood organizations is based on an ethnographic study I conducted in an ordinary long-established población in the Commune of La Pintana, in the southern periphery of Santiago, during 1987, and on subsequent visits in the población, including a 15–day stay in June 1992. By an ordinary población I mean a settlement that does not have a strong history of collective experience, and which therefore has not been studied excessively. For the sake of confidentiality I will call this población the Southern Población. I have also changed the names of those people who participated in the study. I used several methods to gather information, including

participant observation, informal conversations with people over a period of one year, and structured and unstructured interviews. I also rely here on a representative selection of interviews with women who participate in organizations for economic survival in other poor neighborhoods of Santiago, collected by Gloria Angelo and published in her book, *Pero Ellas son Imprescindibles* (Santiago: Biblioteca de la Mujer–Centro de Estudios de la Mujer, 1987). I wish to thank the International Development Research Centre, Ottawa, whose 'Young Canadian Researcher's Award' made my year-long study possible.

21. This is Gayle Rubin's term. See Gayle Rubin, 'The Traffic in Women: Notes Toward a Political Economy of Sex,' in Rayna Reiter, ed., *Toward an Anthropology of Women* (New York: Monthly Review Press, 1975).

22. Compare Lechner and Levy's important study. The main flaw of this study is its failure to grasp disciplining as process and, therefore, to account for women's active relation to the efforts to domesticate them. See Norbert Lechner and Susana Levy, 'Notas sobre la vida cotidiana III: El disciplinamiento de la mujer,' *Material de Discusión*, 57 (Santiago: FLACSO, 1984).

23. A change in the law regulating Mothers' Centers introduced by the military regime prior to the plebiscite of 1988 made it possible for the wives of military officers to continue to control CEMA, the umbrella organization that oversees the Centers. In response to this, and after lengthy debates among women within the coalition government, the Christian Democrats established a new umbrella organization to promote poor women's organizing, by the name of PRODEMU. PRODEMU is headed by President Aylwin's wife (interview with Paulina Webber of MEMCH, Santiago, May 1992).

24. See, 'Estudio sobre violencia doméstica en mujeres pobladoras Chilenas,' edited by Cecilia Moltedo (unpublished paper, Santiago, 1989).

25. The Minister of the Economy, then Jorge Marshall, praised the falling unemployment rate at FESOL 92, the annual fair of micro-enterprises and artisans, and conceded that the challenge remained to improve the quality of work available (*El Mercurio*, November 22, 1992). The minimum wage was raised from 15,000 pesos to 30,000 pesos in 1991, although obviously this did not affect the incomes of thousands engaged in forms of underemployment, including those represented at FESOL 92. Maria Rozas, Vice-President of CUT, reacted to official claims surrounding the falling rate of unemployment. In January 1993 unemployment, at 4 per cent, was claimed by the government to be the lowest in 20 years. According to Rozas, underemployment, not jobs that pay a substantial wage, increases every day: 'there is more work, but the quality and day-to-day conditions of that work have deteriorated more' (*El Mercurio*, February 5, 1993).

26. Campero, *Entre la sobrevivencia y la acción política*, p. 52; Bustamante, 'Algunos antecedentes estadísticos sobre las O.E.P.,' p. 170.

27. Philip Oxhorn, 'The Popular Sector Response to an Authoritarian Regime: Shantytown Organizations Since the Military Coup,' *Latin American Perspectives*, 18 (Winter 1991), p. 86.

28. Hardy, *Organizarse Para Vivir*, p. 51.

29. Some NGOs, notably Programa de Economia del Trabajo, have helped address the technical problems women encounter in the economic type groups. NGOs have also been forced to grapple with the thorny issue of aid dependency. See Angelo, *Pero ellas son imprescindibles*.

30. On this, see Carmen Gloria Aguayo, *Des Chiliennes* (Paris: Des Femmes, 1982).

31. The withdrawal of support for self-help groups by the Church corresponds as well to what one can only call a 'turn to the right' in the Chilean Church in response to Vatican changes. The emphasis of the Church today is on enforcing the new catechism, not on what it terms 'activities of civil society' (interview with members of Tierra Nuestra, a women's NGO, formerly the technical team of the women's program of the Vicaria Sur in Santiago, June 1992). For an excellent discussion of the changing priorities of the Church in Rome, see Ralph Della Cava, 'Vatican Policy, 1978–1990: An Updated Overview,' *Social Research*, 59 (Spring 1992), pp. 169–99.

32. These observations are based on interviews conducted in Santiago with government officials and NGO personnel during May–June 1992.

33. Often, during these events, women complained about the candidates' failure to recognize and address the non-economic dimensions of their collective activities (interviews and observations gathered during attendance at political meetings called by organized women from Santiago's southern periphery in June 1992).

34. For example, this was the topic of a day-long workshop organized by Programa de Economía del Trabajo (PET), which I attended in December 1986. During this meeting, many of the 150+ delegates from economic-type organizations of Santiago confronted the evaluation of their groups offered, among others, by Luis Razeto of PET. Razeto insisted that the groups become more economically self-sufficient, more 'autonomous' or less dependent – an analysis which, in my opinion, seemed to respond more to the institution's own needs in a context of shrinking funding for such activities than to the needs of the organizations themselves. Perhaps this explains the sense of betrayal and anger expressed by many leaders of the groups during the meeting. The issues of self-sufficiency and autonomy are also raised, or at least implied, in most existing studies of economic-type organizations such as those by Razeto et al., *Las organizaciones económicas populares* (1986) and others mentioned throughout this chapter.

35. See Maria Elena Valenzuela, *La mujer en el Chile militar: Todas ibamos a ser reinas* (Santiago: Ediciones Chile América–CESOC–ACHIP, 1987); and Eda Cleary, *Frauen In Der Politik Chiles* (Aachen: Alano Verlag, 1988).

36. Paula Edwards, in 'La mujer pobladora y la TV en el Chile de hoy' (Santiago: CENECA, 1986), discusses the pobladoras' enthusiastic reception of the show *Cagney & Lacey*, where two policewomen face issues ranging from wife-beating to breast cancer and sexuality. Edwards' study suggests that the media participate in domination and create the possibilities for resisting this domination by providing viewers with important cultural resources. My point is based on a cultural studies approach to television and is similar to John Fiske's arguments in *Understanding Popular Culture* (Boston, MA: Unwin Hyman, 1989).

37. This is based on interviews with representatives from a number of NGOs which have worked specifically with women, as well as from so-called solidarity NGOs from the 'North', which suddenly find themselves pressured by the Chilean government to conform to its new strategy. According to these representatives the pressure is often subtle; funding for national NGO work, for example, is now drying up and what little there is is controlled by the government and channeled to projects that fit its strategy. Naturally, frustration is not only felt by women like

Julia and Filomena who, after all, have a vast and rich knowledge of the limitations to participation that women face; it is also shared by those NGOs, both national and international, which have been working for greater popular participation for over a decade and now struggle to make ends meet. The outcome of this trend for NGOs is unclear, and whether or not people, particularly women, in the poblaciones succeed in organizing in a more autonomous manner remains to be seen.

38. See, for example, Maruja Barrig, 'The Difficult Equilibrium Between Bread and Roses: Women's Organizations and the Transition from Dictatorship in Peru,' and Sonia Alvarez, 'Women's Movements and Gender Politics in the Brazilian Transition', in Jane Jaquette, ed., *The Women's Movement in Latin America* (Winchester, MA.: Unwin Hyman, 1989).

39. Based on my own observations of a number of political meetings organized by women's organizations in the southern periphery of the city during the months of May and June 1992. These observations were corroborated by leaders of women's organizations from this area of Santiago, as well as by members of the NGO Tierra Nuestra, whom I interviewed during this period. Tierra Nuestra co-ordinates a vast network of women's organizations in the southern periphery and provided technical help for the groups to organize political meetings.

Part Two

Theme Studies

7

Differential Participation:
Men, Women and Popular Power

Michael Kaufman

The muddy road sloped down towards the gully that carried away the sewage from the surrounding houses. The house we were in, like all those in La Nazareno, was simple but sturdy, built out of concrete and zinc sheets, equipped with electricity and running water. The thing most noticeable was not the house but the tremendous pride of the men and women sitting around the kitchen table. They were from two of the 350 families that had occupied this land several years before and forced the Costa Rican government to buy the land and provide building materials and basic infrastructure. Carlos Corrales was the first president of the community association, a job that was now carried out by Yadira Umaña, his wife. At one point we asked her if she had changed since she joined the urban housing movement. She said no, she didn't think so. Her husband smiled his modest smile at her, and said simply that she had changed, that she was speaking in public, that she was leading a community. She smiled back in acknowledgement.

We asked him if he had changed. He said no. But he hinted at a new found respect for his wife and the women in his community. Women are better leaders in the community, he says, 'because they are closer to the problems of everyday life.' He said, however, that many men try to keep their wives from getting too active.

A couple of thousand miles away, elections were being held for the Executive Assembly in Santa Cruz, a Cuban community to the east of Havana. Following a decade-old model, the Municipal Assembly was choosing its executive and its mayor from among its elected members. One candidate for mayor was a woman who had received the highest vote in the local elections, an acknowledgement of her skills, energy, and supportive style of leadership. Another was a man who was capable – but by many accounts not nearly as capable as the woman – and quite authoritarian in his leadership style. The man was elected the mayor, the woman his deputy. It was hard for Cuban observers from outside the community to make sense of the choice on the basis of the candidates' capabilities.

To the south and east, in a crowded neighborhood of Port-au-Prince, Haiti, a group of men and women gathered outside a house. One person was from one of the many groups within a network of grassroots organizations that had mobilized over the past decade, first against the Duvalier government and then against the military. In this group, as in some community groups in Haiti, there were no leaders, for in a country where two centuries of male leaders have promised solutions and brought only misery, there was a massive distrust of leaders. The women and men were forging a new style of social activism and social leadership.[1]

These stories have some common features. Each is part of an attempt to develop new forms of popular participation and grassroots mobilization, directly aimed, in the first community, at providing housing and a decent life, in the second as part of a delegate system of formal governmental power, and in the third as an attempt to organize and mobilize the poor. Another common feature is that within these structures of power and empowerment, we see an ongoing struggle to define the degree and the style of participation by women and men.

Among activists and progressive intellectuals in much of the world, there is increasing interest and debate on the interlocked themes of democracy, popular participation, and social transformation. Democracy bereft of popular power is better than nothing but is a limited democracy; social transformation without democracy is either impossible or incomplete; development without some form of popular participation has little chance of transforming the relations of socio-economic power. The fundamental issue in emerging conceptions of change is how to build inclusive structures of social, economic and political power, ones that overcome existing inequalities and that fundamentally shift the basis of social power.

Perhaps there really are different problems buried within this one statement. One problem has to do with the need to develop democratic structures of participation and empowerment throughout the society as a whole. Another is to ensure that these new structures are as fully participatory and democratic as possible. This is distinct from the first problem because we can not talk of popular participation or popular empowerment in general. Rather we must acknowledge the existence of what I call *differential participation*.[2]

This chapter explores the problem of differential participation, and defines two aspects of it. The first locates the source of the problem in structures of inequality, the second within the hegemonic definitions of power that exist within patriarchal society. It examines solutions to the first within the framework of participatory democratic or critical liberal democratic theory, while solutions to the latter require a redefinition of power and the development of radically different structures of social power. It concludes by looking not only at how women, but at how men as well, are negatively effected by the very structures in which they have differential power and privilege.

Throughout, I will draw on the case studies presented in other chapters of this book.

The Two Aspects of Differential Participation

Participation does not exist in the abstract. Participation is defined through specific institutions, processes, and ideological and cultural factors. It is defined through the individuals and groups of individuals involved (or not involved) in a participatory process. Within any participatory structure, overall forms of social inequality and oppression are usually reflected and maintained. The challenge we face is to develop not only participatory mechanisms of empowerment but the means to overcome the structured inequalities in social power. These structured differences in participation apply to the many categories of social hierarchy and oppression – relating to class, sex, color, age, religion, nationality, physical well-being, and sexual orientation. These categories are often intertwined and mutually determinant – the categories of race and class in the Caribbean being one obvious example. This chapter will focus on aspects of differential participation between men and women, but we could just as well develop parallel studies of other groups.

Different possibilities, capacities, and modes of participation by men and women are the outcome of the structures of women's oppression and the ideology and practices of male domination. There are two aspects to this problem of differential participation. First are the ways that existing structures and ideologies relating to women's oppression have tended to marginalize women in many economic and political institutions or have shaped the practice of participatory institutions. This aspect, as we shall see, can be addressed theoretically by an extension of a participatory democratic theory, or what we might call critical liberal democratic theory, to deal explicitly with issues of sex.

The second, which we will look at later, is more fundamental. It is my belief that the underlying problem shaping differential participation is not inequality between men and women in the narrow sense but the very conception of power that has become hegemonic in patriarchal societies throughout the world. This is a definition in which power is understood as the capacity of certain humans to control and dominate other humans and control social and natural resources. Such a conception of power is not simply a matter of ideology but is the organizing principle that is embedded in a vast range of political, social, and economic relations. While it shapes the capacity of all humans to participate, men's capacities to exercise power in this form have been less limited than women's. Nevertheless, as we shall see, men's own capacities for participation are distorted and limited through this process. In other words, differential participation negatively affects men as well as women, although differentially of course and, in most cases, not as severely.

Women and the Dynamics of Differential Participation

Men's overall social domination is reproduced within participatory and democratic bodies, bodies which are supposed to be a means for all of the population to be equally represented or involved in democratic processes. In terms of sheer numbers and positions of importance, men control political parties and trade unions, government bureaucracies and many voluntary organizations. Other social institutions that we might like to bring under democratic control – corporations, the media, the education system, and so forth – are similarly controlled by men, although for this chapter I will focus on explicitly political and governmental institutions, especially those at the local level.

This control by men is perpetuated in different ways. The most obvious is that men still tend to be valued more highly as social leaders than are women. For example, in Cuba in 1986, only 17 per cent of delegates to the municipal government – the Organs of Popular Power – were women, a figure typical or even high compared to other countries. Commenting on the results of his study of the electoral process in the municipality of Santa Cruz, researcher Haroldo Dilla suggests with only a little hyperbole that the women who managed to win seats have a level of educational, political and work experience three times as great as their male opponents.[3]

This valuation of men's abilities over women's as social leaders can have the effect of reducing men's participation in organizations where women do play an important role. The Dominican Republic, for example, hosts a range of social movements that carry out organizing work and education in the poor *barrios* of the cities. In some of these groups women make up a majority of the membership and leadership. This majority can be self-reproducing because the response by some men is that they are not interested in participating in what are perceived as women's organizations. These organizations have had to encourage men to participate in spite of the high percentage of women in the membership and leadership.[4]

In societies where the work that men tend to do and the qualities that men have nurtured are valued most highly, men have an automatic advantage in any electoral process for positions of leadership within community and national bodies. In one example, also drawn from our Cuban study, a woman and a man were opponents for a seat in the municipal assembly. The woman had lived in the community only three years but in that time 'had developed a notable prestige for her social sensitivities and her high level of community work.' Her opponent, a man born in the area, was a leader in a factory where many of the people in the area worked. His prestige came basically from this work relationship, according to interviews with voters. The man won the vote. The study doesn't say he was a bad choice, although it is implied that the woman was a better one because of higher capabilities as a community leader. Rather, it is making the point that the existing structures of social prestige and power reproduce themselves within the electoral process: 'the status of leadership in a work center helped reproduce masculine supremacy in the community setting.'[5]

Overall social values shape the conception of the electoral process itself. In Cuba the only written form of campaign literature is a biographical sketch of each candidate, which is posted in the neighborhood to show his or her capacities to carry out the job. Education, work, and political experience form the centerpiece of these sketches. Those capacities that can be quantified in terms of experience will have weight over other qualities that cannot be listed. This format, concludes Dilla and co-researcher Armando Fernández, 'tends to privilege adults and those who are male because they are able to demonstrate the richest level of participation in politics and work and, on the other hand, it tends to penalize women because of their double workday as members of the community and as the ones responsible for the family.'[6]

The same privileging is true in other cases of electoral democracy where the qualities that are valued in a leader have traditionally been those values that men have nurtured or the areas of skill and prestige that men have had greater access to. Such privileging is also seen in cases where substantial financial resources are a requirement of candidacy, a requirement that has a major impact on the possibility of a woman being a candidate (as well as anyone who is working class, a small farmer, poor or young).

This process of penalization of women goes beyond formal electoral processes. If women have most responsibility for child care and domestic work, and especially if they also have work responsibilities outside the home, then they will be hard pressed to find the time or the energy to prioritize leadership roles within the community. If women have to clean dinner dishes and put children to bed at night, or if in some countries they are scrounging for a scrap of food to feed their children the next day, they are less able to participate fully in community meetings which typically happen in the evenings or on weekends. These demands, and the resultant limitations on women's participation, is a story repeated throughout the world and forms the single major impediment to women's participation in political organizations.

Forms of blatant sexism also limit women's participation. In Costa Rica, where a squatters' housing movement arose during the 1980s, land was occupied and the government was pressed to give squatters land and supplies to build modest houses. In the months or years of organizing that would lead up to an occupation, and in the subsequent negotiations with politicians and civil servants, women played an increasingly important role in many communities. Many occupations were backed by road-blocks of key highways – road-blocks staffed by women and children that lasted only a day at a time until the government agreed to negotiate. Despite this role played by women, some men placed limits – or tried to place limits – on their wives' participation. They were jealous of their wife going to town with another man from the community or meeting, and possibly having a meal with, a politician or bureaucrat. Some women struggled against this, others didn't.[7] Similar problems arise in the self-help economic organizations of poor women in the *poblaciones* in Chile. In these communities, where material deprivation is high and the threat of political repression was an ever-present feature for two decades, various forms of workshops emerged to produce goods for consumption or trade. Veronica Schild comments:

> Housewives who decide to join the workshop have, more often than not, done so after having waged a battle at home for 'permission' to join. How very difficult it is for a woman to take part in an organization has been illustrated by Filomena, a young mother of two who is active both in a Church group and in the women's group in the Southern Población: 'when there is a meeting, and the husbands are at home, even if they are chatting at the corner with friends from the club, the women can't go.'[8]

We can also think of the horrible impact that violence against women has on women's participation. If a woman suffers from wife-battering (studies in North America suggest that about one in four women have been hit by their spouse; with a smaller, but still sizeable, number being assaulted on an ongoing basis), her self-confidence and sense of self-worth might well be reduced. As a result, her ability to see herself as a contributor to society, as someone worthy of respect, as someone with a valid voice might well be limited. Or if women in the community are subject to sexual harassment or derogatory remarks in public, this too will reduce their capacity to act as community leaders. Finally, fear for safety in the streets at night will limit women's participation outside the home.

Perhaps the most subtle but also most telling example of differential participation is the extent to which the whole problem is rendered invisible. Of those oppressed, marginalized, or subordinate, their presence or absence in the democratic and participatory organizations is often rendered invisible. Because their specific concerns have been treated as secondary in the dominant economic and political discourses, we cannot assume that their concerns are addressed in existing forms of social expression, including within forms of popular participation.

In spite of such examples, the notion of differential participation isn't meant to imply that men participate and women don't.[9] After all, one of the characteristics of many community-based, grassroots movements of popular power is the high percentage of women among the active membership. The experience in much of the Third World is of women taking a leadership role within community affairs. Some of this might be explained by the greater presence of women within communities during the day. This, however, isn't the only factor, for the communities where grassroots/community organizing is highest are often poor communities with high levels of unemployment among men and, in some cases, a relatively equal level of paid employment among women and men, particularly when one counts the informal sector.

Another factor is thus of importance: the impact of women's traditional role as care-givers to children and as the ones responsible for domestic affairs. For women, these responsibilities can build an awareness of issues concerning health, education, food supplies, water and sewerage, garbage disposal, and community safety. Participation in community organizations is an extension of overall roles and responsibilities. The daily work of making ends meet, the preoccupation with the health and safety of the family, worrying about those unglamorous details of daily life, are matters that many men simply are not concerned about. In some parts of Central America and the Caribbean, for example, this lack of concern has its extreme expression in the large number of men who abandon their families, or who come and go as they see fit.

Women have traditionally created many forms of informal networking to organize matters of daily life: neighbors look after each other's children while one shops or takes a child to a doctor; neighbors shop for each other or sew together; they speak on the street, in the home, or at the market about their common problems; in many countries, women set up informal co-operative savings networks. The very factors of crowding on to small lots, in dwellings, where climate allows, where front doors and windows (if the houses actually have windows) always stay open, can increase informal contact among neighbors. Thus the formal organization of workshops, neighborhood organizations, or community political action groups is a logical extension of these networking activities.

Perhaps another reason for women's high representation in community affairs is that within both the political systems and forms of popular organization in First and Third World countries alike, matters of health, food, social services, and education have tended to be seen by men as less prestigious endeavors for male political leadership than the supposedly gutsy tasks of business and workplace organization, international diplomacy, the army, police, and large-scale economic and infrastructural development. One reason for women's role in community affairs is that men have abdicated responsibility.

If these are some dimensions of the problem of differential, how might they be addressed?

Critical Liberal Democratic Theory and Differential Participation

Emerging within a democratic socialist tradition over the past three decades, a new body of thought has recast the debate on socialism and democracy. Until that time, socialists had been split into two broad camps on this issue; to be rather simplistic:

1. Many Marxists more or less axiomatically equated democracy with socialism. Capitalism could boast only a sham democracy; without state or popular ownership of the means of production, there could be no real democracy; liberal democracy was democracy only for the ruling class. Within this camp were Stalinists who ignored democracy because socialism, *ergo* democracy, had already been achieved in half of Europe and Asia. Others, such as Trotskyists or non-aligned Marxists, argued that these countries were neither socialist nor democratic, but tended to agree that capitalist societies were not democratic either.

2. The other broad camp was the social democratic left, which saw the liberal democratic state as the vehicle for social change and for making gains for working people. This tradition tended to downplay the Marxist critique of the social power of capital and ignored the critique of the capitalist nature of the state. However, the two traditions were united, as Nicos Poulantzas argued, by positing a statist solution and a statist pathway to socialism and democracy.[10]

In the 1960s, the writings of C.B. Macpherson began to recast the debate on socialism and democracy. Macpherson's goal was modest but innovative: to look at the different, and sometimes contradictory, meanings of liberalism and liberal democracy, and to retrieve for socialist theory one strain of liberal democratic thought. Macpherson reaffirmed the liberal democratic goal of individual development, but said that the goal of achieving one's potential was hindered by the socio-economic and political realities of a capitalist market society.[11]

Together, quite a number of theorists and activists – inspired in part by new social movements that stressed issues of democracy and mass participation, and, in the late 1980s, by the upheavals in Eastern Europe and the Soviet Union – have recast the debate on socialism and democracy. Without getting into the differences among these thinkers, or the strengths, weaknesses, and complexity of the debate, we can lump together their work under the rubric of critical liberal democratic theory or participatory democratic theory. Among the elements in this approach that I find most useful is the belief that all societies have at least some degree of democracy at some level of social, economic, or political life. Thus, says Frank Cunningham, we must look at the degree of democracy of any society and not assume, *a priori*, that a certain economic system is, or is not, automatically democratic. Nevertheless, the challenge is to develop what Cunningham calls an extensive democracy.[12]

The point developed in different ways by many thinkers is that a society with an extensive democracy would be one in which democratic control permeates all social relationships: in terms of formal liberal democratic political rights and liberties; within different realms of social life – in education, the family and home, the media, religion, cultural production; and through the control of the economy, in part through public and co-operative ownership and control of the means of production and distribution (although certainly not through complete state ownership and bureaucratic centralization of the economy) and in part through democratic control over whatever forms of private ownership might remain.

This whole approach to the issue of democracy is an attempt to understand the complex of economic, political, and social co-ordinates which structure domination and control in a society. For example, the approach taken by Herbert Gintis and Samuel Bowles, inspired in part by both Gramscian and feminist analyses, seeks to understand the ways in which the economy, the family, and the state all have appropriative, distributive, political, and cultural aspects that need to be brought under democratic control.[13]

The possibility of developing extensive and intensive forms of democracy relies on the empowerment of the population – the word 'empowerment' probably being the most significant contribution of the English language to the radical vocabulary. While most writers tend to shy away from anything that seems overly prescriptive, a common feature of much of the discourse on democracy, socialism, and empowerment is a recognition of the need to develop forms of popular participation. Popular participation, through social activism and forms of direct and representative control throughout the institutions of a society, is seen as a means to tap unharnessed energies of the population, to identify human and material resources, to recognize problems as they emerge, and to mobilize the population to find solutions, whether at a workplace, school, neighborhood, region, or beyond. While popular participation has been a theme with deep roots in the progressive tradition, the failure of state socialism and the limits of state social democracy have given new urgency to this theme. Democratic participation was a means, said Macpherson, to turn people from political consumers into political producers.[14]

But what if everyone cannot participate equally? What if, among the economically oppressed, the existing social structures of inequality and oppression have selectively shaped the nature and structure of oppression? As we have seen, the unevenness of power in a society is reproduced as differences within any neighborhood or workplace. Even when some sort of participatory institutions exist, to the extent that these institutions reflect the overall divisions and contradictions of a society, they do not automatically challenge deeply embedded hierarchies of power and control. This suggests that in any participatory institution there will be differences, large or small, in the nature and type of participation of particular individuals and groups. These differences are based not only on individual capacities, talents, or efforts. They are based on the systemic forms of power and hierarchy that exist within a given community. If new forms of popular participation continue to marginalize the voice of women or certain racial groups or peasants or the young, then we would have to question the extent to which these institutions are truly 'popular.'

The greater these inequalities, the less real is the actual participation. The greater these inequalities, the less is the capacity of a given institution to act as a means of empowerment. The less it can act as a means of participation and empowerment, the less it will be able to confront fundamental inequalities of social power.

In as much as critical liberal democratic theory problematized the issue of economic inequality and differential access to the means of political power, it began to challenge both the theoretical and the structural limits of mainstream liberal democratic theory. But it largely ignored the issue of unequal participation based on sex. Although this is an important oversight, it is one that can be addressed within its own theoretical framework. After all, the aim of this body of theory is to redress inequalities of social power and social voice. The analysis and solutions presented by critical liberal democratic theory/participatory democratic theory are able to address those aspects of differential participation having to do with various forms of inequality or unevenness of power among the oppressed or exploited.

If the goal of a radical, participatory liberal democracy is to develop the social, intellectual, and productive possibilities of all, if it is to be a means of human liberation, then we don't have to go far to see that so long as one group has its capacities limited by being born into one half of humanity rather than the other, then this is not a society of full human liberation. It is consistent with such theory that democratic and participatory bodies address the issues of full participation. Women's equality within such bodies is a requirement if these institutions are to do their basic emancipatory and participatory job. The possibility of such participation hinges on women's equality throughout social and economic structures, the equalization of household responsibilities so that women are able to participate, the de-privileging of the particular skills or capacities that men have excelled in, and conscious programmes to ensure equal participation by women and men.

In reverse, incremental changes in the participation of women can challenge men and can shift other responsibilities. For example, a woman in the small city of Bayamo in the eastern part of Cuba told me of the results of her increased participation in various community and trade union bodies. She went to her husband and said he'd have to take more responsibility around the house. He was reluctant and used the excuse of not knowing how to cook or do this or that. She pushed him and within a few months he was showing considerable pride at his new-found skills. Six months later she heard him arguing with his brother-in-law about how he should be doing his share of the housework. His in-law refused but the husband persisted and finally the brother-in-law broke down and agreed to do some of the cleaning. Similarly, in the Costa Rican example cited at the beginning, the increased role of women as leaders and militants within the neighborhood organizations has led to increased prestige and self-esteem for women.

Patriarchy, Power, and Differential Participation

Equality, though, is not enough. Equality equalizes the chances for participation and individual development. But, narrowly defined, equality doesn't necessarily address the rules of the game. A woman can become Prime Minister or the head of a trade union or corporation – and this may affect certain policies – but her role may not touch the underlying structures and assumptions of that organization or system.

Thus the second aspect of differential participation is that participatory and democratic structures reflect not only the inequality between men and women (or other social groups) but also the centuries-old outcome of that inequality. Patriarchal societies split those values that came to be associated with women and those associated with men. Of these, the outlook and beliefs of men have become hegemonic, reflecting men's overall social power. The conceptions that frame the exercise of power are themselves rooted in a particular structure of oppression. Certain conceptions of power that have been championed by men become part of the common-sense assumptions of a society, the way things are done. Not only would a certain view of power infect the hegemonic social institutions; without a conscious challenge to the exercise of patriarchal power, it will infect counter-hegemonic institutions as well. Let me very briefly address this, the second, aspect of differential participation.

Although we might be creating new structures for the redistribution and exercise of power, we are developing structures that in their very conception will be based on a concept of power we are all familiar with. Power, at least in the way we understand it in developed societies, is shaped by uneven human and social relationships. We think we cannot have power unless we have control either over someone, over our own unruly emotions, or over certain material resources. Power, in this conception, is based on control and domination. It is based on our ability to exploit differences within human relationships; power is a measure of those differences. To have power means to have greater control over resources or greater control over other people or oneself than does someone else. Power becomes the capacity to dominate others, ourselves, and the world around us.

Of course there are alternative ways to understand power; there are other ways that we experience it. Power could be thought of as a positive connection with nature and the world around us; as a fluid understanding of our capacities, abilities and limitations; as a sense of what we can achieve and how we can positively influence and live in harmony with the social and natural world around us. There is the power to meet our basic needs as humans, power to fight injustice and oppression, the power of muscles and brain, the power of love. All men and women, to a greater or lesser extent, experience these other meanings of power. Whatever our individual limitations, we are all complex and diverse human beings.

In spite of these diverse ways to experience power, I believe that the dominant conception of power in our world is a capacity to dominate and control. It is a definition of power that has emerged over thousands of years in societies where a series of divisions have been important bases of social organization: divisions based on the control by certain minority classes over economic resources and politics, control of men over women, and, in some cases, control by one ethnic, color or religious grouping over others. It is only logical that human beings within these societies learn to experience their own power as their inborn or learned capacity to succeed within such a world.[15]

This has important implications for the concept of differential participation. The uneven capacities of men and women to be participants and leaders in democratic and participatory institutions is not only a result of sexism and inequality in the narrow sense. It is also the result of the different values that men and women have internalized as they have created their gendered self-identities. If men are dominant within these societies they will have greater resources, but, just as importantly, they will have a greater stake in achieving and experiencing a certain type of power. Power as control is equated with the hegemonic conceptions of masculinity – however differently masculinity is defined among different classes, national, or color groupings.[16] Achieving and experiencing this type of power becomes a confirmation of one's manhood.

By learning the rules of becoming 'real men' (however our own social grouping defines such a thing) and by going through the prolonged social and psychological process of creating one's masculinity, many men derive a built-in advantage as social actors because they come to embrace, identify with, and celebrate the type of social actor and social action most highly valued in a given male-dominated society. Whether it is expressed through the power of words, force of personality, or physical domination, they embrace a certain definition of power. In turn they create social institutions which embody this notion of power, within which the next generation of men and women are shaped. Because men embody a certain definition of power, they are more likely than women to have the personal attributes and outlook necessary to succeed in the social institutions men have created.

Our social institutions, both more democratic and less democratic, participatory or not, will, to a greater or lesser extent, embody the conception of power that is dominant in society. It is not simply that there exists a hegemonic understanding of power, but that this is part of the basis of the way we conceive of and develop our democratic and participatory bodies. The structure and function of these bodies are themselves a particular discourse on power and its exercise. For example, dominant views of social mobilization reflect this discourse on the exercise of power. Many experiments of more or less radical social change have included elements of popular mobilization. In most conceptions, a radical government or political militants see their role as educators and mobilizers who attempt to draw into action the mass of the population. Radical leaders know that to counter the power of the national and international status quo and the weight of tradition, the energy of the population must be directed towards supporting the new measures being promoted by the government. People are exhorted to work harder and to participate in everything from demonstrations to voluntary work projects.

This type of mobilization can have a positive impact on the process of change, but it remains, essentially, a process in which an enlightened and paternalistic leadership mobilizes a population to follow the well-meaning plans of that leadership. What is lacking is a process in which relations of power are shifted between leadership and led. What is lacking – or at least is kept tightly controlled – is a practice of mobilization in which people are given the tools and the resources to take control and power into their own hands. The population remains political consumers – albeit of a beneficial and often enlightened and popular system – rather than political producers. The result of this is a limitation of the possibilities of social transformation, a huge reduction in the possibility of mobilizing the creative energies that lie dormant in the mass of the population. The result is also that, as circumstances change – for example, as an economic crisis intensifies or as foreign destabilization or war takes its toll, it becomes increasingly hard to mobilize the population behind a government because people's doubts increase and energies wane. Faith in a government, however popular and well-meaning, cannot last forever.

These problems results from many factors, but one of the most important is an essentially paternalistic conception and style of leadership, an approach that sees the exercise of political, economic, or social power as something that can be (and, in some conceptions, should be) in the hands of a skilled technocracy, a powerful bureaucracy, or a trusted political directorate.[17]

What impact does all this have on the differential participation of men and women in participatory bodies? The overall result, as indicated above, is that men more than women come to embody the definitions of power most prized in a society. This not only allows them greater access to positions of leadership, but it gives them a greater personal stake in becoming militants and leaders: after all, if a certain definition of power is equated with masculinity, then social leadership in itself can become a confirmation of one's male power.

Beyond this I am still finding it difficult to be concrete on the impact of a certain definition of power on differential participation. This is an area where more research and thinking need to be done. But it might explain the particular rhythms to women's participation within processes of social mobilization. Magaly Pineda points to a 'higher presence of women in certain violent actions in acute moments of a crisis or in pre-revolutionary situations (such as in the last years of the Somoza dictatorship in Nicaragua, or in April 1984 in the Dominican Republic) but a subsequent reduction of women's presence in the organizational structures that grow out of these actions.'

As with the majority of men, women's participation peaks in periods of extreme social conflict. More particularly, argues Pineda, women seem to participate when 'there doesn't exist any possibility of mediation between civil society and the state.' Perhaps the change in participation is, in part, because women see mediation as a principal means of eliminating conflicts until even that fails.[18] In other words, if women haven't fully embraced or identified with the hegemonic definition of power in patriarchal societies, their interest and identification with certain political bodies and activities may well be limited. Such things may be important to these women, but might seem one step removed from their lived experience and their own social knowledge, which might well be based more on mediation and co-operation than on domination and control.[19] Coupled with this is the outcome of the first aspect of differential participation. Pineda suggests that the structures of participation 'are not sufficiently flexible to accommodate the possibility of women's participation, or that the structures fail to express women's interests, or simply that the roles assigned to women – in particular the care of children and housework – make it impossible for them to sustain their participation.'[20]

These issues of power, and the structures we create for the exercise of power, have implications for other instances of differential participation. For example, although youth may play a prominent role in periods of intense social mobilization, participatory bodies often privilege older people. The lower participation of youth was noted in the Cuban study cited above and also in the study of Community Councils and community-based economic organizations in Jamaica.[21] Young people, by definition, cannot have the same power as adults, if power is understood as control over material and human resources. The same is true of other oppressed or exploited groups.

Men and Differential Participation

Let me conclude with a brief comment on men and differential participation: the problem of differential participation is not just women's problem. Differential participation is a description of the different character, dynamics, and possibilities of men's and women's participation within bodies of political, economic, and social decision-making. It is also a description of the way that these bodies have embodied a definition of power that is rooted within the values of a male-dominated society.

As I have argued elsewhere,[22] the values and structures of men's power have not only been oppressive to women and destructive to the planet, but have been detrimental to men themselves. Men have, I believe, contradictory experiences of power. The very ways that men have defined their power and privileges come with a price to men. That price is alienation from many of our human capacities and possibilities as we try to fit into the straitjacket of hegemonic forms of masculinity. Until recently in male-dominated societies, the powers and privileges of men outweighed the price, or at least made the price feel acceptable. You might have to die in the metaphorical or real battles of life, but what glory and rewards you would reap in the meantime. But with the rise of modern feminism the fulcrum has shifted, certain powers and privileges have been diminished in some societies, and men are increasingly aware of the costs to men of men's power.

Even without self-consciousness of the problem, we could argue that if the hegemonic forms of masculinity include an alienation from our own capacities and possibilities, then the liberal democratic vision of full and free human development is not being fulfilled. This doesn't mean that there is one natural form of human freedom and development, but simply that a vast range of possibilities are shut down for men who must squeeze themselves into the tight pants of masculinity. The developmental objective of liberalism has its gender dimension not only for women but for men.

Men, like women, are affected by the two aspects of differential participation. By privileging 'high' and prestigious positions of state, economic and social power we tend to distance ourselves from the demands of community, children, and domestic life that form so much of the pleasures, difficulties, and texture of human life. By the styles that we use to participate – developing forms based on competition, one-upmanship, and the star system, whether in state bodies, political parties, academia, or popular organizations – we reinforce the competitive, hierarchical, success-oriented, performance-oriented values of class and patriarchal society. We reinforce and validate the characteristics of masculinity that are, simultaneously, the source of our power and of our own pain and alienation as men.

By the way we have come to define power, we set up a situation where most men can't have actual power, something even more true for women, even though men within a given class or social group tend to have power over women of the same group. But because men equate the exercise of a certain type of power with masculinity, to lack power is to be inadequate as a man. The way that we have defined power becomes a source of unconscious insecurity and inner tension. It is the source of anxieties about performance and success that distort men's lives at work, in politics, on the streets, and at home. Men direct these anxieties at women and children in their lives, at other men, and at themselves, as seen in the unconscious doubts or even self-hate, the alcoholism, work-aholism, and ulcers that are part of the lives of many men.

To the extent that participatory and democratic bodies do not break from the hierarchical, competitive forms of the exercise of power, they are not only less functional as participatory mechanisms but they work against the empowerment of the women and men who are supposed to benefit in the first place.

In conclusion, if differential participation is a reality of all existing democratic and participatory institutions, then it is a reality that is in need of change. We are able to address the problem of differential participation partially through an extension of the theoretical and practical frameworks of critical liberal democracy/participatory democracy to include sex and other determinants of inequality. Just as important, though, is to challenge the received conceptions, and institutions, of power. Taken together, this provides a means to reach down to the roots of social disempowerment. It is a step towards developing an extensive and par-ticipatory democracy with a true liberatory potential.

Notes

1. The Costa Rican example is drawn from a November 1990 visit to La Nazareno along with Silvia Lara of the Centro de Estudios para la Acción Social The Cuban example is from a November 1988 visit to the community and from Haroldo Dilla and Armando Fernández Soriano, 'Las elecciones municipales en Cuba: un estudio de caso,' working paper on Organizaciones de Poder Comunal y Democracia Popular en América Central y el Caribe (Centro de Estudios Sobre América, 1990). The Haitian example is from discussions with Rony and Luc Smarth in Port-au-Prince.

An earlier version of this chapter was presented to the workshop 'Alternatives for the 1990s Caribbean' sponsored by the Commonwealth Institute at the University of London in January 1991. My thanks to Jean Stubbs of the Institute for her encouragement.

2. I developed the notion of 'differential participation' in conversation with Magaly Pineda, Director of the Centro de Investigación para la Acción Feminina (CIPAF) in Santo Domingo. In November 1988 we co-authored a working paper, 'Methodological Issues and Research Questions for Studying Differential Partici-pation,' working paper on Organizations of Community Power and Grassroots Democracy in Central America and the Caribbean, (CERLAC, 1988). Some

formulations in this present chapter are taken from my sections of that working paper. I thank Magaly for her contribution to the development of this idea and for permission to draw from our working paper. References to her sections of that document are cited in footnotes.

3. Percentages of women delegates to provincial assemblies and the National Assembly are higher (30.8 per cent and 33.9 per cent respectively in 1986.) This is the result of conscious policies of affirmative action for women. Such policies can work at this level because these elections are indirect; that is, voting is by the municipal assembly and the provincial assembly respectively. Electoral statistics from Asamblea Nacional del Poder Popular, 'Información mínima sobre los procesos electorales en los Organos del Poder Popular' (Ciudad habana, June 1987).

The comment is from discussions with Haroldo Dilla. See also Haroldo Dilla and Armando Fernández Soriano, 'Las elecciones municipales en Cuba: un estudio de caso' (1990), working paper on Organizaciones de Poder Comunal y Democracia Popular en América Central y el Caribe, Centro de Estudios Sobre América.

4. Discussions with César Pérez of the Instituto Tecnológico de Santo Domingo and leaders of various social movements, Santo Domingo, February 1991.

5. Dilla and Fernández, 'Las elecciones municipales en Cuba,' pp. 30–31, my translation.

6. Ibid., p. 24.

7. Discussions with community members and with Silvia Lara, San José.

8. See Chapter 6.

9. This and the following few paragraphs developed in discussion with Magaly Pineda.

10. We can add that both were united by other factors: one was a belief that a capitalist mode of production could be turned into a socialist mode of production by a simple change of ownership (and, in some versions, control) without addressing the technology or what I call the social-ecosystem that emerged with capitalist industry. Linked to this was a rationalist, scientist belief in finding technological fixes to human problems. The other common element was, as I argue below, an acceptance of the concept of power hegemonic within patriarchal societies. On Poulantzas, see his article, 'Towards a Democratic Socialism,' in *New Left Review* 109 (May–June 1978), pp. 75–87.

11. Among Macpherson's works on the subject, see his *Democratic Theory* (Oxford: Oxford University Press, 1973), and his own excellent summary of his thinking, *The Life and Times of Liberal Democracy* (Oxford: Oxford University Press, 1977).

12. Frank Cunningham, *Democratic Theory and Socialism* (Cambridge: Cambridge University Press, 1977).

13. In their excellent book, *Democracy and Capitalism* (New York: Basic Books, 1986), Samuel Bowles and Herbert Gintis have written of 'a mosaic of domination.' This term is inspired by the debates emerging out of a Gramscian position and by the theoretical contribution of modern feminism.

14. Macpherson, *The Life and Times of Liberal Democracy*. Participation, of course, is a handy and rather innocuous term that can mean anything to anyone. Over the past two decades it has become part of the bland language of international aid. Definitions of participation have a hard time twinning the notion of participation with actual control and empowerment. Many conceptions of participation ignore what is for me the key question: not simply whether or not certain groups partici-

pate, but whether the mass of the population has the means to define the terms and nature of their participation.

One of many sources of confusion in the debates on participation is that participation-as-empowerment is both a goal of change and a method of change. As a goal, popular participation ultimately refers to the organization of society in which there no longer exists a monopoly over the means of political, economic, and social power by a particular class, sex, race, social stratum, or bureaucratic elite. As a method of change, participation is a means to develop the voice and organizational capacity of those previously excluded. It is a means for the majority of the population to express their needs and to contribute directly to the solving of social problems.

15. This and the two previous paragraphs on power are based on passages from Michael Kaufman, *Cracking the Armour: Power, Pain, and the Lives of Men* (Toronto: Viking Canada, 1993), and from Michael Kaufman, 'Men, Feminism, and Men's Contradictory Experiences of Power,' in Harry Brod and Michael Kaufman, eds, *Theorizing Masculinities* (Thousand Oaks, CA: Sage Publications, 1994), pp. 142–63.

16. Current research on men and masculinity starts with a concern raised within feminist literature and speaks of different masculinities. Within these different masculinities, one can think of hegemonic versions of masculinity, to use Bob Connell's phrase. See R.W. Connell, *Gender and Power*, (Stanford, CA: Stanford University Press, 1987). See also Brod and Kaufman, eds., *Theorizing Masculinities*.

17. I have written about the themes of the past few paragraphs in my book *Jamaica Under Manley: Dilemmas of Socialism and Democracy* (London: Zed Books, 1985). See especially the concluding two chapters.

18. From Pineda's section of Kaufman and Pineda, 'Methodological Issues and Research Questions for Studying Differential Participation.'

19. Such things are not a biological imperative, nor absolute qualities of all women or all men. To the extent that they exist they are tendencies relating to the power relationships, the psychological realities and the lived experiences of many women in male-dominated societies. I do not believe that females are naturally more peaceful or peace-loving than males.

20. As note 18.

21. In his study of Walkerswood Community Development Foundation, a participatory body open to all members of this small community, Ian Boxhill notes that young people complain that 'not enough consideration is given to their ideas and views.' Ian Boxhill, 'Case Studies of Walkerswood Community Development Foundation and Augustown Community Council,' working paper on Organizations of Community Power and Grassroots Democracy in Central America and the Caribbean, Institute of Social and Economic Research, University of the West Indies, Mona, 1988.

22. Kaufman, *Cracking the Armour*; Michael Kaufman, 'The Construction of Masculinity and the Triad of Men's Violence,' in *Beyond Patriarchy: Essays by Men on Pleasure, Power and Change* (Oxford: Oxford University Press, 1987); and 'Men, Feminism, and Men's Contradictory Experiences of Power.'

8

Political Decentralization and Popular Alternatives: A View from the South

Haroldo Dilla Alfonso

The theme of state decentralization occupies a privileged place in current academic and political debates.[1] Perhaps it is not unrelated to the topic's own conceptual malleability, but the paradigm of a decentralized state has become common ground for those as diverse as international financial agencies, governments and political organizations of left, center and right, and important sectors of the academic world. Such a heterogeneity of advocates – and one can assume major differences between a high official of the World Bank and a community leader in Lima – invites the suspicion that behind this apparent consensus lie substantial differences.

My purpose in this chapter is to explore some of the more relevant issues attached to the debate on decentralization, and I have done so in three main parts. First, I will discuss some theoretical and methodological matters concerning state decentralization, stressing matters of local government. Second, I will present a brief historical overview of the evolution of decentralization proposals and their relationship with the market and the ideal of a participatory democracy. Finally, I will focus on the place of a decentralized state within viable popular alternatives in Latin America.

Defining Decentralization

From the viewpoint of formal logic, decentralization has been perceived as the antithesis of centralization; however, in actual life both conditions are expressed solely as directional principles of organization which are interrelated. A totally centralized or decentralized system – at least, anything complex enough to be called a system – simply cannot exist. From this starting point, we can define decentralization as a process of transferring responsibilities and resources from the decision-making top towards intermediate or base levels. Consequently, whatever its peculiarities, every act of decentralization implies a circulation and redistribution of power. This gives it an eminently political content which not only includes institutional and normative aspects, but other complex issues, such as the transformation of the behavior of individuals (officials, political leaders, citizens) and of the political culture in general. When we speak of decentralization, we are inevitably implying a new way of 'making politics,' which requires a process of socialization of new values and social pedagogy.

State decentralization – even viewed in the narrow sense of administrative decentralization – is an umbrella term used to designate different processes. Within it are posed several key problems, including the role and nature of the agencies involved in such a process, the form in which they supposedly interrelate, and the quantity and quality of decentralized powers. From the start, one distinction to be aware of is whether in the transfer of powers we are dealing with agencies that have a territorial basis (thus, territorial decentralization) or with entities that have specific state functions – that is, functional decentralization. In the first case, *territorial decentralization*, a specific territory – a municipality, region, or in some cases even a nation – is granted a greater level of responsibilities and control than it previously had, through the transfer of such power from a 'higher' or more central level of government. On the other hand, *functional decentralization* refers to the transfer of functions from central agencies to other intermediate or basic levels in a specific sector of public administration.

Territorial decentralization has tended to receive more attention than the functional variety. With the former it is possible to accomplish more important aims in democratization and in finding solutions to basic needs. Functional decentralization has more limited objectives and is usually linked to administrative flexibility or the distribution of state resources for patronage reasons. With functional decentralization, the transfer of responsibility and control – that is, political power – is more constrained than in territorial decentralization. Even considering these suppositions, we must bear in mind that functional decentralization can be linked with complex aims, including democracy-building and social control – such as in the workplace, especially in economies with a preponderance of public enterprises. Thus there are numerous points of relation between the two forms of decentralization. For example, the development of decentralization in public companies takes place in a given territory and involves a human community which acquires a double status as consumer and producer. As we will later see, the effective linkage of both types of decentralization has been a historically conflicting issue, particularly in economies with a strong public sector.

Whether functional or territorial, decentralization also implies the establishment and functioning of a network of channels through which decentralized entities relate to their environment. Even though I will deal only briefly with this matter, I believe it represents one of the essential aspects of state decentralization and of theoretical debates on its pertinence, since it opens a discussion on the issue of planning and the market. Of course, there are simplistic renditions of this debate which irreconcilably oppose the concepts of planning and decentralization, or, in the same sense, reduce the latter to the activity of the market. As we shall later see, the issue is more complex.

In sketching a framework of analysis and action, we find we must define the type of relation between the decentralized entity and the central government. If it is over-regulated, paternalism and re-centralization may follow; if left to itself, it may provoke atomization and uneven regional development. Even considering the fact that decentralized entities can incorporate new horizontal interrelationships, the vertical relation with the central government is necessary as a means of securing the efficiency of certain specialized services, the training of human resources, and institutional development in general. On the other hand, such a vertical relation is also a channel used by the decentralized entity to affect national decisions and make them reflect the particular interests that it represents. Of course, both in its vertical relations with the central government and in the horizontal ones with similar entities, newly decentralized institutions can develop different types of relations, such as information sharing, market ties, programme co-ordination, or co-operation in local planning.

Another aspect for evaluation, and closely linked to these previous points, refers to the amplitude of the powers being transferred. This will affect the capacity of the decentralized organism to operate with sufficient decision-making autonomy in relation to the center. One of the most widely known theories in this regard is that of Dennis Rondinelli and his colleagues at the World Bank, who propose four different levels of decentralized powers. The first and most basic, which they call *deconcentration*, is a redistribution of routine administrative functions between offices dependent on the central organisms. The center retains basic decision-making power in this limited horizontal distribution of functions. The second level, *delegation*, is the transfer of very specific decision-making functions from the immediate and direct control of the central government. The third, *devolution*, implies the creation of autonomous governmental entities with sufficient diversified implementative and decision-making powers, within specific geographical limits. Last, according to

Rondinelli, is *privatization*, which implies the accordance of public functions to private entities, individual or collective. Leaving aside for the moment the last category, the scheme of Rondinelli et al. contains considerable taxonomic utility, particularly in the difference between deconcentration and the other types. Of course, as the authors remark, such ideal types are never found in a pure form in actual life, but appear mingled in complex realities.[2]

Even with its potential for democratization and de-bureaucratization, decentralization is far from being a formula for the solution of the basic problems of contemporary societies. It is not difficult to recognize that state decentralization possesses many virtues, which have been discussed (with few innovations) since the comprehensive report published by the UN in 1962. According to this report, state decentralization encourages quicker and more realistic development decisions, greater flexibility in the co-ordination and offering of services, relief for the congested functions of central governments, and the creation of more adequate political spaces for popular participation in public decisions, especially in matters of everyday life.[3]

Of course, each of these advantages can be offset by undesirable effects such as political atomization, unequal regional development, an impoverishment of social services or the creation of corrupt and authoritarian local elites. The upshot has been that in certain situations, centralization constitutes a more efficient formula for the achievement of political aims, particularly in emergency situations (for example, post-war Europe), or in the often grim structural realities of Third World societies.

In short, every decentralization process results in a complex framework of political, technical, historical, cultural, and social considerations that mark its rhythm, modalities and potential viability.[4] Because of this complexity, a decentralization project may or may not be appropriate, desirable, or possible. As Diana Conyers has declared,

> Most of the objectives which decentralization is supposed to achieve – such as efficiency or coordination, national unity or popular participation – are themselves complex issues for which there are no easy or obvious recipes, and which cannot be achieved by decentralization whatever form it takes. The most obvious implication is the need for a realistic approach to decentralization, one which does not regard it as a panacea for all evils ... but which recognizes that in many situations some form of decentralization can go some way in helping to achieve certain development objectives, although it may also make it more difficult to achieve others.[5]

For obvious reasons, the enterprise and, above all, the municipality[6] have become preferential objects of decentralization. In the specific case of municipalities, decentralization is a direct consequence of the challenges imposed by an uninterrupted urban growth and by the systematic incapacity to satisfy the demands of the complex social subjects inserted in the rigors of everyday life.[7] Particularly in the Third World, the dynamics of urban growth acquires dramatic dimensions considering the deformed characteristics of urbanization and extreme poverty in the cities.[8]

Current tendencies towards the creation of municipalities within varying political systems, for example, originate in the consideration that it is more viable to face such challenges through the use of decentralized decision-making schemes than through a more centralized approach. According to Borja, municipal decentralization constitutes a key part of state decentralization. Strengthening local powers can 'bring administrative functions closer to the citizenship, allow a greater knowledge of citizens' needs and attitudes, improve the efficiency of information and personal services and the implementation of citizen participation in local management.'[9]

Even with varying degrees of decentralization, the municipality is a complex component of the political and state system towards which popular demands often focus. It is where a variety of conflicts, linked with what have been called the 'diffuse rights' of citizens that are derived from the needs of everyday life, are displayed in all their intensity. It is also the municipality – as the political covering for residential communities – which can become an important mediator for the family reproduction process, the socialization of values, cultural standards, and social and political ideas.

The complexity of urban life and the complex relations affected by municipal power raise the question of what is the best balance between the execution of efficient municipal management and the implementation of mechanisms for the construction of an effective participatory democracy. Considering that the municipality constitutes a complex system, a consistent decentralization policy can only become viable if it has an integral vision regarding the types and amounts of power that are transferred, so that the existence of one permits the materialization of others, and, as a whole, has the necessary attributes to achieve an effective mobilization of resources. In this respect, some consider that in a consistent municipalization process such powers should be directed towards strengthening the decentralized entities' capacity to decide not only which are the necessary means to achieve certain goals but also the determination of the goals that are to be set, within the limits of a conclusive, implementative and coercive autonomy.

This presupposes, in the first place, the enjoyment of financial powers, through the municipality's management of its own income and responsible administration of expenses, even in the case of organizations sub-sidized by the central state. Second, it is important that the decentralized entity can establish effective control over its bureaucratic and technical staff and its appointments, promotions or demotions. At the same time, municipalities form part of a political system and a national community. Local power thus exists in reference to its systemic environment. This obviously implies the acceptance that municipal power faces limits in order to guarantee the consistency of central policies with the general interests and aspirations of the national community. This might include the ability of the central or regional government to plan regional develop-ment or to control the basic normative structures.

Whether this inner tension generates conflict or not depends mainly on the capacity of the institutional and normative bodies to guarantee a fluid and reciprocal relationship between the center and local govern-ments, including on matters of central policies. Such relations can refer to representative structures, which could provide municipalities with a permanent presence in national legislative bodies, but they must also include other connections with bureaucratic networks for decision-making and information transmission. This issue becomes especially complex in those countries with an extensive national public sector in which the administrative 'center' physically lies within the municipality's territory, in the form of both public enterprises and delegate or representative insti-tutions. However, the decentralization/centralization equilibrium in a context of municipalization has historically encountered strong bureau-cratic resistance. Frequently this is based on a sort of short-term calcu-lation of costs versus benefits, according to which the decentralized units are incapable of attaining good quality results except at a high cost, or at least at a higher cost than that achieved by centralized entities.

Of course, any political and administrative system is forced to evaluate the effectiveness and efficiency of its structures. But short-term bureau-cratic reasoning omits the long-term requirements of developing a new political and administrative culture. The short-term perspective is a blue-print for bureaucratic inertia: mechanisms in place are always most con-venient. This inertia has repeatedly produced bad co-ordination between national and local institutions, frequently concerning scarce resources and inadequate capacities. This clash provokes an unequal risk distribution between the central state and local governments, a rapid decrease of the legitimacy of basic governmental structures, and higher economic and political costs.

In any case, municipalization does not escape the problems attributed to decentralization in general, already noted at the beginning of this chapter. The creation of municipal governments can encourage participatory and democracy-building projects. However, it can also encourage new forms of authoritarianism because it opens a preferred space for the development of local elites, and also, according to Cerroni, because it can allow fundamental decisions to be taken in a barely controlled manner.[10] We shouldn't forget that one of the most sophisticated institutional exercises of Pinochet's regime in Chile was precisely the development of a consistent project of regionalization and municipalization. Needless to say, that project had nothing to do with strengthening democracy and popular participation, but with the institutionalization of authoritarian patterns.

The transformative potential of decentralization and municipalization does not reside basically in their technical rationality but in the political context that constitutes their environment and to which they relate organically. The issue is highly complicated. Maybe that is why it is appropriate to analyze more deeply the dilemma between the technical imperative and political convenience.

From the Commune to the Market

The idea that a decentralized state has sufficient advantages to be adopted as a practical proposal has a long history in modern times, even though originally this had little in common with the reasons for its current popularity. It is not difficult to find in nineteenth-century political thought – from a revolutionary such as Marx to a conservative such as Charles de Maurras – the idea that a decentralized order has advantages over its opposite. At the time, as in the present, arguments were put forth regarding the advantages of the identification of the citizen with the community, his or her greater political involvement, and the existence of more flexible and cheaper administrative organs.

However, it is not by chance that the challenge to the Leviathan State had its origin among those whose objectives were social and democratic transformations, particularly in non-classist utopian thought and in revolutionary Marxism. As a rule, non-classist utopian experiments in the eighteenth and nineteenth centuries started as small self-administered bodies. These communes were based upon solidarity and were to favor direct democracy with the result of a considerable simplification of administrative functions.[11] The undoubted aesthetic attraction of utopian thought had a considerable effect on later social thought, including the romantic vision which identifies the decentralized state with individual liberties and social solidarity, and its opposite, centralization, with despotism and oppression.

Classical Marxist thought was not immune to this heritage. One of its key starting points was the consideration that class societies, as well as the state, constituted transitional historical entities, doomed to be replaced by a communal order based on the 'self-government of producers.' In the Marxist tradition, therefore, the socialization of power operates as a process of absorption of public functions by a society exempt from antagonistic cleavages. Such a process, preceded by the revolutionary disabling of bourgeois power and its mechanisms of domination, was not guided by the antithetical relation of society to state (so that the former would result as an alternative to the latter), but by a mutual transformation of the character and content of both.[12]

In these various approaches, the commune was the social repository of solidarity and of popular self-management, guaranteed by direct democracy and popular representation based on the principles of accountability and recall. In these approaches the role of the market was seen as limited or non-existent, considering that, especially in Marxism, socialist change was perceived as an alternative to the market's anarchy and its unequal social results.

However, early liberal thought did not put much emphasis on decentralization. This was because early capitalist accumulation needed a strong centralized state as an antithesis to feudal fragmentation, to maintain the territorial space and social control by extra-economic means, to support the accumulation of capital at home and through adventures abroad, and to regulate the newly emergent market. Furthermore, the liberal approach of this era saw private property and the free action of the market as the guarantors of human rights, and so a specific discourse on decentralization was not needed.

The theme of decentralization of the state appeared only in a fragmented form and in relation to well-defined utilitarian objectives which would increase the potential of emergent bourgeois society to integrate subordinated classes. This was the case, for example, with Alexis de Tocqueville and, above all, John Stuart Mill. In de Tocqueville's case, the existence of local government and local liberties would be the best scenario to develop individual liberties and to harmonize 'major private issues' with 'minor public issues.' For Mill, participation in decentralized spaces, in industry or the community for example, was the optimal way to motivate the popular classes to focus on what was at hand as the means to meet their everyday needs, while, at the same time, reserving 'high politics' for the owning classes and the educated elite.[13]

This relative lack of interest in decentralization continued into the twentieth century. Particularly during the period after the Second World War, economic expansion and capital concentration constituted the background for ongoing political and administrative centralization, and favored Keynesian policies and the modernization of state programming and controlling agencies. These changes were made possible by the existence of a large economic surplus which aligned the loyalties of subordinate regional and social actors.[14]

In the second half of the 1960s, the cycle of capitalist economic expansion that had sustained the welfare state was beginning to show its exhaustion. This provoked a shift not only of economic organization and its correlated social policy, but also of the way in which the state was supposed to assume its double role of guarantor of accumulation and legitimizer of the social order. As Curbelo writes, there have been new relations of the internationalization of capital and economic globalization, within which high levels of capital concentration are articulated with decentralized production methods, and where 'the tendency of national states towards decentralization is explained as much by the logic of the demands imposed by accumulation as by the consequent logic of a capitalist state in a period of crisis.'[15]

It is in this context that a new viewpoint regarding state decentralization has gathered force. Of neoliberal inspiration, it is included in the structural adjustment packages favored by the International Monetary Fund, the World Bank, and other international financial agencies. From this perspective, decentralization is a process with a strong technocratic imprint, directed towards the achievement of higher efficiency through the use of de-statization and the disintegration of social activity in the kingdom of privatization and free market.

One of the most illustrative examples of this evolution and of its results is the change of focus that occurred in US aid policy. In a certain way, the perception of decentralized political-administrative models as a proper background for development had been a constant component of US foreign aid policy since the end of the Second World War. This was exemplified by the implementation and development of community projects in more than 25 Third World countries. However, such projects were conceptually guided by a strong ethnocentrism which consisted of transferring North American experience regarding local leadership and institutions to peripheral countries.

From the last years of the 1950s, these programmes were subjected to severe criticism by many developmental theorists in that the programmes seemed more oriented towards the performance of macro-economic variables than in local development. Even though such a community perspective was in decline towards the middle of the 1960s, it had a considerable and tragic impact during the Vietnam War where the communal development experiences of the US Agency for International Development (AID) were used for the implementation of counter-insurgent strategic hamlets.

At the end of the 1970s, the decentralization proposal was again strengthened in AID programs, and by 1979 almost half of its projects were concentrated at local levels. Two years later, during the Reagan administration, AID offered a more explicit formulation of its policy based on the construction and reinforcement of a decentralized organization system capable of offering services through the invigoration of market incentives, as well as through an increase in the capacity of non-governmental organizations to assume a larger number of functions in place of traditional public administration structures. 'During the early 80s,' says Rondinelli, 'AID further focused its assistance on transferring appropriate technology to improve productivity and raise the incomes of the poor, on promoting private enterprises as an alternative to direct government provisions of goods and services, and on institutional development as a way of increasing the capacity of a wide variety of private, voluntary and local organizations.'[16]

Democratization and the extension of participation entered through the back door: in this framework, participation was considered as a more responsible relation between a diminished state and a stronger private sector. There was also the notion that private interests would assume new roles in a free market unhindered by governmental interference. In essence, democracy is here considered, as Von Hayek defined it almost half a century ago, as 'a utilitarian device for safeguarding internal peace and individual freedom.'[17]

The limits and rather perverse effects of the neoliberal proposal deserve a more detailed comment. One point refers to the role of the market and privatization. Truly, it is now difficult to conceive of a practical process of decentralization, be it territorial or functional, that doesn't imply the existence of market relations and even the privatization of certain areas and functions. There can be a considerable advantage to the creation of a competitive framework that stimulates resource mobilization, an increase in the quality of services and production, and a more dynamic circulation of information between buyers and sellers. As has been widely acknowledged, the failure to recognize this advantage remained a permanent economic and social bottle-neck in the 'actually existing socialism' experiences.

But this practical advantage should not lead us to ignore the negative consequences of those processes, such as an increase of social inequality and regional imbalances. We mustn't forget that we are not speaking about an ideally competitive market but of one which takes place in a world marked by the prevalence of oligarchical interests and by an internationalization process advantageous to world capitalist centers.

Consequently, neoliberal decentralization can only lead, and in practice has led, to the strengthening of the existing power structures, a technocratic centralization policy and a deepening power asymmetry between ever-weaker Third World countries and stronger transnational blocs.[18] We should remember that the most successful development experiences that have taken place during the post-war period, even in capitalist economies, have counted in their favor a strong state presence in planning and economic regulations, and even in the property system.

Socialism, Decentralization and Market: Guides to a Mistaken Dilemma

The consignment of decentralization to the laws of the market, with the perception of the latter as the ideal space – or at least a more propitious one – for democratic realization, has not been the exclusive territory of neoliberalism and capitalist restructuring projects. In fact, with a different emphasis and perspective, it has also gained a considerable space in recent Marxist thought and in debates on socialist strategy.

One of the peculiarities of the debate about decentralization in socialist projects has been the considerable emphasis put upon what we have already called functional decentralization. In a pragmatic sense this is linked to the demands inherent in economies in which the state and planning play – or are supposed to play – a leading role. But even beyond the boundaries of this relationship, the predominance of the functional criterion has its roots in the core of the classical Marxist tradition, in which 'producers' self-government' was a formula used to challenge the primary niche of bourgeois power – that is, the enterprise. It was also seen as a means to overcome the liberal division between politics and economics and to substitute the concrete notion of worker for the abstract one of citizen. In this context, the workers' council, a crucial issue of Marxist discussions since the 1905 Russian Revolution and a central idea in the work of Lenin, Trotsky, Gramsci, Luxemburg, Korsch and Adler, became the theoretical touchstone of the democratic construction process in the framework of new power relations. It was also the original conception behind the Soviet institutional model, based on decentralized governmental units with a singular combination of geographic and workplace communities.

As we may suppose, emerging conceptions of municipalities or smaller communities as significant areas for the consolidation and institutionalization of democracy and popular action had at that time very little space within revolutionary Marxist thought. It is even possible to find within the Bolshevik tradition a purposeful banishment of the issue, unless it dealt, as Bukharin used to present it, with a clear distinction between 'proletarian municipalities' and 'bourgeois municipalities', whatever this was supposed to mean.[19]

In any case, decentralization was always linked, at least in theory, to democratization and the consolidation of workers' power, with very little or no space for a mercantile scenario. It was only after the victory of the Russian Revolution, when the theory had to submit to the tests imposed by the tough real world, that the market was included in this discussion, even though it was done in a utilitarian and tactical way, as one concludes from the debates in the 1920s about the New Economic Policy.

It wasn't until well into the 1930s that the market, as an organizational principle, acquired an organic space in Marxist thought. This was partly because, in Stalinism, the three paradigmatic pillars of socialism – equality, socialization of property, and democracy – suffered, shall we say, a severe erosion. Whatever might have been positive about democratic centralism became obliterated by bureaucratization.

One of the first to propound this new perspective, and probably the most prolific and well-known, was the Polish Marxist economist Oscar Lange. For Lange, the centralization/decentralization relation constituted a basic dilemma for socialism. He did not hesitate to recognize the relevance of planning in the socialist economy, even though he discussed its magnitude and the temporality of its constitution. He considered that during the first stages of a transition to socialism, the plan should be extremely centralized, with a strong political component, in order to solve the initial tensions of the transition. But in a second stage, it should advance towards a decentralized phase in which 'extra-economical forces' must give way to 'economic laws' in order to produce a gradual separation of the national economy administration and the extra-economic state activities.

According to these considerations, decentralization offered a relevant space for the market, even though it also appeared in combination with an active non-detailed planning (of major importance for the construction of the new society), and above all with the construction of effective workers' participation. Lange conceived this decentralization process as the beginning of the communist dream of the disappearance of the state.[20]

Lange's work, as well as that of other contemporary economists such as Dickinson and Lerners, had a germinal effect in the enrichment of the debate regarding the viability of socialism as a system whose ethical values, economic efficiency, and forms of participative democracy either seemed like contradictory goals or as impossibilities within extreme centralization and bureaucratization. A considerable part of the rich theoretical discussions on the issue of economic reforms in the USSR and Czechoslovakia during the 1960s, as well as the postulates of Yugoslavian self-management, reflected this search for new avenues.

It wasn't until the following decade that the market erupted into socialist theory with an emphasis that transcended its earlier utilitarian

meaning and historical temporality. It was increasingly seen as an organizational principle of society and of democratic construction. This theoretical
perspective – generically called 'market socialism' – was an attempt to
present a pragmatic, 'feasible socialism' as an alternative to the Soviet
centralized bureaucratic model. But it has also been a challenge to traditional forms of participatory democracy. Here, the emphasis on producers
has been transferred to the consumers, so that to a certain extent the
realm of democracy is narrowed to relations between buyers and sellers
in the marketplace.

According to Alec Nove, one of the best-known and most consistent
supporters of 'market socialism,' in order to achieve the construction of
'feasible socialism' it is necessary to face the technological and consumer
challenges imposed by the world capitalist economy. This is possible only
through intensive and rational economic growth. Consequently, after
exploring the weaknesses of Eastern Europe's centrally planned economies and of the USSR, he concludes that only the market (to which he
attributes great potentialities for the rational distribution of resources
and for the stimulation of efficiency) can confer to socialism the necessary
levels of efficiency and competitiveness to guarantee its continued existence. State property, centralized planning and popular participation assume
a significant role, but always in subordination to the variations of the
market. Consequently, 'market socialism' deals with a decentralized social
model that occurs in, and is created for, a market context. The only kind
of decentralization that works automatically is the market, says Nove, and
it has to be competitive. Accordingly, when the issue under discussion is
decentralization, it becomes a discussion about decentralization of types
of markets.[21]

Nove's work, like that of other Marxist theoreticians in this tendency,
constitutes an intellectual challenge which should not be dismissed out of
hand. It contains novel proposals based on the knowledge of a socialist
reality which was to demonstrate a fragility that not even Nove could
foresee. But it is also necessary to recognize that the socialist market
model is open to many doubts about its capacity to achieve key socialist
goals, particularly when we consider not only the industrialized North
but also the underdeveloped South – markedly dissimilar scenarios for a
'feasible socialism.'

Every society, regardless of its political system, is sustained by something more than calculations of technical efficiency; this is especially true
of the complexity (political, ideological, cultural, and international) of the
socialist project. The market is a mechanism too powerful to be considered as a docile instrument of socialist advance. It would be naive to
think that a market society could produce adequate levels of social equity,

rational consumer patterns, co-operative relationships, a healthy ecosystem, or an effective framework for popular participation. But it is essential not to confront the market socialism proposal with one of bureaucratic centralized state omnipotence; the authoritarianism, relative economic inefficiency, ecological breakdown, and spiritual dissatisfaction of the latter are well known.

At the same time, just as decentralized management cannot be equated with the distribution of resources as a function of price fluctuations in the market, planning (even that which takes place centrally) is not necessarily a synonym for bureaucratization. As Lukács pointed out, it is necessary to transcend the oppressive dilemma between the 'substance of Stalinist methods' and the 'introduction of the methods that rule in the West.'[22]

I would like to believe that between centralized bureaucratic planning and the supposedly unfettered market there exist many intermediate levels of decentralized planning, technically efficient and democratic, that can process market signals and involve a transparent network of administrative and political relations of co-operation that go beyond the simple criteria of competitiveness. That would be a true political economy of a viable socialism.

Back to the Commune?

This discussion on the range of meanings attached to the notion of state decentralization raises the possibility of considering to what degree it can be conceived as a crucial component of a popular political alternative not only to 'actually existing capitalism' but also to known socialist experiences.

From my point of view a popular alternative in Latin America and perhaps elsewhere in the Third World must plan for and bring about a society capable of avoiding the omnipresence of a powerful central bureaucracy, a socialist leviathan. The goal of socialism is inseparable from democracy, and democracy means, among others things, the right of common people to participate in the decision-making process, to decide how to participate and to control their own lives and destinies. Stimulated by the frustration with the social change 'models' of past decades, support for the paradigm of a decentralized state (either as a means or as an end) has rightly gained ground in the Latin American popular movement.

The importance of decentralization of the state in the context of building new social movements becomes polemical, however, when it is turned into an extreme 'localist' approach – as Carlos de Mattos has critically named it.[23] In this sense, some grassroots leaders and theoreticians are returning to the idea of a sort of utopian commune, with its invitation (charged with a heavy ethical load) to question the prevalent notions of development and to rescue traditional patterns of social life. In this context, the building of a participatory democracy is being conceived as a combination of forms of economic self-management and grassroots democracy drawing on regional corporations, plebiscites, popular assemblies, open chapter councils, sectoral citizens' councils, local elections, and so forth. Such things are seen to exist in an environment dominated by 'public spheres' opposed to both the state and to private activity.[24]

None of these proposals is irrelevant. If brought into existence, such instruments might well manage to improve self-confidence and the sense of a participatory political culture among people who have long been socially and culturally without power. Such proposals should be considered a fair reaction against corruption, anti-democratic practices, repression and other long-standing features of Latin American states. But, unfortunately, they remain at best primary steps and very partial solutions.

At the end of the twentieth century it is impossible to discuss development without questioning the predominant paradigms. As Wolfgang Sachs has pointed out, 'the idea of development was once a towering monument inspiring international enthusiasm. Today, the structure is falling apart and in danger of total collapse. But its imposing ruins still linger over everything and block the way out. The task, then, is to push the rubble aside to open up new ground.'[25] Undoubtedly, this process is one of the most relevant points in any popular agenda. But 'to open up new ground' cannot ignore the complexity and interconnections of world economic, social, and political affairs. And to downplay capital's tendencies towards power centralization (independent of the degree of decentralization of the institutional forms) is to engage in a useless intellectual exercise. The goal of sustainable development cannot be reduced to a sort of splendid self-sufficiency and to a belief that we can reproduce atavistic patterns of social life. This is all the more true when we consider that the globalization of the world economy is an ongoing design of a 'market colonialism' affecting the livelihoods of more than 80 per cent of the world's population.[26]

Lastly, so long as central states – even decentralized states – remain at the core of political power, the state must remain a strategic target of the popular movement. As I discussed previously, the central state is a unique ensemble of relations able to carry out a set of important tasks concerning development planning, distribution of national revenue, international negotiations, and national defense, among others. Consequently, grassroots democracy, the relevance of which I do not doubt, appears to be an indispensable but partial way to achieve a meaningful democratization of the political system and the society as a whole. Without a clear reference to the central state and to 'high politics,' grassroots democracy will reverse into a niche of self-management of minor themes, prone to be subordinate to clientelistic relations.

The pertinence of decentralization as part of a perspective for change continues to be secondary in my mind to the well-aimed Marxist perception of power and domination as a chain that reproduces itself. Even though a break-up of the political logic of peripheral capitalism is not sufficient for a substantive decentralization and for a democracy-building process, as Slater has stated, it remains a necessary historical condition.[27] Only with a challenge to this logic can the state become not an antagonist of the self-expression of civil society, but its supporter. And through this, we will overcome the irrational, or at least counter-productive, antagonism of state versus society.

The challenge of decentralization is not simply the option of putting power 'closer' to the citizens (which in any case leaves a breach between the two), or of creating niches of self-sufficient reproduction of the necessities of daily life. The ultimate goal must be to allow the reappropriation of power by concrete and diverse individuals and their collectivities. A real process of popular empowerment will convert the ordinary citizen from a passive political consumer into an active political producer. But more than this, it will be a process of re-evaluating the very concept of power. Macpherson's views of the potential power of humans to develop their own abilities and capacities for self-definition will be instructive in this context.[28]

Searching and finding realistic means along this pathway is an intellectual and practical challenge bordering on conceptual subversion. We must be capable of producing adequate responses to the increasingly complex, interrelated problems of our era. Although it was fashionable a few years ago to speak of the end of history, I would prefer to see this as a new beginning.

Notes

1. I would like to thank Michael Kaufman, Gerardo González, Ana Teresa Vincentelli, Stanley Malinowitz, and Juan Valdés for their comments and help. An earlier version of this chapter was published in 1991 as a working paper for the CERLAC community power project, and then, in a somewhat different version but under the same title in William Carroll, ed., *Organizing Dissent: Contemporary Social Movements In Theory and Practice* (Toronto: Garamond Press, 1992).

2. D. Rondinelli, J. Nellis, and S. Cheena, 'Decentralization in Developing Countries,' World Bank Staff Working Papers, no. 581 (Washington DC: World

Bank, 1984). A more detailed account of Rondinelli's scheme is found in Gregory Schmidt, *Donors and Decentralization in Developing Countries* (Boulder, CO: Westview Press, 1989).

3. United Nations Technical Assistance Program, *Decentralization for National and Local Development* (New York: United Nations, 1962).

4. I will not linger on these national historical considerations that constitute the frame of every decentralization process. But we must recognize their decisive weight, a fact which has not always been noticed by institutional designers or by the international agencies that promote state decentralization. Some writers have even suggested that the viability of a state decentralization process is in direct relation to a nation's age, its economy, and particularly its industrial development, among other factors. See Rondinelli et al., 'Decentralization in Developing Countries'. See also G. Cochrane, 'Policies for Strengthening Local Governments in Developing Countries,' World Bank Staff Working Papers no. 528 (Washington DC: World Bank, 1983) for a discussion on the impact of authoritarianism on decentralization possibilities.

5. D. Conyers, 'Decentralization and Development: A Framework for Analysis,' *Community Development Journal*, vol. 21, no. 2, 1986, p. 97.

6. Using the term 'municipality' as a basic government unit doesn't ignore the existence of smaller territorial units with administrative or mobilizing powers. In this sense, the term is more closely related to Iberoamerican than to Anglo-Saxon traditions. It is also the terminology most suited to Cuba's experience.

7. Castells, in his already classic works on the issue, has defined the root of the urban crisis as 'the growing incapacity of capitalist social organization to guarantee the production, distribution, and management of the collective consumer products necessary for everyday life' (from houses to green areas), owing to the fact that those services 'are not sufficiently cheap so as to be produced by capital with a profit expectation.' See Manuel Castells, *Ciudad, Democracia y Socialismo* (Mexico: Siglo XXI Editores, 1977), p. 82.

8. 'The proportion of inevitably poor in a society with two-thirds of satisfied citizens, which seems to characterize the North, is inverted in the South, where only one in three human beings enjoys [entrance into] the legitimate circle of civilization.' Pancho Liernur, 'Requiem para la plaza y la fabrica,' *Nueva Sociedad*, no. 114, July–August 1991, pp. 28–9.

9. Borja Jordi, 'Dimensiones teóricas, problemas y perspectivas de la descentralización del estado,' in *Descentralización del Estado* (Santiago, Chile: FLACSO, 1987).

10. Umberto Cerroni, *Teoría política y socialismo* (Mexico: Ediciones Era, 1984).

11. For Rousseau, they were societies organized in bodies 'not too big so that they can be governed, nor too small so that they have their own life.' J.-J. Rousseau, *El Contrato Social* (Havana: Editorial de Ciencias Sociales, 1973).

12. See Karl Marx, 'The Civil War in France,' *Selected Works*, Vol. 2 (Moscow: Progress Publishers, 1977).

13. Alexis de Tocqueville, 'La Democracia en América,' in W. Ebestein, ed., *Los grandes pensadores políticos* (Madrid: Revista de Occidente, 1965); John Stuart Mill, *Representative Government* (London: Everyman, 1910).

14. The pertinence of centralized states, or at least their emphasis by political designers, was not limited to capitalist centers. In the former Eastern European

and Asian socialist blocs, centralization represented the only opportunity of mobilizing human and material resources to achieve the planned development goals, and it represented a guarantee for national defense. Such considerations were often extended to emerging Third World countries, whose development paradigms often adopted the socialist experience.

15. José Luis Curbelo, 'Economía política de la descentralización y planificación del desarrollo regional,' *Pensamiento Iberoamericano*, no. 10, 1989, p. 57. According to the author, 'the restructuring of the economic order through the intensive application of new technologies and the internationalization of capital operations on a world sc ale runs parallel to the process of loss of confidence and functionality by the state, not only as a producer of products and services but as the agent that makes possible the reproduction of the economic system.'

16. Dennis A. Rondinelli, *Development Administration and US Foreign Aid Policy* (Boulder, CO: Lynne Rienner, 1987), p. 29.

17. F.A. von Hayek, *The Road to Serfdom* (London: Routledge & Kegan Paul, 1962). The neoliberal omission of democracy and participation is inherent to Hayek's conception of politics and of the relations that exist between the public and the private. This last distinction is vital to understanding Rondinelli's proposal. For reasons of space, I will not linger on this discussion, which has been explored extensively elsewhere. See, for example, C.B. Macpherson, *Democratic Theory* (London: Oxford University Press, 1977).

18. Recent Latin American experience attests to the perverse results of the mercantile-privatist perspective of decentralization. Not only was there the repressive authoritarian content of the territorial and functional decentralization in Chile during the military dictatorship (as mentioned above); other experiences, even in countries as relatively democratic as Costa Rica, show a similar character. See Hernán Pozo, 'La participación en la gestión local para el régimen actual chileno,' in *La Descentralización del Estado* (Santiago: FLACSO, 1987); Maria E. Trejos and M. Pérez, 'Descentralización y democracia económica en el marco del ajuste estructural: el caso de Costa Rica,' in *Estudios Sociales Centroamericanos* 52, January–April, 1990.

19. N. Bukharin, *The Politics and Economics of the Transition Period* (London: Routledge and Kegan Paul, 1979). Also see Lenin's polemic with Maslov that appeared in 'Revisión del Programa Agrario del Partido Obrero,' *Selected Works*, Vol. 3 (Moscow: Progress Publishers, 1976).

20. Lange's work is of vast proportions. A good selection of his articles and more recent talks may be found in *Papers in Economics and Sociology* (Oxford: Pergamon Press, 1979).

21. Nove wrote voluminously about Eastern Europe's economies. For our purposes his most important book is probably *The Economics of Feasible Socialism* (London: George Allen & Unwin, 1983), which gave rise to a rich polemic among various theoreticians in *New Left Review* during 1987 and 1988. See also Nove's *Socialism, Economics and Development* (London: George Allen & Unwin, 1986).

22. Georg Lukács, *El hombre y la democracia* (Buenos Aires: Editorial Contrapunto, 1989). For a criticism of market socialism, see Ernest Mandel, 'The Myth of Market Socialism,' *New Left Review* 169, May–June 1988.

23. Carlos de Mattos, 'Falsas expectivas ante la descentralización,' *Nueva Sociedad* 104, November–December, 1989.

24. Orlando Fals Borda, *El nuevo despertar de los movimientos sociales* (Medellin,

1986). For a novel view on the issue, see Juan Carlos Portantiero, 'La múltiple transformación del estado latinoamericano,' *Nueva Sociedad* 104, November–December, 1989.

25. Wolfgang Sachs, 'Development: A Guide to the Ruins,' *New Internationalist* 232, June 1992.

26. Michel Chossudovsky, 'Global Poverty and New World Economic Order,' *Economic and Political Weekly*, November 2, 1991.

27. David Slater, 'Territorial Power and the Peripheral State: The Issue of Decentralization,' *Development and Change*, vol. 20, 1988.

28. C.B. Macpherson *Democratic Theory* (Oxford: Oxford University Press, 1973). The English language has seen the introduction of the term 'empowerment', which has not yet been adequately translated into Spanish (see Chapter 6). For Dharam Ghai, the term means 'the strengthening of the power of the dispossessed masses' and is a necessary component of any participative development experience, obtained through decentralization but not limited to it. D. Ghai, 'Participatory Development: Some Perspectives from Grass-Roots Experiences,' *Journal of Development Planning* 19, 1989.

9

New Social Movement Theory and Resource Mobilization Theory: The Need for Integration

Eduardo Canel

Two distinct theoretical paradigms dominate the study of social movements (SMs) in contemporary societies: the first is the European *new social movement* approach (NSM); the second is the North American perspective known as *resource mobilization* (RM).[1] Both seek to explain the emergence and the significance of contemporary social movements in (post-)industrial societies. In so doing, both approaches have reformulated traditional theories of collective action on each side of the Atlantic.

The theoretical issues each perspective addresses are to a great extent determined by the different scientific traditions and contemporary debates in each region. NSM theory, for instance, questions reductionist Marxism, which assigned the working class a privileged place in the unfolding of history. RM theory, in contrast, criticizes Durkheim's view of collective action as anomic and irrational behavior resulting from rapid social change, and it questions 'relative deprivation' theory, which assumes a direct link between perceived deprivation and collective action. Each perspective developed in relative isolation from the other, and until recently there was little theoretical interaction between them. It is commonly assumed that the theoretical premises of these paradigms are incompatible, but a close examination indicates otherwise. Although there are significant theoretical differences, these are partly due to the fact that each approach examines SMs at different, but complementary, levels of analysis.

The NSM perspective emphasizes the cultural nature of the new movements and views them as struggles for control over the production of meaning and the constitution of new collective identities. It stresses the expressive aspects of SMs and places them exclusively in the terrain of civil society, as opposed to the state. This approach also emphasizes discontinuity by highlighting the differences between the new movements and traditional collective actors. RM theory, in contrast, stresses the political nature of the new movements and interprets them as conflicts over the allocation of goods in the political market. Hence, it focuses on the strategic-instrumental aspects of action and places social movements, simultaneously, at the levels of civil society and the state. It also places emphasis on continuity between the new and the old collective actors.

Reactions against Traditional Paradigms

Both the NSM and RM theories point out that traditional theories explained collective action in reference to structural dislocations, economic crisis, and exploitation. The older theories assumed that the passage from a condition of exploitation or frustration to collective action aimed at reversing the condition was a simple, direct and unmediated process. The new paradigms, in contrast, proposed that this passage from condition to action is a contingent and open process mediated by a number of conjunctural and structural factors. NSM and RM theories differ, however, in their definition of which central factors mediate the transition from condition to collective action.

NSM theorists suggested that two types of reductionism prevented Marxism from understanding contemporary SMs. The first, economic reductionism, is the assumption that a single economic logic provides the unity of a social formation and determines its political and ideological processes. Thus economic reductionism gives theoretical primacy to economic factors and treats politics and ideology as epiphenomena of the economic realm. The second reductionism in Marxism is class reductionism: the assumption that the identity of social agents is given to them overwhelmingly by their class position. Thus all social actors are, ultimately and fundamentally, class actors, and their identity only reflects economic class interests (Mouffe, 1979: 169; Laclau & Mouffe, 1985: 76).

The two reductionisms have prevented Marxism from understanding the new conflicts in modern societies. NSM theorists argued that new collective actors had moved to the center of contemporary conflicts and displaced traditional working-class struggles. These new actors were not class actors as their identity was not constituted by their place at the level of production. Their primary concern was not with economic issues but with collective control of the process of symbolic production and the redefinition of social roles. They raised non-class issues related to gender, ethnicity, age, neighborhood, the environment, and peace. Their identity was defined in relation to these issues and not by class position. Thus the identities of contemporary SMs could not be a mechanical reflection of economic interests. They were themselves the product of ideological and political processes. NSM theorists made it clear that economic and class reductionism had prevented Marxism from explaining the mediated nature of the passage from condition to action. In the new framework this transition was said to be mediated by ideological, political and cultural processes.

Resource mobilization theory challenged the functionalist basis of collective behavior theory – which emphasized integration, equilibrium and harmony – and proposed a conflict model of social action. Collective action, they argued, is triggered by well-entrenched cleavages in society, not by short-term strains resulting from rapid social change. They also pointed out that in traditional studies of collective behavior the object of analysis was not the social movement itself but the system's sources of disequilibrium which led to the rise of collective actors. Resource mobilization theorists, for their part, made social movements the object of analysis.

While collective behavior theory viewed collective action as non-institutional, irrational responses by those displaced by social change, the new approach suggested that participants in the new movements were rational, well-integrated individuals or groups developing strategies in pursuit of their interests. They theorized that collective actions operated at the political-institutional level so that the distinction between institutional and non-institutional action was not pertinent to the study of social movements. Rational actors, employing strategic and instrumental reasoning at the political-institutional level, replaced the irrational crowd as the central object of analysis in studies of collective action (Cohen, 1985: 674–5).

The critique of relative deprivation theory centered on the relationship between condition and action. Relative deprivation studies assumed that collective action resulted from perceived conditions of deprivation and the feelings of frustration associated with these perceptions. RM theory pointed out that grievances and inequalities could only be considered a precondition for the occurrence of social movements. Relations of inequality and domination, they argued, were found at every level of social life, but only in some instances would the legitimacy of these relations be questioned, and even when this occurred, the formation of organized movements aiming to change these relations was only one possible outcome. The existence of inequalities and/or the subjective perception of these inequalities were not enough to explain why social movements emerge. RM theory proposed that the passage from condition to action was contingent upon the availability of resources and changes in the opportunities for collective action (Tilly, 1978: 99).

New Social Movement Theory: Explaining the Emergence of Social Movements

A number of theorists – Habermas and Offe, rooted in German critical theory; Laclau and Mouffe, with their synthesis of post-structuralism and neo-Gramscian Marxism; and Touraine with his sociology of action – explain the emergence of SMs in reference to structural transformations and long-range political and cultural changes which created new sources of conflict and altered the process of constitution of collective identities. Habermas views new social movements as struggles in defense of the 'life world.' Offe explains SMs within the context of late capitalist societies and focuses on the contradictory role of the capitalist state, as it must ensure, simultaneously, the conditions for capital accumulation and bourgeois legitimacy. Some authors (Habermas, Offe, Laclau and Mouffe) highlight the notion of *crisis* (of hegemony and legitimation) in contemporary capitalist societies and conceive collective actions as rational responses to such crisis. Laclau and Mouffe explain SMs in terms of the availability of democratic discourse and the crisis of the hegemonic formation consolidated after the Second World War. Touraine focuses on the emergence of a new societal type, post-industrial society, characterized by increased levels of reflexivity.

The crisis of legitimation

Habermas argues that system integration and social integration possess distinct logics that require different types of rationality: system integration (the steering mechanisms of a society) results from mechanisms of domination, such as the state and the mass media; social integration (the legitimating normative structures) is obtained through socialization and the creation of a 'life world' of meaning (Cohen, 1982: 203–5). A crisis develops when the expansion of steering mechanisms (system integration) disturbed the processes through which norms, values and meaning were produced (social integration). Habermas identifies the present intrusion by the state and the market into areas of private life – the 'colonization of the life-world' – as the source of the present crisis of legitimation (Habermas, 1981: 35). NSMs, he argues, represent defensive reactions seeking to retain or re-create endangered lifestyles. They operate at the level of social integration and are concerned less with redistributional issues than with the 'grammar of forms of life' (33–4). Thus the new movements arise 'at the seam between system and life-world' (36).

Offe explains the rise of new movements within the context of the crisis of legitimation resulting from the new relationship between state and society in late capitalist societies. He views the state as a network of steering mechanisms, whose role in securing system integration, given the inadequacy of market mechanisms, has greatly increased. The capitalist state must secure, simultaneously, the conditions for capital accumulation and for bourgeois legitimacy. Offe argues that given this new role of the state as regulator of social and economic processes, the administrative and normative subsystems acquire greater autonomy from the economic level. Thus, since the economic subsystem cannot be isolated from political and administrative mediation, conflicts cannot emerge from purely economic concerns.

The basis for the present 'crisis of crisis management' is found in the irony that state regulation can secure the stability of the capitalist system only through 'non-capitalist' means. The state must 'compensate for the failures of the market mechanisms' without infringing on 'the primacy of private production,' but it cannot do so without expanding 'non-commodity forms of social relation[s].' (Jessop, 1984: 108–9). The 'decommodification' of growing areas of social life – which results from the expansion of non-productive forms of labor and the increased provision of 'public goods' by the welfare state – threatens capital accumulation and bourgeois legitimacy. The conditions for capital accumulation are affected by the withdrawal of capital from productive activities, resulting in fiscal crisis. The expansion of non-commodity relations erodes bourgeois legitimacy because it politicizes economic relations, making it possible to challenge the view that market forces should be the main allocators of wealth and resources in society.

Given its role as a 'crisis manager,' the state has become a central source of inequalities and power differentials. As Cohen (1982: 198) explains, Offe sees the political system as a 'filtering mechanism' that determines what interests and demands can be selected for political articulation. The interests and demands which are excluded are those that cannot be associated with specific interest groups, or those coming from sectors that are not fully integrated into, or do not have functional significance for, the economic and political system. This filtering process has important consequences for the legitimacy of the 'crisis manager.' The inability of political parties and trade unions to meet and/or to articulate the multiple demands raised by numerous interest groups produces a 'crisis of mass loyalty' and contributes to the emergence of new collective actors.

For Offe, the emergence of new social movements must be understood as a reaction against the deepening, broadening, and increased irreversibility of the forms of domination and deprivation in late capitalist societies. The deepening of the mechanisms of social control and domination – the expansion of steering mechanisms – takes place as more and more areas of private life come under state regulation 'through the use of legal, educational, medical, psychiatric, and media technologies' (Offe, 1985: 846). This process, paradoxically, has contradictory effects on state authority: on the one hand, it strengthens it as more areas of civil society come under state regulation and control; but, on the other hand, state authority is weakened as 'there are fewer nonpolitical – and hence uncontested and noncontroversial – foundations of action to which claims can be referred or from which metapolitical (in the sense of "natural" or "given") premises for politics can be derived' (818).

Following from the above, contemporary conflicts center around two different projects. Neoconservatives fight for a restrictive redefinition of the political and the reprivatization of issues and conflicts that political authority cannot satisfy. NSMs, by contrast, expand the political by politicizing civil society and reconstituting it in ways that make it 'no longer dependent upon ever more regulation, control, and intervention' (820). The negative effects of existing economic and political arrangements have been broadened as feelings of deprivation have expanded from the work role to other social roles such as citizen, consumer, client of bureaucratic decisions, and so on. The increased irreversibility of forms of domination and deprivation refers to the 'structural incapacity' of existing political institutions to reverse the problems and deprivations that they have caused (844–7).

The emergence of post-industrial society

While the conditions for the reproduction of capital are the starting point in Offe's discussion of SMs, Touraine relates the rise of NSMs to the emergence of a new societal type, post-industrial or programmed society, which has brought 'a new culture and a field for new social conflicts and movements' (Touraine, 1985: 781). This said, Touraine is against any type of reductionism, and rejects the view that society is driven by a single inner logic. Social relations, he argues, cannot be understood only in reference to position in the process of production, since they are a 'normatively oriented interaction between adversaries within a cultural field open to opposed interpretations' (Cohen, 1982: 212). Society is a 'hierarchized system of systems of action' of actors defined by cultural orientations and social relations; the key to understanding it is to focus on the origins of norms and the conflicts over their interpretation (Touraine, 1981: 61).

A central concept in Touraine's sociology of action is *historicity*, a property of modern societies. Historicity refers to the capacity of society to 'act upon itself' in order to reshape the set of cultural models that guide social practices. It is 'the set of cultural, cognitive, economic, and ethical models by means of which a collectivity sets up relations with its environment; in other words, produces ... a culture' (Touraine, 1988: 40). But for Touraine a culture is more than a general framework of social relations: it is the fundamental object of historical contestation. A culture is 'a stake, a set of resources and models that social actors seek to manage, to control, and which they appropriate or whose transformation into social organization they negotiate among themselves' (8). Culture, in other words, is a product, the result of social conflict over the appropriation of historicity.

Touraine's typology of modern societies divides them into three discontinuous types – commercial, industrial and post-industrial – each with its own cultural model, type of investment and central conflict. The central conflicts in commercial societies (which are culturally oriented to exchange, and possess a type of investment in the sphere of distribution that includes goods and rights) involve struggles for civil liberties and political rights. The central struggle of industrial societies (which are culturally oriented to production and have a mode of investment that transforms the means of production and the organization of work) is between capitalists and workers. Class domination in industrial societies is based on Taylorism and the ownership of capital, leading to conflicts around questions of material production, such as control over the forces of production, the organization of the labor process and other economic issues.

In post-industrial societies investment is made at the level of production management, and class domination is based on the monopoly over the supply and processing of data and on the control of the ways of organizing social life and the production of meaning. Hence, the central conflicts of post-industrial societies are no longer over political rights or material concerns, but rather over the 'production of symbolic goods' – in other words, over the appropriation of historicity (Touraine, 1985: 774). The central actors engaged in these struggles are those who control the production of meaning, the technocrats, and those who resist it and struggle for the collective reappropriation of historicity (Touraine, 1981: 62; Cohen, 1982: 219).

In contrast to other NSM theorists (who argue for dispersion and plurality in contemporary social conflicts), Touraine proposes that in any society there is a central conflict, and that the 'greater the diversity of struggles, the more each society is animated by a single social movement for each social class' (Touraine, 1981: 94). The term 'social movement,' indeed, must be reserved for these 'truly central conflicts' which call into question the social control over historicity (1988: 26). Touraine's use of the concept of social class is designed to stress the centrality of certain conflicts and the consequent division of society into two opposing camps. While retaining the basic language of class theory, however, Touraine transforms the reductionist meaning given to it by Marxism. Classes are not defined in reference to position at the level of production, but rather by being in a position of dependency or domination *vis-à-vis* the appropriation of historicity. Thus he expands the concept of class conflict to include the question of control over cultural models (Arnason, 1986: 144).

From Touraine's perspective, a social movement is, therefore, the action of a subject calling into question the social form of historicity (Touraine, 1988: 68). If historicity is the set of cultural models (cognitive, ethical, economic), SMs are the groups that 'contend in order to give these cultural orientations a social form,' to transform them into concrete forms of social organization (42). This is why SMs are central to the functioning of society and to the process through which it is created (Cohen, 1982: 213). They are 'the fabric of social life' (Touraine, 1981: 94).

Touraine makes a sharp analytical separation between the diachronic and synchronic axes of a social system, or between its pattern of development and its mode of functioning. Changes from one societal type to another, system contradictions, revolutions, development and steering mechanisms are located at the diachronic level. Touraine argues that the transition from one societal type to another – which implies a radical break with the logic of the existing social system – requires an agent and a logic of action from outside the system. Such an agent, Touraine explains, can only be the state (1981: 104). The state, therefore, is the central actor at the diachronic level and becomes the 'central agent of development' (117). The functioning of a social system – the self-production of its historicity – is located at the synchronic level (104). It includes the conflictual generation of norms, social institutions and cultural patterns. Touraine argues, like Habermas, that this is the terrain where SMs operate. The state is marginal at this level because it is located along a different axis. Thus, while SMs deal with the production of meaning at the synchronic level, other actors deal with politics and the state at the diachronic level.

Decentered subjects and political articulation

In contrast to Touraine's view, which sharply separates the social from the political, Laclau and Mouffe assert the primacy of political articulation and the broadening of politics. For them, the unity of a social formation results from the contingent and open process of political articulation (Laclau and Mouffe, 1985: 76–7; Laclau, 1981: 45). Identities and interests do not have a pre-discursive existence; nor do they derive their unity from a single economic logic (Laclau and Mouffe, 1985: 90).

Laclau and Mouffe suggest that social agents are 'essentially decentred' (that is, they do not possess an essential unity), given that they are the locus of multiple subject positions 'corresponding both to the different social relations in which the individual is inserted and to the discourses that constitute these relations' (90). Because the identity of these agents is contingent upon political processes, it can be nothing more than an 'unstable articulation of constantly changing positionalities' (Laclau, 1983: 23). For Laclau and Mouffe, hegemony is the process of discursive construction of social agents. But hegemonic practices can never fully fix these identities because the social, by its very nature, is always 'open.' Since each subject position has the potential for multiple constructions, the subjectivity of every subject position will always be provisionally fixed (Laclau and Mouffe, 1985: 86–7).

Laclau and Mouffe explain the emergence of new social movements in reference to the availability of the democratic discourse and the consolidation of a new hegemonic formation following the end of the Second World War. According to them, 'the democratic revolution' that began with the French Revolution of 1789 made possible the proliferation of new antagonisms by extending the democratic principles of liberty and equality to new areas of social life. This democratic revolution constructed individuals and groups as subjects in a democratic tradition, placing the values of equality and liberty at the center of social life. The 'subversive power' of the democratic discourse was to spread these values into increasingly wider areas of social life. Hence, the availability of the democratic discourse permitted the emergence of collective actors who challenged the view of society as a natural and rigid hierarchical system of differential positions.

The significance of the democratic revolution to explaining the origins of social movements becomes clearer when Laclau and Mouffe introduce the analytical distinction between relations of subordination and relations of oppression. The former refers to a situation where an agent is subjected to decisions of others without questioning the power relation; relations of oppression refers to a condition where the agent challenges these relations of subordination, turning them into sites of antagonism (1985: 153–4). What are the conditions whereby a relation of subordination constitutes itself as the site of an antagonism, thus giving rise to a social movement? Laclau and Mouffe suggest that an antagonism may emerge when the identity of a given subject is negated by other discursive practices. This negation of subjectivity could take two forms: one, negation of rights, when acquired rights are called into question; two, contradictory interpellation, when, as a result of social transformations, certain social relations which previously had not been constructed as relations of subordination begin to be constructed as such (Mouffe, 1988: 94; Laclau and Mouffe, 1985: 159).

Laclau and Mouffe also link the rise of SMs to structural transformations. They view them as responses to antagonisms which developed with the consolidation of a 'new hegemonic formation' after the Second World War.[2] The new formation brought about fundamental changes in production, in the nature of the state and in culture, which resulted in an increased *commodification, bureaucratization* and *massification* of social life. Unlike Offe, they argue that there is an increased commodification of social life resulting from the penetration of capitalist relations into wider spheres of social life (Laclau and Mouffe, 1985: 160–61; Mouffe, 1988: 92). Changes in the labor process brought about by 'scientific management' led to increased productivity and created the basis for the transformation of society into a big marketplace in which new 'needs' were constantly created and more and more products of human labor were transformed into commodities. The rise of the welfare state led to an increased bureaucratization of social relations and a deeper penetration, by the state, of a growing number of spheres of social life, thus blurring the distinction between the private and public spheres and giving rise to a variety of new areas of conflict. The process of massification of social life resulted from changes in the modes of cultural diffusion and the establishment of a mass culture presenting a homogeneous way of life and cultural pattern (Mouffe, 1984: 140–41; Laclau and Mouffe, 1985: 163–4).

Social movements as discontinuity

In spite of the wide array of theoretical propositions among them, NSM theorists converge in their emphasis on rupture and discontinuity when comparing the new movements with traditional struggles and collective actors. These new actors are said to be at the center of contemporary conflicts, to raise new issues, to be the carriers of new values, to operate in new terrains, to employ new modes of action and to have new organizational forms.

The first aspect of rupture with traditional collective actors is that in contemporary struggles the contending actors do not constitute fundamental (economic) social classes; instead they are aggregates of various social groups whose identity is not defined by their place in the process of production or with reference to traditional ideologies of left, right and center. As Offe puts it, 'the universe of political conflict is coded in categories taken from the movement's issues: gender, sexual orientation, locality, etc.' (Offe, 1985: 831).

Discontinuity with previous struggles is also seen in the issues and values raised by the new movements. NSM theorists stress that the new actors struggle for collective control over the process of meaning-production and are primarily concerned with symbolic issues and the constitution of new identities. In contrast to traditional actors, political parties and trade unions – which operate at the strategic-instrumental level of action and are concerned with material reproduction and distri-bution – the new movements operate at the communicative level of action and are concerned with cultural reproduction, social integration and socialization (Cohen, 1983: 106; Habermas, 1981: 33). They fight for the right to realize their own identity, for 'the possibility of disposing of their personal creativity, their affective life, and their biological and interpersonal experience' (Melucci, 1980: 218). They are struggles for 'the reappropri-ation of time, of space, and of relationships in the individual's daily experience' (219).

The movements raise a wide array of issues: the eradication of discrimi-nation and oppression, the rejection of traditional roles (worker, consumer, client of public services and citizen), the reappropriation of physical space (neighborhood, locality, the city), the cultural and practical redefinition of our relationship with nature (environment, consumerism, productivism) and the constitution of new identities (based on gender, age, locality, ethnicity, sexual orientation). They advocate the values of equality and participation, autonomy of the individual, democracy, plurality and differ-ence, rejection of manipulation, regulation and bureaucratization. One effect of bringing to public discussion issues which were previously con-sidered private – like sexual orientation, interpersonal relations, biological identity, family relations – has been to blur the traditional lines of demarcation between the public and private spheres (Offe, 1985: 817; Melucci, 1980: 219; Laclau and Mouffe, 1985).

Another sign of rupture with traditional conflicts is observed in the field of action of contemporary collective actors. NSM theorists point out that the creation of new meanings and the reinterpretation of norms and values take place at the level of social integration, not at the level of steering mechanisms (the state). Thus, they argue, the field of social conflict has shifted from the political sphere to civil society and the cultural realm (Touraine, 1985; Melucci, 1985: 789). They say that new movements are transforming civil society by creating 'new spaces, new solidarities and new democratic forms' (Cohen, 1983: 106). It is in the context of these 'liberated' spaces, where alternative norms and values guide social interaction, that new identities and solidarities are formed. This reasoning resembles Gramsci's discussion about the need to move from a war of maneuver to a war of position. In this case the new spaces would be the new trenches that Gramsci said had to be conquered and secured in the process of building a counter-hegemonic project.

There are differences, however, in how each theorist assesses the linkages between the new movements and the political system. Touraine places SMs at the level of civil society (social integration) and excludes them from the political realm (system integration). Movements operating at the political level are not SMs proper: they are either historical movements (fighting for historical change) or struggles operating, according to him, at lower levels of social action (politico-institutional). Laclau and Mouffe, in contrast, argue that the multiple points of antagonism that have emerged have led to the expansion of the political through the proliferation of political spaces. As social conflict expands into new areas of social life, the field of politics is enlarged (Mouffe, 1988: 96). These new movements, they explain, are contesting the state's redefinition of the public and private spheres and thus transforming private issues into political issues (Mouffe, 1985: 161–3; 1988: 93).

Other theorists (Habermas, 1981; Offe, 1985; Melucci, 1985) place SMs in an intermediary space between civil society and the state. For Habermas they operate in a sub-institutional, extra-parliamentary terrain located at the 'seam between system and life world' (Habermas, 1981: 36). Offe argues that the new movements challenge 'the boundaries of institutional politics' by tearing down the traditional dichotomies between private and public life, institutional and non-institutional action, political and civil society. In doing so they politicize civil society 'through practices that belong to an intermediate sphere between "private" pursuits and concerns, on the one side, and institutional, state-sanctioned modes of politics, on the other' (Offe, 1985: 820). The actions of SMs, Offe argues, politicize civil society but in ways that do not reproduce existing forms of control, regulation and state intervention.[3] Melucci also refers to an 'intermediate public space' where SMs make society hear their messages and where these messages enter the process of political articulation. The movements, however, retain their autonomy: they are not institutionalized; nor do they become political parties. All they seek is control of a field of autonomy *vis-à-vis* the political system (Melucci, 1985: 815; 1980: 220).

The organizational structures of NSMs are said to have features different from those of traditional collective actors. While most NSM theorists tend to neglect the organizational dimension of SMs, Melucci argues that movements do not exist only in their cultural dimension: they also assume organizational forms (Melucci, 1985: 813). But these forms are different from traditional formal organizations. They are loosely articulated networks of participatory democratic organizations permitting multiple membership and part-time or short-term participation and demanding personal involvement both inside and outside the organization. These organizational forms and modes of action de-emphasize other traditional dichotomies, such as the distinction between leaders and led, members and non-members, private and public roles, means and ends, instrumental and expressive action (Offe, 1985: 830; Melucci, 1985). The distinction between leaders and led is undermined by a strong emphasis on democratic participatory structures, the absence of elected officials for regular intervals, and minimal organizational bureaucracy (Melucci, 1980). Limited formal requirements for membership allow for a loose definition of who belongs to the movement. Since participants are expected to 'practise' what the movement 'preaches' in their day-to-day life, the distinction between private and public roles is also diffused.

NSM organizations are not instrumental in the sense that they are not conceived as means to achieve broader political goals: they make no clear distinction between the movement's goals and means. Thus the distinction between instrumental and expressive action ceases to be relevant. The organization is itself an integral component of the message. Melucci explains that, since 'the action is focused on cultural codes, the form of the movement is a message, a symbolic challenge to the dominant patterns' (Melucci, 1985: 801). In other words, 'the medium … is the message' (801). The movements challenge established cultural codes and show, by the things they do and how they do them, that an alternative is possible (812). This makes the categories of success or failure inappropriate for assessing the impact of SMs, because their very existence is a gain in itself (813).

Assessment of the NSM paradigm

The NSM perspective presents a non-reductionist approach to the study of modern societies, offering important insights into the nature of contemporary social conflicts. By moving beyond economic and class reductionism, the new perspective can identify new sources of conflict that give rise to new actors. The emphasis on processes of constitution of new identities and on the novelty of some features of contemporary movements has allowed NSM theorists to underline the degree to which these movements represent a break with past traditions.

The strength of Offe's model is that it explains the 'crisis of crisis management' in reference to structural factors and political and cultural processes. Offe highlights the politically mediated nature of social relations, including economic ones, and offers a non-reductionist approach to the constitution of conflicts and identities in modern societies. Steering mechanisms (the state) are presented as sources of power and conflict, and not as mere epiphenomena of the economic base. New actors emerge, therefore, as a result of the growing intervention of steering mechanisms in regulating economic and social life. In consequence, their identity is constituted in the intersection between the state and civil society.

Laclau and Mouffe's analysis focuses on the process of constitution of new identities. By reformulating the concept of hegemony, they highlight the open, contingent and relational nature of social identities. In explaining the rise of NSMs they point to the emergence of new antagonisms created by the new hegemonic formation consolidated after the Second World War. The new conditions are given by a reorganization of the production process and the expansion of capitalism into wider areas of social life, the emergence of a new type of state and new mass culture, plus the availability of the democratic discourse. As a result, the field of social conflict is enlarged, and multiple new sources of social antagonisms give rise to a multiplicity of social movements.

Touraine's action theory attempts to rescue the subject from all forms of reductionism and seeks to achieve a balance between structure and actor. Post-industrial society, with new technology and increased reflexivity, gives rise to new conflicts and actors. His emphasis on the functioning of society (the synchronic dimension) and on normative contestation highlights the significance of the new movements. The emergence of new actors struggling over non-economic, non-political themes demonstrates the increased reflexivity of post-industrial society regarding the social construction of reality. There are, however, five important shortcomings in this approach.

First, NSM theory offers an incomplete account of the origins of SMs and neglects to identify all the processes which intervene in the passage from 'condition' to 'action.' It explains the meaning of SMs in reference to structural, historical, political and ideological processes, but it does not integrate into its analysis the strategic-instrumental dimension of social action – that is, the processes by which individuals and groups make decisions, develop strategies and mobilize resources. The emphasis on identity comes at the expense of considering strategic questions. It is assumed that a given social group develops an identity first, and only subsequently engages in strategic-instrumental action. NSM theorists study only the first stage, which they consider to be the most important. This stage conception of the development of SMs and group identity is flawed. Identity develops only in the process of interaction with other social forces, and organizational and strategic concerns are an integral part of it. It is simplistic to see these two levels as sequential.

Offe's powerful analysis, for example, limits itself to identifying the 'structural potential' for SMs by focusing on how structural transformations and political intervention create the conditions for the rise of new actors. Laclau and Mouffe rightly suggest that the transition from condition to action is not explained by structural potential or by the condition of subordination itself. Yet, is the existence of the democratic discourse a sufficient condition for the emergence of new forms of collective action? Reference to the democratic imaginary alone cannot explain why the new movements emerged during the 1960s and not before. Moreover, in their effort to emphasize the openness of the social they fail to point out that the constitution of social agents is not an arbitrary process. Shared experiences, imposed by structural conditions, set limits to the possible group identities that might emerge. This neglect of extra-discursive elements leads Laclau and Mouffe to replace economic and class reductionism with 'discourse reductionism' (Assies, 1990: 57). Yet, when it comes down to explaining the rise of the new movements, they are forced to refer to (new) structural conditions: the expansion of capitalism and the welfare state.

In assessing Touraine's analysis of the origins of SMs the circularity in his argument is clear: on the one hand, NSMs are new actors because they express new conflicts corresponding to a new societal type – that is, post-industrial society; on the other hand, post-industrial society is new because it has led to the rise of new collective actors who fight over historicity (Cohen, 1985: 702). Moreover, Touraine's sharp distinction between synchrony and diachrony prevents him from addressing the dynamics of mobilization, in which collective actors emerge (or fail to do so) as a result of decisions, strategies, organizational structures and changes in the opportunities for collective action. By placing structural factors, system change and the state on another axis, he only displaces this strategic-instrumental component of social action to another level. SMs are left, by definition, without any instrumental or political dimension. The question of the relationship between actor and structure does not find an adequate solution (Cohen, 1982: 216).

Second, the various definitions of NSMs are based on a radical, and untenable, opposition between SMs and politics, civil society and state. This results from an exclusive focus on the cultural aspects of the new movements and on the proposition that civil society is the only arena for SM activity. This way of defining social movements has stripped them away from their political dimension. It has also inhibited NSM theorists from exploring the connection between civil society and the state, and between SMs and political reform. Thus NSM theory cannot explain the processes and the mechanisms that intervene in the institutionalization (or the absence of institutionalization) of the new values and social practices that NSMs are said to be developing within civil society.

Laclau and Mouffe, for example, insist that every new social conflict is political, as politics expand to civil society, but fail to discuss the institutional aspects of politics, the relationship between NSMs and political parties, and the institutional process through which the democratization of the state can be achieved. Such separation between SMs and the political system can potentially contribute to the de-politicizing of SMs. This is most ironic, given that the purpose of their argument is to demonstrate the expansion of the political. Likewise, Touraine's radical oppositions (diachrony versus synchrony, pattern of development versus mode of functioning, state versus civil society, organizational and institutional levels versus historicity, historical movements and struggles versus social movements) fail to realize that SMs are more than cultural phenomena: they are also struggles for institutional reform. In other words, Touraine focuses on normative contestation, but excludes from his analysis what is actually institutionalized.[4]

Third, NSM theory has tended to ignore the organizational dimension of SMs. NSM theorists have little to say about organizational dynamics, leadership, recruitment processes, goal displacement, and so on. Given their emphasis on discontinuity (de-differentiation of roles, participatory democracy, etc.) no attempt has been made to compare SM organizations with more formal organizations and to apply organizational theory to the study of SMs.

Fourth, NSM theory does not explore all aspects of continuity between the new and the old actors in terms of their modes of action, organizational structures and their relationship with political institutions. A closer examination shows that the rupture is not as radical as some suggest. Thus it is perhaps more appropriate to replace the term 'new SMs' with 'contemporary SMs,' as suggested by Cohen (1983).

Touraine's sharp separation between struggles over civil and political rights, material production, and historicity, which is said to characterize each societal type, cannot easily be found in practice. Isn't the common denominator of these struggles, old and new alike, that they seek to democratize political, economic and social life? Labor struggles of the past were not restricted to redistributional questions. They were also struggles for the constitution of new collective identities (Thompson, 1975).

Other NSM theorists, however, explore the question of continuity. For Laclau and Mouffe, contemporary SMs contain aspects of continuity and discontinuity. Continuity is provided by the permanence of the egalitarian imaginary which links the struggles of the nineteenth century with those of contemporary SMs. There is discontinuity because SMs extend the democratic revolution to new social relations by challenging the new forms of subordination created by the new hegemonic formation. Offe argues that what is least new in contemporary SMs is their values. According to him, there is a growing awareness of the contradictions that exist within the modern set of values, but this does not lead to a rejection of these *in toto*. Rather, some values are emphasized over others. SMs, therefore, do not represent a value change but a selective radicalization of these values and a change in their mode of implementation (Laclau and Moufe, 1985: 849–54).

Fifth, the emphasis on theorizing the 'why' of SMs has come at the expense of empirical studies (Touraine being an exception). Most NSM theorists have concentrated on developing general theoretical postulates on NSMs but have neglected the micro-contexts where these movements operate. More empirical studies can help to show the wide variety of forms and orientations displayed by contemporary SMs. More comparative studies, across Eastern and Western Europe, between Europe and North America, could offer new insights.

In summary, the strength of NSM theory is in identifying long-term transformations that create new conditions – structural, political, cultural – which affect the potential for the emergence of SMs. Its central contribution is to stress the cultural dimension of these movements, as processes of constitution of new subjects and new identities, and to identify the newness of contemporary movements. As we have already mentioned, Melucci argues that this paradigm is oriented to explaining the 'why' of SMs, at least in so far as the answer is restricted to broad structural conditions and does not include how the actors mobilize resources. It does not, however, explain the 'how' of SMs; that is, how strategies, decisions, resources, opportunities and other factors converge to give rise to an SM. NSM theory excludes from its analysis the dynamics of mobilization, the instrumental level of action, political action, the relationship between SMs, political reform and institutionalization of civil society and organizational dynamics. These are precisely the aspects in which RM theory is strongest.

Resource Mobilization Theory: Its Explanation of the Emergence of Social Movements

While NSM theory explains the origins of social movements with reference to macro-processes and identifies the structural potential for social movement activity, RM theory, in contrast, focuses on a set of contextual processes (resource management decisions, organizational dynamics and political changes) that condition the realization of this structural potential. It takes the issues, the actors and the constraints as given, and focuses instead on how the actors develop strategies and interact with their environment in order to pursue their interests. RM theory, therefore, employs a 'purposive model' of social action and explains social movements in reference to the strategic-instrumental level of action (Tilly, 1985: 740–41; 1978: 228–31). The emergence of social movements, and the outcomes of their actions, are treated as contingent, open processes resulting from specific decisions, tactics and strategies adopted by the actors within a context of power relations and conflictual interaction.

There are two main approaches within RM theory: the 'political-interactive' model (Tilly, Gamson, Oberschall, McAdam) and the 'organizational-entrepreneurial' model (McCarthy and Zald). The first employs a political model to examine the processes that give rise to social movements. It focuses on changes in the structure of opportunities for collective action and on the role of pre-existing networks and horizontal links within the aggrieved group. It examines issues of political power, interests, political resources, group solidarity, and so on. The second model focuses on organizational dynamics, leadership and resource management. It applies economic and organizational theories to the study of social movements and, metaphorically, makes reference to such concepts as social movement industry, resource competition, product differentiation, issue elasticity, packaging, social movement entrepreneurs, social movement organizations, and so on. (Perrow, 1977: 201). Organizational theory has been applied as researchers in this tradition argue that formal organizations act as carriers of social movements (Zald and McCarthy, 1987: 12). Researchers have focused on two aspects of organizational analysis: the interaction of social movement organizations with their environment, and the organizational infrastructure which supports social movement activity (Gamson, 1987: 2–4).

RM theorists argue that affluence and prosperity tend to foster SM activity. Prosperous societies generate a number of resources (such as means of communication, money, intellectual classes) that can aid SM mobilization (McCarthy and Zald, 1973; 1977b). These societies also open opportunities for 'grievance entrepreneurs' to develop and market new SM 'products.' Affluent societies also give rise to 'conscience constituents' who donate resources to SMs (McCarthy and Zald, 1973; McAdam et al., 1988: 702–3). The growth of the welfare state is also identified as a source of increased social movement activity. Yet, while NSM theory refers to the penetration of the life world by steering mechanisms, RM theorists argue that state agencies facilitate mobilization by providing resources to grassroots organizations (money, manpower, facilities) through community development programs.

The dynamics of mobilization

Resource mobilization theory focuses on how groups organize to pursue their ends by mobilizing and managing resources. A 'resource management' perspective views resources as being permanently created, consumed, transferred and lost (Oberschall, 1973: 28). Social conflict, therefore, is conceived as the struggle for the appropriation of existing resources and the creation of new ones. Resources can be of a material or non-material nature: the former include money, organizational facilities, manpower, means of communication, etc.; the latter include legitimacy, loyalty, authority, moral commitment, solidarity, etc. (Jenkins, 1981: 117).[5] Mobilization is the process by which a group assembles resources (material and/or non-material) and places them under collective control for the explicit purpose of pursuing the group's interests through collective action. But mobilization is more than resource accumulation; for mobilization to take place, these resources must be placed under collective control and must be employed for the purpose of pursuing group goals. As Tilly explains, without mobilization 'a group may prosper, but it cannot contend for power [since] contending for power means employing mobilized resources to influence other groups' (Tilly, 1978: 78). According to RM theory, four central factors condition the process of mobilization: organization, leadership, political opportunity and the nature of political institutions.

Organization and leadership

Oberschall (1973) argues that social networks providing group coherence and strong horizontal links are key facilitators of collective action. These links promote the development of group identity and group solidarity. They also foster communication and encourage the development of organizational skills and leadership experience. In other words, they facilitate mobilization by providing precarious organizational bases from which more complex forms of organization can develop. It has been argued that these semi-informal networks, or 'micro-mobilization contexts,' provide the linkages between the micro- and macro-levels of group formation, and constitute the basic 'cell structure' of collective action (McAdam et al., 1988: 711).[6]

RM theory stresses the importance of leadership in the emergence of SMs. Leaders identify and define grievances, develop a group sense, devise strategies and facilitate mobilization by reducing its costs and taking advantages of opportunities for collective action. While RM theorists agree that outside leaders will tend to play a central role in mobilizing groups with low organization, power and resources, they disagree in their assessment of the relative role of leaders and masses in initiating mobilization and sustaining SM activity. For instance, McCarthy and Zald (1973) argue for the centrality of leaders and suggest that in many cases leadership availability takes precedence over grievances in facilitating SM mobilization. They even argue that issues and grievances may be manufactured by 'issue entrepreneurs' (1977b: 1215). Gerlach and Hine (1970) say that the masses play a more fundamental role than leadership availability in the emergence of social movements. Freeman (1983: 26) argues that the relative weight of leaders and masses will vary from case to case.

The structure of political opportunities

Resource mobilization theorists point out that opportunities for collective action come and go. The challenge for social movements is to identify and seize opportunities for action. This implies a cost–benefit assessment of the likelihood of success, given their evaluation of the possible outcomes of their actions and the responses of their adversaries as well as those of their allies. In their day-to-day activities, collective actors develop strategies, make tactical decisions, form new alliances and dismantle old ones. But the environment in which social movements operate is not passive: it is composed of social forces which are actively trying to influence, control or destroy the social movement (Gamson, 1987: 2). This means that the outcomes of their interventions in the social and political fields face 'considerable uncertainty' (Oberschall, 1973: 158).

The structure of political opportunities refers to the conditions in the political system which either facilitate or inhibit collective action. Political and cultural traditions, for example, will determine the range of legitimate forms of struggle in a given society. The degree to which civil liberties and individual rights are respected in a given society will also facilitate or inhibit collective action. But repression and facilitation are not determined unilaterally by sympathizers or enemies of social movements: they are the result of conflictual interaction and political struggle. According to Tilly, many of the changes in the patterns of collective action result from drastic changes in the structure of repression–facilitation. He also argues that the *scale* of the action and the *power* of the aggrieved group will determine the degree to which these actions will face repression and/or facilitation. In general terms, the broader the scale of the action and the less powerful the group the more likely it will suffer repression (Tilly, 1978: 115).

The nature of the political system

Tilly's work has focused primarily on the political sphere and the mobilization of political resources. He views collective actions as efforts by new
groups ('challengers') to enter the political system (Tilly, 1978: 52). He
explains that the relative openness of the political system to incorporating
the interests of new groups will affect the emergence of SMs. Tilly's
model has proved useful for historical studies and could be applied to
contemporary exclusionary political systems. It is, however, less germane
to the study of modern SMs. Participants in these movements are not
challengers in Tilly's terms, because they come from well-integrated social
groups that are already members of the polity. What they seek is not
entry into the polity but access to decision-making spheres to influence
policy-making.

By drawing attention to the nature of political structures at the national
and local levels, RM theorists have assessed the differential potential for
SM activity among industrial societies, in contrast with NSM writers who
seem to assume a certain similarity of conditions and SMs across industrial
(or post-industrial) societies. Ash-Garner and Zald (1987) suggest that
the emergence and nature of SMs are conditioned by the size of the
public sector, the degree of centralization of the state and governmental
structures, and the nature of existing political parties.

The relative size of the public sector will influence SM activity in at
least two fundamental ways. First, a large public sector places resources
(employment and/or grants and social action programs) in the hands of
the state; these resources can then be used to co-opt, neutralize or destroy
SMs, and/or to promote SM activity by channeling resources to grassroots organizations. Second, the size of the public sector determines the
potential politicization of issues and the legitimacy of various courses of
action available to SMs. Societies with less interventionist states with
smaller public sectors are more likely to have more autonomous and less
politicized SMs (Ash-Garner and Zald, 1987: 311).

Ash-Garner and Zald also suggest that the greater the spatial and
functional decentralization of a given political system, the more likely it
is that SMs can be effective and autonomous (310). For instance, SMs
can more effectively press for their demands at the local or regional
level in countries with powerful local or regional governments. Similarly,
the effectiveness of SMs will be increased in those political systems
which provide some degree of autonomy to various branches of government. In these cases, the target of mobilization can be more clearly
identified, as SMs make demands to specific branches of government.

Political systems that most encourage SM activity are those with multiclass parties, with diffuse ideological views and weak party discipline, representing large combinations of interest groups (312). This type of political structure is found, primarily, in societies with a low degree of political polarization along class lines. In highly polarized societies, by contrast, political parties take a central role in mediation, thus reducing the space for SM activity. These features also influence the degree of SM autonomy. In societies where political parties do not tightly control the elaboration and transmission of demands, SMs tend to enjoy a high degree of autonomy in their membership, strategies, and policy decisions, and in the selection of channels to place their demands in. In contrast, in societies which are highly politicized and mobilized by parties and corporatist groups, SMs tend to be aligned along party lines and enjoy limited autonomy from the political system (295).

Social movements as continuity

In contrast with NSM theory, which focuses on social integration, normative contestation, control of cultural production and expressive action (constitution of new identities), RM addresses themes of system integration, political processes and instrumental action. While the NSM paradigm concentrates on discontinuity by highlighting the 'newness' of SMs, resource mobilization focuses on continuity in organizational forms and action.

For Tilly, contemporary social movements are no different, in the form and content of their actions, from early-nineteenth century collective actors, since they both employ the same 'repertoires' – that is, the limited range of legitimate actions available to collective actors. The consolidation of capitalism and the growth of the national state in the early nineteenth century caused a shift from communal to associational forms of collective action. The emphasis on democratic freedoms (to assemble, to speak, to demonstrate, to organize) encouraged the creation of special-purpose organizations and voluntary associations and the consolidation of civil society. These transformations gave rise to the forms of collective action that characterize representative democracies: rallies, strikes and demonstrations (Tilly and Tilly, 1981: 19–23; 44–6 and 99–101; Tilly, 1978: 151–71).[7] In contrast to European collective protests in the eighteenth century, collective struggles in the nineteenth century became proactive as they sought access to new rights or resources (Tilly, 1978: 143–51). According to Tilly, these basic features and repertoires still characterize collective action.

Organizational dynamics

The emphasis on continuity has directed RM theorists to explore similarities between SMs and formal organizations. The foundations for this line of research were provided by Zald and Ash (1966), McCarthy and Zald (1973, 1977a, 1977b) and Zald and McCarthy (1987). By applying theories of formal organizations to the study of SMs they have exposed the wide variety of organizational arrangements that modern SMs have developed. They suggest that the development of democratic-participatory organizational forms, which is almost taken for granted by NSM theory, is only one possible outcome among many. The main variables that affect the organizational structures of SMs are the following: the nature of the movement and of its goals (expressive/instrumental, single/multiple issue), the type of recruitment process (individual or bloc), the role of leaders in the formative stages, and the influence of third parties.

McCarthy and Zald distinguish between SM and social movement organization (SMO), or preference for change and organized action for change. A social movement is 'a set of opinions and beliefs in a population which represents preferences for changing some elements of the social structure and/or reward distribution of a society' (McCarthy and Zald, 1977b: 1217–18). A social movement organization is the 'complex, or formal organization which identifies its goals with the preferences of a social movement ... and attempts to implement these goals' (1218). They suggest that SMs are never 'fully' mobilized, because those holding opinions and beliefs favouring change will always outnumber those who participate in SM activities and SMOs. They argue that, in most cases, formal or complex SMOs will become the carriers of SMs, as informal networks (so essential in the formative stages) cannot co-ordinate the complex challenges facing SMs after their emergence. Thus the task of determining the movement's goals and program, strategy and tactics, will tend to be carried out by formal SMOs.

McCarthy and Zald (1973) argue that the more typical contemporary SMO is formally structured, with centralized, hierarchical structures and a clear division of labor and roles, and that the trend of SMs (in the United States) is towards greater professionalization of structures and leadership. 'Classical SMOs,' they explained, had part time, volunteer indigenous leadership and membership. In contrast, present-day SMOs are 'professional SMOs' because they rely on a small group of full-time leaders, 'social movement entrepreneurs,' who usually do not belong to the aggrieved group. These leaders are professionals from the new middle class who possess the necessary skills to lead SMs in contemporary 'organizational societies': they know how to deal with the state; they can create images and symbols and handle the communications media.[8]

The nature and goals of the SM will affect organizational forms and leadership structures. Zald and Ash (1966) argue that different tasks demand different types of organizational structures. Centralized structures can be more effective for institutional change, but have more difficulty in promoting grassroots participation. Decentralized structures can obtain more membership involvement, greater satisfaction and group maintenance, but will tend to score low in strategic-goal attainment (329). Instrumental movements seeking to achieve short-term goals will tend to develop centralized, hierarchical organizations possessing a clear division of labor and roles. In this case, organizational survival will not be a concern, beyond obtaining the movement's goals, and all resources will be invested in goal-attainment. Expressive movements seeking attitudinal and value transformations and the re-creation of collective identities will tend to have long-term goals and emphasize organizational survival. In this case, the SM will develop decentralized, segmented and reticulate organizational structures with a vaguely defined division of labor and roles (Freeman, 1983: 204).

According to Oberschall (1973), organizational structure is also determined by the nature of the recruitment process to collective actions. 'Bloc recruitment' (the integration of whole organizations into the group seeking collective action) will be more typical among constituencies possessing strong organizational networks (Oberschall, 1973: 125).[9] In this case, each organization will bring into the movement its own leadership structures and resources. As various types of leadership coexist within the same SMO, they will establish a number of checks and balances, and consequently the organizational structures will tend to be more democratic and decentralized. 'Individual recruitment' will be more typical when pre-existing organization is weak or non-existent. In this case, individual leaders will play a central role in the formative phases, and consequently the organizational structure will tend to be more hierarchical and centralized.

Resource mobilization theorists warn that the goals, strategies and actions of SMOs are not always those of the social movement as a whole. Several studies have found discrepancies between the leaders' beliefs and motivations and those of SMOs' rank and file. Jenkins warns that because SMOs enjoy relative autonomy from the movement's membership, 'the convergence between SMO program and membership interests ... should be assumed to be problematic' (Jenkins, 1981: 126). Furthermore, SMs are 'rarely unified affairs' because they are integrated by diverse SMOs pursuing different goals and employing different tactics. Possibly these SMOs can engage in 'all-out war against each other' as they compete for limited resources and support (Zald and McCarthy, 1987: 161). Common interest, therefore, does not necessarily lead to co-operation.

Endogenous factors alone cannot account for the rise of SMs. RM theorists also assess the role of outside forces, or third parties, in the development of SMs. McCarthy and Zald argue that 'conscience constituents' (individuals and groups who share the movement's goals and donate resources, but who do not stand to benefit directly from goal-attainment) play a central role (McCarthy and Zald, 1977b: 1221). The flow of resources from these sectors to SMOs is of crucial importance in the process of mobilization, especially in cases where the aggrieved group comes from the lower end of the social ladder (Oberschall, 1973: 159).

Assessment of the RM paradigm

The main contribution of RM theory is to explain the dynamics of mobilization, to identify the type of resources and organizational features that condition the activities of SMs, and to focus on the relationship between the movements and the political system. By focusing on resource management, tactics and strategy, it calls attention to the importance of strategic-instrumental action. It examines a level of social action where the actors' decisions affect the outcomes of conflicts, and influence the future and the effectiveness of SMs. By focusing on social networks, organizational dynamics and political processes, it successfully identifies elements of continuity among contemporary collective actors. As mentioned earlier, Melucci argues that this approach is useful to explain the 'how' of social movements; that is, how strategies, decisions and resources are combined to determine the emergence of an SM.

McCarthy and Zald's useful distinction between SMs and SMOs permits us to examine the organizational dynamics of social movements by applying organizational theory. Their analysis of the role of SM 'entrepreneurs' and the trend towards 'professionalization' highlights tendencies in SMs that remain unexplored in NSM literature. By taking into consideration strategic-instrumental action, they can argue that the search for effectiveness (at this level of action) can undermine potential democratic-participatory tendencies. Thus, the degree to which SMs develop democratic structures – something taken for granted by NSM theorists – becomes a contingent matter.

The emphasis on 'political processes' provides useful insights into the relationship between SMs and the political system. The focus on the 'structure of opportunities' makes it possible to identify a set of political factors that constrain or facilitate the emergence of SMs. Moreover, this approach makes it clear that SMs engage in politics, although sometimes employing 'different means,' and therefore the field of operation of SMs includes both civil society and the political system. RM theory sees social movements as political actors that operate side by side – sometimes in competition, sometimes in collaboration – with traditional political institutions, an aspect neglected in the NSM literature.

The usefulness of Oberschall's work is its focus on the relationship between social networks, group identity and solidarity, and collective action. It calls attention to the importance of shared experiences in the emergence of social groups and collective action. It also highlights the potential mobilizing role of tradition and organization in closely knit communities.

Resource mobilization theory has five basic weaknesses.

First, by focusing exclusively on rational-instrumental action and limiting the actions of SMs to the political realm, RM theory neglects the normative and symbolic dimensions of social action. SMs tend to be reduced to political protests. As Gamson points out, collective actors are presented as managers of resources in pursuit of common material interests, but their actions are devoid of cultural meaning (Gamson, 1987). Contemporary SMs are more than political actors pursuing economic goals and/or seeking to exchange goods in the political market and/or to gain entry into the polity. As NSM theory points out, they are concerned with control of symbolic production, the creation of meaning and the constitution of new identities.

Second, exclusive focus on the 'how' of social movements – on how strategies, decisions, resources and other elements converge to give rise to an SM – has been detrimental to explaining the 'why,' or the meaning, of collective action. Touraine has argued that by neglecting structural problems, RM defines actors by their strategies and not by the social relationships, especially power relationships, in which these actors are involved (Touraine, 1985: 769). Absent from this tradition are explanations of SMs by reference to systemic contradictory developments (such as the penetration of the life-world by steering mechanisms, crisis of legitimacy and/or of hegemonic formation, multiplication of points of antagonism, increased reflexivity, and so on.) This prevents RM theory from assessing the full significance and the stakes of contemporary conflicts.

Third, RM theory employs an individualistic conception of collective action and a restrictive view of rationality. It assumes that collective action is an aggregate of multiple individual decisions based on a cost–benefit assessment of the chances of success. But these individuals appear to be socially isolated and, as we explained, broader macro-processes are not taken into account. To be sure, the emphasis on rationality was a healthy antidote against collective behavior theory, which conceived collective action as irrational. Yet RM theory reduces the rationality of collective action to the ability to maximize the strategic accomplishment of interests in a given context. This narrow focus on rationality precludes any assessment of the advantages of collective action from a non-strategic standpoint. Only if one identifies 'solidarity and identity as goals of group formation, in addition to other goals, can one see that, with respect to these goals, collective action is costless. One cannot, however, simply add a consideration of solidarity, collective identity, consciousness, or ideology to the RM perspective without bursting its framework' (Cohen, 1985: 687).

Fourth, RM theory does not fully account for the passage from condition to action. RM theory cannot explain the processes of group formation and the origins of the organizational forms it presupposes; it fails to explain how a social category – an aggregate of people with shared characteristics – develops a sense of identity and become a social group. RM theory assumes that collective actors have common interests and focuses instead on the processes that hinder or facilitate collective action in pursuit of those interests. This conception is not very different from that of simplistic Marxism or relative deprivation theory. The processes of definition of common interest are not determined by objective conditions alone; interests are constituted and articulated through ideological discourses and therefore do not have a prior existence independent of the awareness of social actors.

Fifth, by placing so much emphasis on continuity, on political-institutional processes and instrumental action, RM theory misses the differences between the new movements and traditional collective actors. Similarly, it does not clearly define the distinction between SMs and interest groups, because these two categories are placed together as 'consumer movements,' or forms of goal-oriented action, in a pluralistic, organizational society. Tilly's discussion of 'challengers' and 'contenders' points out that what distinguishes SMs from interests groups is that the former lack institutionalized access to the political system. Yet even Tilly's work does not include the idea of SMs as collective actors struggling for control of historicity, operating in new terrains and developing new modes of action and organization.

The Two Paradigms

In spite of the existence of significant differences between the two paradigms, there are some important points of agreement. Both paradigms have criticized traditional theories of collective action and made SMs the object of their theorizing. These are no longer perceived as reflections of structural dislocations, economic crisis or class exploitation. Neither are they discussed as the irrational behaviour of anomic masses or the rational outcome of 'natural' laws. For both paradigms, SMs involve modes of action and organization which are specific to advanced industrial societies. Collective action is the normal form of contestation in modern pluralistic civil society, and participants are rational, well-integrated members of organizations. The two theories agree that the passage from condition to action cannot be explained by the objective conditions themselves, because these conditions are mediated by discursive practices, ideologies, political processes, or resource management.

Writers working within each tradition have begun to bridge the gap between the two approaches. Some NSM theorists, for example, have discussed the importance of the instrumental, goal-oriented dimension of social movements (Cohen, 1985; Melucci, 1985). Melucci has commented that RM theory opens up important theoretical space to explain how movements produce themselves. He also suggests that this theory has provided useful insights in the study of SMs with its 'intelligent and fruitful' application of organizational theory (Melucci, 1989: 193–4). Some writers in the RM tradition have recently emphasized discontinuity by linking the emergence of SMs with new features of contemporary capitalist societies (Zald and McCarthy, 1987: 294–304).[10]

Nevertheless, significant differences remain. Each paradigm, as we have seen, tends to stress the opposite features of social movements. These differences in emphasis can be summarized as follows:

Resource Mobilization	New Social Movement
Continuity	Discontinuity
System integration	Social integration
State	Civil society
Political realm	Cultural realm
Instrumental action	Expressive action

RM theory emphasizes continuity. It explains SMs in relation to resource management, organizational dynamics, political processes, strategies, social networks, and so on. It highlights the instrumental aspects of SMs as they address their demands to the state. SMs are said to seek transformations in the reward-distribution systems of modern societies, to operate at the political level, and to be concerned with system integration and strategic action.

NSM theory stresses discontinuity. It identifies the structural potential for collective action by focusing on macro-structural analysis, which explains modern society's increased capacity for self-production, the constitution of new identities around new points of antagonism, and crisis of legitimation. It emphasizes the expressive nature of SMs and points out that their field of action is civil society. They are concerned with cultural issues, symbolic production, normative contestation and social integration.

Studies from the two perspectives have shown the variety of forms, orientations and modes of action found within and across contemporary SMs, which indicates that the new movements should not be seen as unified and coherent actors. It is more useful to assume that ambiguity and contradiction will be integral features of contemporary collective actors and that aspects of the oppositions (polarities) presented above (continuity–discontinuity, system–social integration, state–civil society, political–cultural, instrumental–expressive) will coexist, sometimes in harmony, most often in conflict, within SMs. The specific mode of co-existence and the relative weight of each of these factors *vis-à-vis* its opposite vary across movements and can be determined only through careful empirical research.

Thus contemporary SMs, which are primarily concerned with social integration, also operate at the level of system integration. They deal with symbolic production and the constitution of new identities, but they also direct their demands to the state and political institutions. They do not deal exclusively with historicity, as Touraine suggests, because they also operate at the institutional and organizational levels. Thus they combine expressive and instrumental action and operate simultaneously at the cultural and political levels. Some organizational structures stress partici-patory democracy and de-differentiation of roles, but others will develop centralized organizations with clear division of labor and roles. SMs stress autonomy from traditional political actors, but they do not operate in isolation from political institutions, and from time to time they enter into alliances with traditional actors. The degree of autonomy they will obtain will vary from case to case. Hence, each SM possesses a specific combi-nation of new and traditional features and of continuity and discontinuity.

Given this ambiguous and contradictory nature, SMs can best be studied through a more eclectic approach that borrows from both new social movement and resource mobilization paradigms. The analysis must account for structural constraints and the range of possibilities available to SMs, but it must also examine how the actors interact with their environment, manage resources, and devise strategies in order to pursue their goals. SMs must be explained in reference to six factors operating at two distinct levels of analysis.

The first set of factors deals with *macro-processes*. At this level of analysis a theory of SMs must explain the following: first, the structural potential for SM activity, identifying systemic tensions, contradictions, and conflicts that can give rise to new actors; second, the nature of the political system and the relationship between the state and civil society, including such factors as political processes and changes in the structures of political opportunities; third, the processes through which collective identities are constituted and legitimized, including political and cultural traditions, common sense, ideology, and hegemonic practices.

The second set of factors refers to *micro-processes* and to factors that involve strategic-instrumental action. At this level of analysis the theory must explain: first, the dynamics of mobilization – resource management, strategies and tactics, the role of leaders, responses of adversaries and allies; second, organizational dynamics – the nature of recruitment processes, the role of leaders and of third parties, type of goals, and goal displacement; third, existing social networks – the nature of these networks, the degree to which they have helped the group develop new leaders, communication channels, and a sense of group identity.

Only a theory that takes these factors into account can provide an adequate explanation of SMs and explain the linkages between micro and macro, civil society and the state, instrumental and expressive action, politics and culture. Neither NSM nor RM theory can, on its own, address all of these six factors, which makes the argument to integrate the two approaches more compelling: NSM theory is better equipped to deal with the first set of factors, while RM theory can best explain the second set.

Notes

1. For a comparison of the two approaches, see Cohen (1985); Klandermans (1986); Melucci (1984); and Salman (1990). An earlier version of this chapter was published in 1991 as a working paper for the CERLAC community power project, and then, in a somewhat different version but under the same title, in Carroll (1992).

2. Mouffe defines a hegemonic formation as 'an ensemble of relatively stable social forms, the materialization of a social articulation in which different social relations react reciprocally either to provide each other with conditions of existence, or at least to neutralize the potentially destructive effects of certain social relations on the reproduction of other such relations' (Mouffe, 1988: 90).

3. A movement is political or has political significance only when it places two types of demands on other social and political actors: one, when it demands recognition of its means of action as legitimate; two, when it seeks to ensure its goals become binding for the wider community (Offe, 1985: 826–7).

4. Cohen (1982: 227) argues that SMs must address institutional questions if they are to have long-lasting effects. Civil society is more than a field of operation for SMs: it represents the institutionalization (as sets of rights) of certain associational forms and conventions for public life. The institutions of civil society

provide a normative framework that conditions the actions of the state and forces it to operate within legally defined spaces, sharing power with non-state elements, and controlled by political rights. Thus collectivities cannot build democratic forms without being bound by organizational and institutional imperatives. This is why any attempt to reconstitute social spaces without reference to further institutional reform would be politically naive and condemn social movements to political marginality.

5. Rogers (1974) differentiates between 'instrumental' and 'infra-resources'; Jenkins (1982) makes a distinction between 'power' and 'mobilizing' resources; Tilly (1978: 69) refers to 'land,' and 'technical expertise'; Freeman (1979: 172–5) distinguishes between 'tangible' and 'intangible or human' assets (see Jenkins, 1983: 533).

6. Micro-mobilization contexts are defined as 'any small group setting in which processes of collective attribution are combined with rudimentary forms of organization to produce mobilization for collective action' (McAdam et al., 1988: 709).

7. The eighteenth-century repertoire, in contrast, was composed of public festivals and rituals, assemblies of corporate groups, food riots, land invasions, and rebellions against tax collections (McAdam et al., 1988: 709).

8. While McCarthy and Zald argue for the 'professionalization' of SMs, others point out the variety of organizational forms and leadership structures. Freeman (1983: 9) suggests that SMs have a center and a periphery. At the center of a movement there will be a core of groups or organizations with greater influence in determining policy and goals. Gerlach and Hine argue that SM structures are segmentary, decentralized, polycephalous (more than one head) and reticulate (network-like) (Gerlach and Hine, 1970: 55).

9. Freeman (1983) has argued that the existence of these networks is not sufficient, as they must also be co-optable to the 'new ideas of the incipient movement' (9).

10. Since this chapter was first published as a working paper for the CERLAC community power project in 1991, a number of publications have attempted to integrate the two theoretical perspectives. See Escobar and Alvarez (1992) and Morris and McClurg Mueller (1992).

References

Arnason, J. (1986) 'Culture, Historicity and Power: Reflections on Some Themes in the Work of Alain Touraine,' *Theory, Culture and Society*, vol. 3, no. 3.

Ash-Garner, R. and M. Zald (1987) 'The Political Economy of Social Movements,' in Zald and McCarthy (1987): 293–317.

Assies, W. (1990) 'Of Structured Moves and Moving Structures,' in Assies et al. (1990).

Assies, W., G. Burgwal and T. Salman (1990) *Structures of Power, Movements of Resistance: An Introduction to the Theories of Urban Social Movements in Latin America*, Amsterdam: CEDLA.

Carroll, William, ed. (1992) *Organizing Dissent: Contemporary Social Movements in Theory and Practice*, Toronto: Garamond Press.

Cohen, J.L. (1985) 'Strategy or Identity: New Theoretical Paradigms and Contemporary Social Movements,' *Social Research*, vol. 52, no. 4 (Winter).

———— (1983) 'Rethinking Social Movements,' *Berkeley Journal of Sociology*, vol. 28: 97–114.

———— (1982) *Class and Civil Society: The Limits of Marxian Critical Theory*, University of Massachusetts Press.

Escobar, A. and S. Alvarez, eds. (1992) *The Making of Social Movements in Latin America. Identity, Strategy and Democracy*, Boulder, CO: Westview Press.

Freeman, J., ed. (1983) *Social Movements of the Sixties and Seventies*, New York: Longman.

———— (1979) 'Resource Mobilization and Strategy,' in Zald and McCarthy (1987).

Gamson, W. (1987) 'Introduction,' in Zald and McCarthy (1987).

Gerlach, L.P. and V.H. Hine (1970) *People, Power and Change: Movements of Social Transformation*, New York: Bobbs-Merril.

Habermas, J. (1981) 'New Social Movements,' *Telos*, no. 49: 33–7.

Jenkins, J.C. (1983) 'Resource Mobilization Theory and the Study of Social Movements,' *Annual Review of Sociology*, vol. 9: 527–53.

———— (1982) 'The Transformation of a Constituency into a Movement: Farmworker Organizing in California,' in Freeman (1983): 52–70.

———— (1981) 'Sociopolitical Movements,' *The Handbook of Political Behaviour,* vol. 4: 81–153.

Jessop, B. (1984) *The Capitalist State*, Oxford: Basil Blackwell.

Klandermans, B. (1986) 'New Social Movements and Resource Mobilization: The European and the American Approach,' *Journal of Mass Emergencies and Disasters* 4: 13–37.

Laclau, E. (1981) 'The Impossibility of Society,' *Canadian Journal of Political and Social Theory*, vol. VII, no. 1–2.

———— (1983) 'Transformations of Advanced Industrial Societies and the Theory of the Subject,' in Sakari Hanninen and Leena Paldan, eds., *Rethinking Ideology: A Marxist Debate*, New York: International General/IMMRC.

Laclau, E and C. Mouffe (1985) *Hegemony and Socialist Strategy: Towards a Radical and Democratic Politics*, London: Verso.

McAdam, D., J.D. McCarthy and M.N. Zald (1988) 'Social Movements,' in Neil Smelser, ed., *Handbook of Sociology*, Sage Publications: 695–737.

McCarthy, J.D. and M.N. Zald, eds. (1977a) *The Dynamics of Social Movements*, MA: Winthrop Publishers.

———— (1977b) 'Resource Mobilization and Social Movements: A Partial Theory,' *American Journal of Sociology* 82 (May): 1212–39.

———— (1973) *The Trend of Social Movements in America Professionalization and Resource Mobilization*, Morristown, N.J.: General Learning Corporation.

Melucci, A. (1989) *Nomads of the Present: Social Movements and Individual Needs in Contemporary Society*, Philadelphia: Temple University Press.

———— (1985) 'The Symbolic Challenge of Contemporary Movements,' *Social Research*, vol. 52, no. 4 (Winter).

———— (1984) 'An End to Social Movements?', *Social Science Information*, vol. 23, no. 4/5: 819–35.

———— (1980) 'The New Social Movements: a Theoretical Approach,' *Social Science Information*, vol. 19, no. 2: 199–226.

Morris, A. and C. McClurg Mueller, eds. (1992) *Frontiers in Social Movement Theory*, New Haven, CT: Yale University Press.

Mouffe, C. (1988) 'Hegemony and New Political Subjects: Towards a New Concept of Democracy,' in C. Nelson and L. Grossberg, eds., *Marxism and the Interpretation of Culture*, Chicago: University of Illinois Press: 89–101.

——— (1984) 'Towards a Theoretical Interpretation of New Social Movements,' in *Rethinking Marx*, New York: International General/IMMRC.

——— (1979) 'Hegemony and Ideology in Gramsci,' in C. Mouffe, ed., *Gramsci and Marxist Theory*, London: Routledge & Kegan Paul.

Oberschall, A. (1973) *Social Conflict and Social Movements*, Englewood Cliffs, NJ: Prentice-Hall.

Offe, C. (1985) 'New Social Movements: Challenging the Boundaries of Institutional Politics,' *Social Research*, vol. 52, no. 4. (Winter).

Perrow, C. (1977) 'The Sixties Observed,' in McCarthy and Zald (1977a).

Rogers, R. (1974) 'Instrumental and Infra-Resources,' *American Journal of Sociology*, 79: 1218–1433.

Salman, T. (1990) 'Between Orthodoxy and Euphoria: Research Strategies on Social Movements, a Comparative Perspective,' in Assies et al. (1990).

Thompson, E.P. (1975) *The Making of the English Working Class*, Harmondsworth: Penguin.

Tilly, C. (1985) 'Models and Realities of Popular Collective Action,' *Social Research*, vol. 52, no. 4 (Winter).

——— (1981) *As Sociology Meets History*, Academic Press Inc.

——— (1978) *From Mobilization to Revolution*, Reading, MA: Addison-Wesley.

Tilly, C. and L. Tilly (1981) *Class Conflict and Collective Action*, Sage Publications.

Touraine, A. (1988) *Return of the Actor*, Minneapolis: University of Minnesota Press.

——— (1985) 'An Introduction to the Study of Social Movements,' *Social Research*, vol. 52, no. 4 (Winter).

——— (1981) *The Voice and the Eye: an Analysis of Social Movements*. Cambridge: Cambridge University Press.

Zald, M. and R. Ash (1966) 'Social Movement Organizations: Growth, Decay and Change,' *Social Forces* 44: 327–40.

Zald, M. and J.D. McCarthy, eds. (1987) *Social Movements in an Organizational Society*, New Brunswick, NJ: Transaction Books.

About the Contributors

Michael Kaufman is the former Deputy Director of the Centre for Research on Latin America and the Caribbean at York University in Toronto. He now works full time as a writer and public educator on gender issues. (Dr Kaufman can be contacted at 'mkmk@yorku.ca' or at CERLAC, York University, York Lanes 240, 4700 Keele Street, Toronto, Canada M3J 1P3, or by fax at (416) 736-5737.)

Eduardo Canel is an assistant professor in the Division of Social Science at York University in Toronto, where he is also co-ordinator of the Latin American and Caribbean Studies Programme. (Dr Canel can be reached at 'ecanel@yorku.ca' or at the Division of Social Science, York University, 4700 Keele Street, Toronto, Canada M3J 1P3.)

Haroldo Dilla Alfonso was a senior researcher at the Centro de Estudios Sobre América and senior adjunct professor in the Faculty of Philosophy and History at the University of Havana, Cuba. (Prof. Dilla can be contacted at Calle 31A, No. 3011, Entre 30 & 34, Aptdo 5, Miramar, La Habana, Cuba.)

Silvia Lara, a sociologist, is a program co-ordinator for Centro Mujer y Familia in San José, Costa Rica, with specialities in gender and political participation. Until it disbanded, she was an executive member of the Centro de Estudios para la Acción Social (CEPAS) in San José. (Ms Lara can be reached at Box 3820, 1000 San Jose, Costa Rica.)

Gerardo González Núñez is an economist; previously he was a researcher at the Centro de Estudios Sobre América in Havana. (Mr Gonzalez can be contacted through Haroldo Dilla.)

Eugenia Molina is a doctoral student in sociology in Belgium and is working in Costa Rica as a consultant in communications and the environment. (Ms Molina can be contacted through Silvia Lara.)

César Pérez is Profesor of Urban Sociology and Underdevelopment at the Instituto Tecnologico de Santo Domingo (INTEC) as well as at the Universidad Autónoma de Santo Domingo. (Prof. Pérez can be contacted at EQUIS, INTEC, Aptdo 342–9, Santo Domingo, Dominican Republic.)

Veronica Schild was born and raised in Chile, and is currently an assistant professor of political science at the University of Western Ontario. (Prof. Schild can be reached at 'schild@sscl.uwo.ca' or through the Dept of Political Science, UWO, London, Ontario, Canada N6A 5C2.)

Luc Smarth is the Director of the Centre de Recherches Sociales et de Diffusion Populaire (CRESDIP) in Port-au-Prince, where he also teaches sociology at the Université d'État d'Haiti. Until the coup of 1991, he worked with the Aristide government. (Prof. Smarth can be reached at CRESDIP, rue Babiole No. 25, Babiole, Port-au-Prince, Haiti. Phone and fax: 509–453–973.)

Index

Aguilar, Oscar, 49, 50
alcoholism, 167
Allende, Salvador, 129
Alvarez, Virtudez, 89
Arias, Oscar, 14, 32, 34, 35, 36, 43, 44, 51
Ariel Darce *barrio* (Nicaragua), 20
Aristide, Jean-Bertrand, 1, 2, 102, 103, 107, 108, 115, 119, 120, 121, 122, 123; inaugurated as president, 105
Ash, R., 211, 212
Ash-Garner, R., 209
Asociación Nacional de Vivienda (ANAVI) (Costa Rica), 29, 31, 44, 50
Association of Haitian Writers, 103
Azieri, Max, 56

Balaguer government (Dominican Republic), 85, 86
basic needs strategy, 7
Bayaguana municipality (Dominican Republic), 87
Bayamo municipality (Cuba), 60, 61–2, 161
Bel Air neighborhood (Haiti), 117
black markets, 117
Bobbio, Norberto, 28, 34
Borja, Jordi, 174
Bosch, Juan, 86
Bowles, Samuel, 159
Boxhill, Ian, 18
Bukharin, Nikolai, 180
bureaucracy, 10, 11, 15, 55, 77, 120, 154, 175; power of, 3
bureaucratization, 181; of life, 198

Caisses Populaires (Haiti), 117
Canada, 2
Candelier, Pedro, 95
Canel, Eduardo, 21
Carmen Lyra community, 29, 34–7, 39, 40, 42, 43, 44, 46, 49, 50
Carter, Jimmy, 102
Castillo, Luis Mora, 19
Catholic Church, 103, 104, 120, 121, 130, 131, 135, 136, 139; militants, 92
central planning, 4, 57
Central Unica de Trabajadores (CUT) (Chile), 134
centralization, 75, 79, 183, 184
Centre de Recherches Sociales et de Diffusion Populaire (CRESDIP) (Haiti), 17
Centre for Research on Latin America and the Caribbean (CERLAC) (Canada), 12
Centro de Estudios Para la Acción Social (CEPAS) (Costa Rica), 14
Centro de Estudios Sobre América (Cuba), 15
Centro Habana municipality (Cuba), 60, 61, 62, 69, 81
Cerroni, Umberto, 176
Chambas municipality (Cuba), 60, 63–4, 81
Charlemagne, Emmanuel, 118
child care, 13, 165
Chile, 2, 18, 126–47, 176
Christian Base Committees (CBCs): in Haiti, 17, 103, 108, 109; in Dominican Republic, 84, 86, 89